I AM NOT A NUMBER!

Freeing America from the ID State
Revised and Expanded Second Edition

by Claire Wolfe

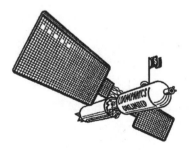

Loompanics Unlimited
Port Townsend, Washington

I AM NOT a NUMBER!
Freeing America from the ID State,
Revised and Expanded Second Edition
© 2003 by Claire Wolfe

Published by:
Loompanics Unlimited
PO Box 1197
Port Townsend, WA 98368
Loompanics Unlimited is a division of Loompanics Enterprises, Inc.
Phone: 360-385-2230
E-mail: service@loompanics.com
Web site: www.loompanics.com

Cover Artwork by Knoll Gilbert

ISBN 1-55950-232-0
Library of Congress Card Catalog Number 2002113491

"I am not a number;

I am a free man."

Patrick McGoohan, "The Prisoner" (also known as Number Six)

• • • • • •

The Prisoner: "What do you want?"

Number Two: "Information."

The Prisoner: "You won't get it."

Number Two: "By hook or by crook, we will."

Opening dialog between The Prisoner and his chief warden, Number Two

• • • • • •

Number Two: "I'll kill you."

The Prisoner: "I'll die."

To the Fighters:

Cyndee, Scott, Jackie, Linda
and others whose names I may never know.
On the day you stop being nice, tyrants should tremble.

Acknowledgments

To thank everyone who contributed to this book would be impossible. I would have to start by thanking the entire Internet, that wild, global swirl of information that is remaking the very concept of communities and nations.

Many of the ideas expressed here germinated from the thousands of messages that have crossed my computer in the last few years. Where possible, I've acknowledged individuals who've e-mailed ideas, personal stories, and news articles. In other cases, snippets of information have arrived uncredited — cross-posted so many times it was impossible to tell their origin. In still other cases, attitudes and ideas from the net have simply soaked through my intellectual skin, becoming "mine" (and others') in the way that any culture imparts certain assumptions to its members. So, to the Internet, thank you.

Thanks also to Charles Curley, who not only put up with a crazed writer, but who did it through Thanksgiving, Bill of Rights Day, the anniversary of the Boston Tea Party, Yule, Solstice, Hanukkah, Christmas, New Year, and the beginning of Ramadan. The book is done, Charles! Happy Chinese New Year and beyond!

And in no particular order, but with much gratitude, thanks to:

Vin Suprynowicz for his innovative thinking and his generosity with ideas;

L. Neil Smith for sheer curmudgeonly inspiration;

Pat Henry, for living free and sharing his experiences; also for thoughts on electronic privacy and identity;

John Greenley, for his views on community and for many kindnesses;

Patricia Neill, for sisterhood, laughter, otters, more laughter, and monkeywrenches;

Bill Evans, for moral and other support and for his undying crusade against four-putting;

Todd Gillespie and Ed Wolfe, the rest of the Sacred Bull Gang, on general principles and for the humor;

Mary Lou Seymour, Liberty Activist, for her thoughts on organization and for giving my work a forum;

Cyndee Parker, Scott McDonald, Linda Muller, and Jackie Juntti, who've done more than anyone to alert Americans to the dangers of federal ID and tracking legislation;

Mike Kemp, for taking a principled stand even when it could have cost him everything, and for being a good Idea Guy;

Deborah Marie Pulaski (1943-1997), for inspiration and bravery;

Sam Hall, also for inspiration;

Members of the Conspiracy for humor and general conniving, especially the Frog Proctologist, the Old Polish Woman, the Priest's Rowdy Wife, and Mr. Justice;

Cousin Michael Voth, scofflaw and poet, for being among the first to start building the Future Underground;

Wendy McElroy, for pointers toward information on past & contemporary communities;

Bob Kephart, for information on the Sovereign Society and offshore banks;

Jim Davidson, for information on several free nation projects;

Sunni Maravillosa, for her thoughts about children and free families;

All the unshy folks who attended the November 1997 meeting of the Wyoming Libertarian Party, with particular thanks to Don Lobo Tiggre, Mary

Sunderman, Dennis Brossman, Jim Brady, Ed Cassidy, and Dave Dawson;

Gene Hahn, for the reminder about Fidonet;

Intel96B, for writings on underground communications;

Eric Gray, for sharing experiences with alternate ID and more;

Carl Alexander, for helping me claireify my ideas and for forging swords and cattle prods;

The mysterious Badsheep;

Woody Hassler, for the cute envelope trick;

Sarah Thompson, who suggested the addition of a communications chapter;

Internetizens Rick Rabbit, Steve Washam, Doc Memory, and Don Cline;

Keith Justice, Steve Stroh, and the Tucson Amateur Packet Radio Corporation, for information on the technology and use of packet radio. And David Pinero, for information about scanners and open broadcasting. These people might not approve of the uses to which I have put their information, but they were most helpful in setting me straight on technical questions.

Thanks to my editor Gia Cosindas and publisher Mike Hoy, without whom there would be no book — and without whom the entire world of publishing would be far less interesting. Thanks to the rest of the Loompanics gang, especially Gina, Jan, Audrey and everybody in the world's most efficient shipping department.

Finally, extra thanks to Scott McDonald, Charles Curley, and Mike Kemp, each of whom reviewed a draft chapter of this book. Your help was invaluable, guys.

Being mentioned in these acknowledgments does *not* imply that any of the above folks endorse the message of this book or share my assumptions or attitudes.

Also, any errors anywhere in this work are purely mine, and not the fault of any of the people who gave so generously of their time and their thoughts.

Contents

Part I
Rule and Resistance

Part II
Free Nation America

Part III
Times of Trouble

Author's Foreword

to the 2002 Edition

When *I Am Not a Number!* first came out in July 1998, the legal groundwork for a vast national ID and citizen-tracking system had recently been laid. Several 1996 laws, along with a growing web of dependencies on government, had spurred a huge "advance" in the long-term process of turning free people into chattel — herd beasts, to be monitored, controlled, and effectively owned by the government, just as herds of cows and sheep are owned and scientifically managed by modern farmers with the aid of computers.

This type of passive, malleable, well-cataloged, and constantly observed population is what every tyrant in history has desired and what no government of the free would ever wish for.

But few knew and fewer cared about the ominous new laws. "Privacy" — a hot topic now — was nearly a nonissue when this book first came out. Not only did the TV-dulled millions not hear, know, or care about what was being engineered for them, but neither did most political activists.

Now that has changed. But the recent focus on "privacy" as the central issue in these questions of who controls and maintains data on us is itself a tragic misdirection. Privacy is important *not primarily* because it's embarrassing if some marketer learns from our druggist that we've got hemorrhoids and *not* because some thief might steal our identity if he's able to access too much information about us and not even because the government might snoop into our computers and learn we're having an affair, dealing dope, or skimping on our tax payments. Privacy matters because it's a mainstay of self-ownership. It's

a sign that individuals are important in and of themselves and that they are important *to* themselves and each other. It says that we have individual rights to own and control our own lives, that we are not mere "taxpayers," "corporate citizens," "consumers," or "aggregate statistics," to be examined, profiled, and managed by the state or corporations.

The real question isn't how to protect our privacy; it's how to retain ownership of our lives.

And on that question, the whole future of freedom stands or falls. If we accept the kind of numbering and tracking now being imposed upon us, freedom falls. If we effectively say no, freedom can be regained and privacy will be a given.

What to expect in this book

When it first came out, this book was ahead of its time. It still is in some ways. It sold modestly, not brilliantly, a few thousand copies. It went into a second small printing and in November 1999 was scheduled for a third. But when Loompanics asked me to make the updates and revisions for that third printing, I looked at the book and said, "No way."

The slave-making ID laws, regulations, and technologies were coming too fast and heavy to keep up with. It was true then and it's true now that anything you write about the legal or technological aspects of citizen-tracking may be obsolete before it's published. And even though the rumblings of concern for privacy were growing louder, I still believed that few people cared enough to take the radical steps required to take ownership of their identities and their lives back from government. So I felt that the task of re-vising *I Am Not a Number!* was futile.

I asked Loompanics to take the book out of print.

Things have changed, and now, three years later, this book is coming back. I doubt that attitudes have changed enough for *I Am Not a Number!* to have any great impact on the world. I'm not a Pollyanna about the future of freedom. I only hope this book will help the few thousand who read it. I believe it *will* help those few who have the integrity to use it or be inspired by it to find their own methods to resist numbering, surveillance, and regimentation.

I will tell you right up front that this book does not emphasize "Fast, EZ Solutions!" for preserving your privacy (though you will find a few such tricks inside).

Nor is this book for the risk-averse. *You are not going to get your freedom back without taking risks, re-examining what you really value, and changing the way you live.* You will probably also have to break laws — although which laws and in what manner is always up to you.

If you imagine you can have both freedom and a convenient, secure, go-along-to-get-along life, then save your money, save your time, put this book down, go back to watching reruns of *Seinfeld.* Your children and grandchildren may damn you for having sold them into slavery, or having lazed as they were sold, but hey, you'll have had a nice, smooth life and who really cares about the little rugrats, anyway?

If you think convenience is the most important thing in life, *I Am Not a Number!* isn't for you. If we restore freedom, then our kids and grandkids can have a nice, smooth life. But it's not for us, not for this generation.

On the other hand, this book is also not about *fighting* for freedom — neither with the ballot box nor the cartridge box. It is about *living* for freedom, which is both harder and easier than voting or shooting the bastards.

I doubt that one in a hundred self-proclaimed freedom lovers is willing to live free if it means giving up certain perks, or facing uncertain outcomes. But if you are that one in a hundred, or one in a thousand — welcome, welcome, welcome and bless you for the potential you bring to humanity. I hope that *I Am Not*

a Number! will help you change the world by changing individual lives.

Why is *I Am Not a Number* back in print now?

Sometime early in 2002 a friend pointed me toward Amazon.com's page on *I Am Not a Number!*. (That giant seller-of-everything maintains pages on out-of-print books and offers possessors of used books the chance to sell their copies through its site.) Someone was offering a copy of *I Am Not a Number!* for $90.

My friend, who had loaned her copy out and never gotten it back, laughed and said, "Sorry, Claire. I love you — but not *that* much!" I had to agree; even *I* didn't love me that much, although I'd lost my last copy of *I Am Not a Number!* myself. I expected that book to sit there unsold for a long, long time.

(One of my little dreads as a writer is that I will someday come across one of my books at a thrift store, selling for a quarter in a bin filled with dog-eared copies of *Return to the Son of Valley of the Dolls the Sequel, Part III* and *Chicken Soup for the Soul of Nauseatingly Sentimental Morons.* So I admit that it was flattering, as well as a vast relief, to find that one of my books had met an opposite fate. But I still thought it was nuts.)

Just weeks later another friend dropped me an e-mail. A different vendor on Amazon.com was now selling a copy of *I Am Not a Number!* for $197.12. Don't ask me why such an odd price; I haven't got a clue. But the $90 copy had apparently sold.

I never went back to see whether the second grandly inflated copy of *I Am Not a Number!* found a buyer. That would be tempting fate. But I did drop a note to Gia Cosindas, my editor at Loompanics, laughing (and yes, okay, boasting a little) about this bull market in *I Am Not a Number!*. And instead of laughing back at me, Gia went to Mike Hoy, the boss, and they came back to me and said, "Hey, stupid, can't you see that people want this book — and that the world *needs* this book, and needs it *now*?"

With the world rapidly surrendering even more of itself to governments in the aftermath of September 11, 2001 ("Trust us, we'll save you."), they were right. They still had to twist my arm pretty hard to get me to update and rerelease it.

Clearly Gia and Mike realize that more people now understand that if the government can require you to carry its number and endure its scans, warrantless searches, and inspections everywhere you go, then the government can control the most fundamental parts of your life — where and how you travel, how (or whether) you earn a living, your communications, and even whether or not you can get medical care.[1]

In rereleasing *I Am Not a Number!* I don't hope to make the Big Bucks or the best seller lists. I'm grateful that I have a devoted, intelligent readership — including someone who'll pay $90 for a used paperback book[2] — but I've always known that the numbers of my readers are small. What I do hope is to encourage those who have the courage to resist, to give them some ideas, and to keep alive an idea that has always been at the center of this book: building freedom communities.

Retaining full self-ownership in this day and age is almost an impossible task for an individual alone or for a family. You have to be willing either to live in primitive, privacy-protecting ways that not one in a 100,000 folks would tolerate or you have to be willing to spend your life keeping one step ahead of the government's ever-changing rules on various privacy-protection dodges.

The former means not having a conventional job, refusing to use a Social Security number, not paying taxes, owning few possessions, not using credit cards, never accepting government services, keeping children out of state schools, avoiding banks, doing without drivers' licenses, auto registrations, or insurance, etc. The latter means an eternal scramble to stay ahead of new laws, regulations, and brutal enforcement methods that are forever being levied against offshore banks, trusts, corporations, and even against such ordinary businesses as private mail-receiving companies.

Both primitive living and sophisticated hiding methods are an option for some — for millions, I hope. But these are no way to run a society. If we want freedom on a large scale, we may have to begin by creating free mini-societies to provide the basic functions communities are designed to serve. That may still mean living primitively or dangerously in the short run, but with the goal of changing the culture in the long run (or being ready when the damn fool Big Brother state collapses around us). If we can't change the culture, or if the sheep never decide to break out of the pen, then at least we've created freedom networks to provide services and protection for those who resist government might. That's what this book is really about.

What's changed lately?

A lot has changed since *I Am Not a Number!* went out of print. Or not much has changed, depending on how you look at it.

The biggest change of course began on the morning of September 11, 2001 when three jets slammed into their American targets and one — thanks to the courage of passengers — slammed into a field in Pennsylvania. For a time thereafter, most Americans were willing to tolerate nearly all government violations of their privacy and their individual rights. Six months later, about the time people began remembering that you can't protect freedom by destroying it, a myriad of truly un-American policies had already been put into law (particularly in the inappropriately named USA-Patriot Act) and into practice (a Soviet-style Homeland Security bureaucracy, federalization of airport searches, etc.).

This is the wonderful thing for governments. Whether the crisis is as real as 9-11 or as mythical as the Clintons' Great American Childcare Crisis or the media-hyped "torpedoing" of the battleship *Maine* a hundred years earlier, all the statist control freaks need is a short period of panic to push through their "reforms" and "emergency measures." By the time people return to their senses it's too late; the new controls are a done deal. Rarely are the "emergency measures" ever repealed. And never, but never, do the new laws and regulations actually solve the crisis

---

[1]   For more on this terrible trend and what it might hold for us in the near future, read *The State vs. the People* by Claire Wolfe and Aaron Zelman (Mazel Freedom Press, 2002), available through the Loompanics catalog.

[2]   If you paid $90 or more for a copy of *I Am Not a Number!*, I'm sorry if this re-issue diminishes its value. If you'll get in touch with Loompanics and show them evidence you paid that much, I'll autograph your copy for you.

at hand. (No, it requires yet *more* new laws to do that. And when *those* also fail to solve the problem...)

Public outcry may cause the tyrant wannabes to move more slowly, or even temporarily to back off on certain policies (as has happened in the case of one or two of the horrors exposed in *I Am Not a Number!*). But governments always move in the same direction — toward total power — as far and as fast as the people will let them go.

Since *I Am Not a Number!* last appeared, there've been some terrible, terrible developments, as we shall see. There have also been a few that looked good. But while bad policy is always as bad as it looks, "good" news is harder to evaluate.

For instance, the George W. Bush administration shot down Oracle CEO Larry Ellison's plan to establish, in a ninety-day rush, a true and comprehensive nationwide ID system, preloaded with revealing information about everything from our education to our tax returns. Civil libertarians cheered. And the Bush administration went on developing a quieter, slower, but no less outrageous plan of its own. In the end, our freedom will get fried just as badly, but because they're turning up the heat more slowly, we'll go more quietly to our doom.

Still, there has been genuine good news, some of it perfectly charming.

Facial-recognition cameras — a looming, but barely implemented threat when *I Am Not a Number!* was last in print — became a genuine menace on the streets, and a well-publicized menace at "Snooper Bowl XXXV," where 100,000 football fans were involuntarily put through an electronic criminal lineup. But shortly thereafter the cameras became a laughingstock as it turned out that the almost supernaturally accurate technology (allegedly able to unerringly recognize even a face obscured by sunglasses, a false mustache, and the shade of a baseball cap) actually had a thirty-forty percent error rate, resulting in millions of wasted tax dollars, harassment of innocent people, the identification of a few dozen people with petty criminal records (but no obvious current criminal intent), and not a single arrest of a dangerous villain.

And so it goes. Conditions continue to change rapidly (so rapidly that, during the six weeks it took to update this book, several items had to be rewritten as much as three times, simply to cover new developments and new discoveries).

The worst news is usually followed by at least a little governmental back-pedaling ("Oh, no, we really didn't mean we were going to do *that*..."), but the overall trend continues to be toward government (and hand-in-hand with that, state-corporate) control of our lives. The plain fact staring us in the face is that for all the soothing talk about "privacy czars" and "privacy policies" and "respect for privacy," both our privacy and our self-ownership will go on disappearing until we put a flaming, adamant, don't-tread-on-me halt to it.

As Frederick Douglass warned us, people will always get exactly as much tyranny as they're willing to put up with.

This book is for people who won't put up with it any more. People who aren't going to beg an uncaring government to give back what it has absolutely no intention of restoring. People who are willing to take risks, to innovate, to make connections, and to build a different sort of future.

You'll find as many questions as answers here. Nobody, and certainly not I, an ordinary woman of limited means, has *the* secret to restoring self-ownership.

It's up to us all to figure out how to get from here to a free land — helping each other along, sharing ideas, sharing risks, and sometimes paying consequences. There is no single thing we absolutely *must* do to restore freedom and self-ownership, except, of course, to resist as intelligently and adamantly as we know how. But there is absolutely one thing we must *not* do.

We must not sit on our backsides and let this terrible thing sap the human race of its individuality and freedom.

How this book is structured

In re-issuing *I Am Not a Number!*, Loompanics and I have opted to leave most of the existing chapter text unchanged, except for updated URLs, addresses, and any needed error correction. We've also deleted a few bits that have become so obsolete they weren't even worth a backwards glance. (If anyone ever reminds me that the original *I Am Not a Number!*

contained a word about the Y2K bug-that-wasn't, I'll deny it with great ardor and a completely straight face.)

Revisiting *I Am Not a Number!* after several years, I was astonished to find it still fresh (and, to my delight, a piece of writing I still felt proud of). Nevertheless, many things have changed. So while the text itself is substantially as readers last saw it, at the end of each chapter I've added a brand-new section, sometimes long, sometimes brief, of news, updates, and personal observations.

One reason for this approach is to drive home just how much has changed in three short years. Look at the way things were in 1999; look at the way they are today — and mourn.

There's another reason that, even with all the changing laws and regulations, this book actually didn't require a top-to-bottom updating. It's because *I Am Not a Number!* isn't about what the government does. And it isn't about surveillance technology, current events, or past ones, or how to finagle your way around the latest roadblock to privacy.

It's about building the future. Let's go and do it now.

● ● ● ● ● ● ●

I Am Not a Number!

Ozymandias

by Percy Bysshe Shelley, 1818

I met a traveler from an antique land
Who said: Two vast and trunkless legs of stone
Stand in the desert…Near them, on the sand,
Half sunk, a shattered visage lies, whose frown,
And wrinkled lip, and sneer of cold command,
Tell that its sculptor well those passions read
Which yet survive, stamped upon these lifeless things,
The hand that mocked them, and the heart that fed:
And on the pedestal these words appear:
"My name is Ozymandias, king of kings:
Look on my works, ye Mighty, and despair!"
Nothing beside remains. Round the decay
Of that colossal wreck, boundless and bare
The lone and level sands stretch far away.

Introduction
Toppling Ozymandias

It's time to take our freedom back. Not to ask for it. But to take it.

Some of us have spent a lifetime politely begging politicians to return our stolen freedom. The politicians' response: to take more. We have raised our voices. They have taken more. We have pointed out our rights. They have taken more.

In the 1994 national elections, we sharpened our tone. We imagined we issued a peremptory and unmistakable *demand* for the return of our freedom. The politicians' response?

The Congress that promised to "get government off our backs" established the largest citizen-control and tracking system ever known to mankind. They did it secretly, sneakily, and in a firm spirit of bipartisanship. They gave themselves what Stalin and Hitler could only dream of having.

They declared their ownership of the last thing we can ever afford to let them have: our privacy, our very identity. And some of us will not *let them have it, as long as we live.*

Now we face three choices: to bow and be slaves, to rebel… or simply to live free, in spite of their rule.

It may come down, someday, to a choice between rebellion or slavery. But I believe our best hope lies in simply withdrawing our consent and living free, right under their noses.

Some of us have been practicing free life for decades. I now think it's time for the next logical step.

Radical Free America

We can create an entire Free America right under the eyes of — right inside the gaping maw of — the growing ID State. It is an America that can offer prosperity, excitement, comradeship, freedom and free markets. It's an America that also offers risks — in some cases grave risks. But some of us will prefer any risk to the abasement of slavery.

Until now, we freedom seekers have been isolated. But our numbers are shifting, and that's going to make all the difference in the world. If I'm right and millions of Americans have now reached their line in the sand, a new, free, underground country will almost build itself. We just need to be aware and flexible when the opportunity arises.

There are many thinkers and doers working on new concepts of the individual's relationship to government. These concepts often involve removing oneself and one's assets from the jurisdiction of ravening governments. They're useful and we should take advantage of them to whatever extent we can.

This book is primarily for Americans (though I hope it will be useful to freedom seekers in other countries, as well). Even with new horizons opening to mobile, independent people, some of us prefer to stay in the United States. Some of us feel that we *must* or *should* stay here, for various reasons. So even while we use burgeoning new methods to move our privacy and assets out of the jurisdiction of rapacious governments, we ourselves will remain, for good or ill, in this land.

I Am Not a Number!

But we don't have to submit as subjects to a boundlessly controlling government. We have the opportunity to build a Free America, Our Own Private America, even while "mainstream" America remains in bondage.

A huge task? Of course. But many of us have been flinging ourselves into a larger and more futile task for decades.

We've been trying to free America through voting, letter writing, petitions, lobbying, contributions — in short, by attempting to change huge systems and to move inert masses of people. We've been thinking we have to alter (somehow) the whole nation or a majority of legislators.

We don't. In fact, we can't. We've been using the wrong paradigm and wasting a shameful amount of energy.

All we need to do — the most powerful thing we *can* do — is change our own choices.

A million... two million... three million... individual choices become the invisible hand that writes a new course for the land. Individuals acting alone. Individuals joining into cooperative business efforts. Individuals helping each other — and themselves — to become more free. We don't have enough strength or determination to move a whole nation. But we do have the ability and the urgent need to create better, safer, saner lives for ourselves and the people we care about.

If the rest of the nation chooses not to be free, that is their choice.

Of course, it will be dangerous co-existing with an unfree nation ruled by violent power-seekers. But there is no choice we face today that *isn't* dangerous.

If we are very fortunate, the American Ozymandias will topple under its own weight and the weight of destiny. That is, after all, the message of Shelley's poem quoted at the beginning of this book. Perhaps by living free, however, we can give the idol of government an extra push. If nothing else, we can take steps to get out from under the tumbling, crumbling stones that will crush naïve fools who thought the Great and Powerful Ozymandias would take care of them as it ruled them forever.

But in a sense, it doesn't matter whether Ozymandias stands or falls. The government of America is a fact we have to live with for now. What matters is *how* we choose to live.

The beginning of an answer

The first part of this book talks about the problem — the laws excreted by Congress, the technologies that help implement them, the life we can expect to live under them, and other new laws and technologies on the horizon.

The second, and much larger, part of the book proposes a solution. It's a solution of nonviolent, but adamant noncooperation.

The final chapter looks at ways we might have to protect ourselves when the rulers of America interfere with our right to live free, as they certainly will.

This entire book is nothing more than a beginning. No one writer and no one book could do justice to the topic of creating a Free America. I may be raising more questions than I answer. From the point of view of any individual reader, my proposals may even be the *wrong* solutions.

If that's your reaction as you read this book, then I urge you to ask the new questions. Raise the objections. Find what works and what doesn't — for yourself. The best way to answer the questions of creating a Free America is — to *create a Free America*. Live it.

Do what you must to free yourself and help other freedom seekers to release themselves from bondage. But don't ever, ever, ever, ever yield to enslavement, however benign your master's face, however well he promises to take care of you if you submit.

Do not accept his mark of ownership. His brand. His Number.

Sudden change has come upon us. The laws to enslave us were passed so quietly that many of us are just now waking up to what's been done. We are about to be numbered like prisoners and tracked like cattle in a herd.

But we are waking up and saying, "No. I am not a number. I am a free human being."

As enough of us free ourselves, new markets, new communities, new styles of commerce, new forms of communication will grow out of *necessity*.

I Am Not a Number!

Necessity is a mother. We know that. But we have a shot at making it the mother of a world of new hopes.

The usual disclaimer:

This book talks about "illegal activities." It doesn't advocate committing crimes. Never do anything that is against your own conscience or your own better judgment, and certainly never break a law because someone else gets the bright idea to do so.

I believe, unfortunately, that in today's America the only way to live free is to live as an outlaw. And I express that opinion pretty blatantly throughout this book. But it is just one person's opinion. If you see a better option, pursue it.

Please make your own careful choices. But please, whatever you do, choose freedom.

I Am Not a Number!

Interlude
Other Scenarios of Collapse

This book is primarily for those who oppose Big Brotherish ID and tracking schemes. However, it could also be useful to anyone envisioning economic or social collapse. No matter what the scenario, if it involves any degree of remaking life in America, this book might have something to offer.

A mega-collapse of the economy

An economic collapse is long overdue. And as I write this, most of Asia is teetering economically, and Argentina has virtually gone down the tubes. The IMF and other global bodies keep pumping out the assistance to forestall catastrophe. How many bailouts can there be before the boat sinks? If a market collapse is followed by any great degree of social or governmental breakdown, it could be an opportunity for freedom.

Plague, war, or other catastrophe

If this happens and you need to run to safe territory, only your own wits and preparations are going to help you in the short term. But once it comes time to rebuild, this book could help you and other free people begin to do so.

Or just plain being sick of it all

Maybe nothing catastrophic is going to happen to the world or the country in the immediate future. Maybe you've just had enough and want, dammit, to live free.

Welcome to the book. Our reasons don't matter as long as we all agree that we will live free and accept nothing less.

Part I
Rule and Resistance

Chapter One
The Orgy of Enslavement

"We federalize everything that walks, talks, and moves." — *Senator Joe Biden, Democratic chairman of the Senate Judiciary Committee, 1986 to 1994.*

"Give the government an inch and they'll think they're rulers." — *Archie Bunker*

It began with a whimper. Or was it a soft moan of perverted power lust?

In September 1996, the Republican-dominated Congress, writhing with Bill Clinton in a coprological orgy of legislation, let loose its collective sphincter and excreted a stinking heap now known as Public Law 104-208.

The ominous bludgeon bill

Public Law 104-208, also known as HR 3610, began life as a relatively innocuous Defense Appropriations Act. That's what it remained as it moved through both houses of Congress, was passed, and made its way into conference committee. If you believed your civics teacher, you probably thought the conference committee process simply enabled the House and Senate to work out differences between their versions of the same bill, to let them take a final vote on a unified measure. That's the theory.

Rushed through the 104th Congress in the heat of the 1996 election season, HR 3610 became a piece of classic "kitchen sink" legislation. Dozens of other bills were tossed into it before it re-emerged from committee. Some were also routine appropriations bills. (Bundling these is a common practice.) Others were completely unrelated to appropriations — like the already huge "Illegal Immigration Reform and Immigrant Responsibility Act of 1996." Then there were amendments. They represented the whims of powerful legislators. So in they went.

In short, when HR 3610 emerged from conference committee as House Committee Report 104-863, it contained hundreds of pages of unknown and unexamined provisions. With Congress in a hurry to go home to campaign for re-election, your alleged representatives voted on this monster bill without having read it.

There were two other reasons why they couldn't have read it, even if they'd cared to. There was only one copy of the bill available for each house at the time the vote was taken. And at more than 468,000 words, the bill was four times the length of the average novel.

There was, nevertheless, some debate on the bill in the days before it emerged from committee. The bill contained three anti-gun provisions, two of them blatantly unconstitutional. These were hotly — though futilely — opposed by the gun owners who had been largely responsible for putting the Republican majority in place.

But the Republicans had no stomach for voting against a budget bill in 1996. They had let the government shut down late in 1995, after refusing to approve earlier appropriations bills. The ensuing PR war had been resoundingly won by the Clinton administration.

In 1996, the Republicans would have done anything — anything — to keep the federal government operating.

What they did was dramatically expand the size and power of the federal government once again. The House passed the measure 370-37. The Senate didn't bother counting; it passed HR 3610 on a similarly lopsided voice vote.

Freedom activists were furious. But it would be months before they learned how deep their betrayal had truly been.

A little law in Georgia

Early in 1997, a handful of activists in Georgia became alarmed when their state legislature passed, very quietly, a law to require digitally encoded fingerprints and other Big Brotherish features on state drivers' licenses. When they learned that New Jersey was contemplating turning its driver's license into a so-called "smart card," that Washington state was attempting to pass legislation requiring a dozen forms of "biometric data" on its licenses, and that more than twenty state governments around the country were suddenly, sometimes furtively, trying to impose similar requirements, they realized something was very, very wrong.

Somewhere, behind this frenzy of state obsession with ID, national legislation had to lie.

Georgia's Cyndee Parker and her friends in the Georgia Coalition to Repeal the Fingerprints Law got to work... and *bingo!*

There it was, in Public Law 104-208, DIVISION C, TITLE VI, SUBTITLE D, SEC. 656:

IMPROVEMENTS IN IDENTIFICATION-RELATED DOCUMENTS (b)(1)(A)

...A Federal agency may not accept for any identification-related purpose a driver's license, or other comparable identification document, issued by a State, unless the license or document satisfies the following requirements...
(ii) Social security number. — Except as provided in subparagraph (B), the license or document shall contain a social security account number that can be read visually or by electronic means.[1]

(iii) Form. — The license or document otherwise shall be in a form consistent with requirements set forth in regulations promulgated by the Secretary of Transportation after consultation with the American Association of Motor Vehicle Administrators. The form shall contain security features designed to limit tampering, counterfeiting, photocopying, or otherwise duplicating the license...

Translation of the lulling legalese: The federal government will no longer recognize any form of ID that does not contain this universal citizen ID number and meet other federal specifications. This law (originally part of the Illegal Immigration Control and Immigrant Responsibility Act) was scheduled to take effect on October 1, 2000.[2]

The national ID card — discussed for decades, but always rejected as an intolerable intrusion on freedom — had been passed without even a moment of public debate. And it is based on your Universal Citizen Identification Number — your Social Security number.

Congress had taken a lesson from the Hillary Care fiasco of 1993; there would be no more attempts to remake American society head-on. The most draconian federal controls would henceforth be engineered in secret.

And that was not the only game they'd learned how to play. By making their national ID card your state driver's license, they had attained deniability. "What, national ID card? No, not us!"

The national ID card is now a reality every American must face. It will look different in all fifty states. But it will contain the same federally mandated features and be the key to access your "right" to federal government services, such as passports and Social Security.

Unless you bear its Number, unless you present its Number upon your Card, the federal government will no longer even pretend to "serve" you.

---

[1] The "exception" noted in subparagraph (B) is actually no exception at all. It enables some states to exclude the SS number from the face of the card as long as the number is available in a database. There is no escape provided in this law for people who do not possess a social security number or who have religious or philosophical objections to the use of universal identifying numbers.

[2] Some readers may be aware that this law was eventually repealed. Read on and learn the story of why we got a national ID driver's license *anyway*.

But this was just the beginning. Other deceptive laws were being passed by the "get the government off your back" Republican Congress. Together they created a trap in which to capture the last of our freedoms.

Laws closing like a vise

The national ID card is only a single claw on the vise the 104th Congress created to close around us. Quietly, they slipped a paragraph here, a provision there, into a variety of laws passed during 1996.

All were passed in secret (although, in one case, a kind of bizarre open secret) by the same group of Republicans, trading perverse strokes with the same group of Democrats. All can be verified by anyone with the inclination to uncover them. But all must be uncovered within the depths of huge bills.

Remember, the people who voted for these bills often didn't know — and certainly didn't care — what they were actually voting for. Members of Congress habitually vote on what "sounds" good (welfare reform, tax relief, keeping the government operating). Or they vote according to political deals and party pressures. But the various agencies that got the secret provisions written into the laws (federal police agencies, executive branch bureaucracies, government lobbying groups or industry lobbying groups) certainly knew and cared what was in these laws. It may be years before the true impact of some of their handpicked provisions is known.

In any case, the related laws *that have been uncovered so far* are:

The "Deadbeat Dads" database

This one was created in HR 3734 (now Public Law 104-193)[3]. The bill breezed through Congress as the "Personal Responsibility and Work Opportunity Reconciliation Act of 1996," also known as the Welfare Reform Act. No secrets here. The Republicans patted themselves on the back for "ending welfare as we know it." And the liberals, while grousing about the "mean-spiritedness" of some provisions, applauded the creation of a national database to catch

those notorious "deadbeat dads." It's just that no one in government or the media talked about the real implications of what Congress was engineering.

Don't skip this section just because you aren't a dad or a deadbeat. This is actually a national database of *all* employed people. The information in the database is to be shared with a truly vast and comprehensive network of state and federal agencies. Officially known as "The New Hires Database," it is rapidly becoming what it was intended to be — the foundation for a huge, nationwide tracking system. This data on your life, you suspect-deadbeat you, is filed under your Universal Citizen ID Number — your Social Security number, again!

In an interesting aside for the religiously inclined or those who follow eerie coincidences: Public Law 104-193 amends 42 USC (United States Code) — Section 666(a)(13).

Want to go fishing? Want to get married? Not without an SS number!

There were more tricks hiding in the "Personal Responsibility and Work Opportunity Reconciliation Act of 1996." According to Scott McDonald of Alabama's diligent "Fight the Fingerprint" organization:

> Sec. 317, of the Act amended Title 42 U.S.C. 666(a)(13) to require that, as a condition to receiving federal funds States must — "establish procedures requiring that the Social Security number of any applicant for a professional license, commercial driver's license, recreational license, occupational license, or marriage license be recorded on the application"

Bad, yes? But it gets worse. Again, according to McDonald:

> Here's where you must pay special attention to the details. Notice that it does not say "driver's license." Notice that the second type of license for which the States must obtain a SSN is a "commercial driver's license". It just so happens that there is a 170 million license difference between "commercial" drivers and regular non-commercial drivers!
>
> Back in 1996 when HR 3734 was being debated it was much easier to overcome opposition to the SSN requirement with it applying

---

[3] The Deadbeat Dad's database was defined in Title III, Subtitle B, Section 313 of the bill. Other sections of interest include 311-317, 369 — nearly everything in the 300s.

to only the 10 million or so "commercial" drivers in the country. There's simply fewer numbers of negatively affected subjects out there to raise objections when the legislation only imposes upon a relatively small segment of the population as this bill first did.

However, just one year after the SSN requirements were implemented, Congress DELETED the word "COMMERCIAL" from this section of the Act. Thereby, they changed the scope of the SSN requirement so that now ALL 180 MILLION LICENSED DRIVERS in the country must give a SSN in order to get a driver's license. By deleting that one word: "commercial" the "Balanced Budget Act of 1997" served to expand the scope of Title 42 U.S.C. 666(a)(13) from what *was* a relatively small group of about 10 million commercial drivers so as to now include all of the nearly 180 million non-commercial licensed drivers in the U.S.

DO NOT THINK that the people responsible for drafting this legislation just "forgot" to include the additional 170 million drivers on the first go-around.... not on your life. They intended to enact the softly worded version first. Then, they simply waited a year and surreptitiously modified the wording to consummate their dirty deed. It was intended all along.

P.S. Just to cheer you up even more, the alleged welfare reform law also calls for utility companies — water, electric, phone, cable TV — to report customers to the government. And guess what they'll use to identify you? Your Number.

The Kennedy-Kassebaum health care data "transmission standards"

True stealth legislation. Not only did few people know this little time-bomb was buried in the "moderate" health care bill (HR 3101, now PL 104-191), but the beastie was couched in language making it seem harmless — even protective.

This law requires that all health care data transmitted in the U.S. conform to federally established standards — and that each person whose medical data is transmitted anywhere, by anyone in the health care industry, be coded with a "unique identifying number." (This may be your SS number, though the pro-

posed "regulation" defining the standards has not been published on schedule.)

The states make it worse

Under the Tenth Amendment, the federal government can't actually require the states to do its wishes. While it used to get away with trying, both the states and the Supreme Court have begun getting tetchy lately about the federal government imposing "unfunded mandates" and otherwise intruding on the territory of state governments.

So the federal government doesn't "require" anything. It either bribes the states with development money or threatens to withhold federal money from those who don't obey.

State governments, of course, rush to comply.

Unfortunately, when the states pass the enabling legislation that puts the federal laws in force, they often add even worse provisions of their own.

Here's another report from Scott McDonald on one state's implementation of the alleged Welfare Reform Act:

South Carolina enacted new legislation this year [1997] that implements the federal Social Security number registering, reporting, locating, and tracking requirements. The South Carolina law (S532) was signed into effect by the governor on June 10, 1997. The Act implements at the state level the federal funding requirements imposed by the recently amended federal Social Security Act. Pursuant to S532, all state agencies must now obtain Social Security numbers for divorce decrees; administrative and judicial orders; marriage licenses; occupational and professional licenses; business licenses; drivers' licenses; hunting, fishing, or trapping licenses; paternity orders and acknowledgments; and birth and death certificates.

In other words, in South Carolina you can't work, drive, get married, get divorced, fish, hunt or even DIE...; in fact YOU CAN'T EVEN GET BORN unless you (and your parents) have a Social Security number!!! But don't feel like it's only South Carolina residents who'll be confronted with this problem... you too will be subjected to the same SSN reporting requirements if you live in any state in the United States that receives federal child support grant money — which happens to be... all of them!

Since insurance companies have always had their own requirements and procedures for conveying data, no "unique [national] identifying number" was ever necessary, even though companies used your SSN for their own convenience. So what's the function of the "unique identifier" now?

Well, first of all, with medicine becoming increasingly federalized, the One Master Payer in Washington, DC, needs to keep your records straight. But secondly, even where your entire health history legitimately remains a matter for you, your doctor, and your insurance company — the fedgov simply wants to know.

You are, after all, its "resource."

These "transmission standards" for health care data quite simply end all privacy between physicians and patients forever, and put the most intimate observations about your health into the hands of researchers, bureaucrats, police agencies, and any snoop with access to a database.

As is usual in these cases, we were told (when we were told at all) that these "standards" were needed to make your medical data "more secure" and to "end abuses." And certainly there have been abuses of privacy in private insurance data systems. Now, however, the possibility — nay, the certainty — of abuse has expanded a hundredfold. Because your records are that much easier to find, and that much more freely and easily shared.

A pilot program to give the Social Security Administration prior approval before you can be hired by a private company.

Public Law 104-208 (Division C, Title IV, Subtitle A, Sections 401-404) also called for pilot programs in which private employers are required to "procure" a document reader linked to the Social Security Administration and prospective employees are required to present scannable, SSN-based cards before being allowed to work. The card is swished through the electronic scanner. Then the federal government decides whether or not it will give you permission to have a job.

What if there's an error in the Social Security Administration's records? Ever tried to straighten out an error made by a federal bureaucracy? Have a nice time.

What if someone in Washington, DC, doesn't like you? What if you're a political dissident or have made a personal enemy? Want a job? Not in this country you don't…

It's all true

None of this is fantasy. This is not rumor. This is law.

It doesn't take much imagination to see how these programs, passed at different times but by the same politicians, fit together. We'll be looking at some of those links — and their potential consequences — in Chapter Two.

In the meantime, keep your eyes open. The Republicans and their Democratic partners aren't through yet. Florida Republican congressman Bill McCollum has sponsored legislation (HR 231) to turn the SS card into a photo ID.

And that isn't all. Here's another report from Scott McDonald and "Fight the Fingerprint."

Almost weekly someone will e-mail to the "Fight the Fingerprint" web page wanting to know if they can claim the federal tax credit for their children without having, (or using), a Social Security number.

Typically, these people don't want to number their children and want to know what the law says. Since the law doesn't say that everyone must have a Social Security number, the question regarding claiming children who don't have numbers is an important one. …Here is a quick update on some of the new and proposed requirements for SSNs that we may expect to see in the near future.

Tax credits for children

The requirement to supply a SSN in order to receive the tax credit has steadily increased over the years. And, this year Congress passed the "Taxpayer Relief Act of 1997" (HR 2014) which certainly will serve to "relieve" you of more of your money if you don't use numbers to identify your children. Again our "conservative Congress" as part of the continuation of the "Contract on America" has imposed a new tax stipulation designed to prod all parents who haven't done so already to number their children.

The law, which goes into effect this year, states:

"(e) No credit shall be allowed under this section to a taxpayer with respect to any qualifying child unless the taxpayer includes the name and taxpayer identification number of such qualifying child on the return of tax for the taxable year."

The IRS Code states that the "taxpayer identification number" is a Social Security number. Many people are opposed to numbering our children due to religious beliefs. How much more "relief" can we stand?

And how much more numbering can we stand? We may find out soon enough. Two bills currently being considered by Congress will add still more requirements for using Social Security numbers in order to... VOTE... or to OWN A FIREARM!

Scott goes on to describe the "Voter Eligibility Verification Act," HR 1428, which would, among other provisions "...amend the Social Security Act to permit States to require individuals registering to vote in elections to provide the individual's Social Security number." This act, if passed, would also establish a national "Voter Eligibility Confirmation System" to be maintained by the Attorney General's Office and the Social Security Administration. Then Scott continues as follows:

Perhaps you can be comforted by the following statement which is mockingly included as part of the Act. Section 2(h)(2) states:

"Nothing in this section shall be construed to authorize, directly or indirectly, the issuance or use of national identification cards or the establishment of a national identification card."

This exact same comment about "not establishing a national ID" is also included in the "Illegal Immigration Reform and Immigrant Responsibility Act of 1996," P.L.104-208. Why has our "conservative Congress" felt it necessary to include in two major Acts within a year of each other statements denying that they are establishing a National ID System? The reason is simply that they actually ARE establishing a National Identification System — and they know it — but they think that telling the American People they're NOT will make it so...

Classic "Double Speak."

Scott continues with a description of HR 1998, the "Yates Firearm Registration and Crime Prevention Act of 1997." The act, if passed, would require registration of all firearms in the U.S. — with SS number, photo and fingerprints. And he concludes:

I wonder if this bill could be said to also "not establish a National ID System"? I may be from Alabama but.... If we have to use Social Security numbers to: get a driver's license, register an automobile, establish credit, get a job, get tax relief, obtain a professional business license, get a hunting license, get utility service, and now potentially register a gun and vote — don't we already have a National ID in the form of a Social Security number?

Contact information for "Fight the Fingerprint" is found in the Appendix.

What about fighting within the system?

Activists all over the USA are trying to fight their own states' implementations of these national ID laws and the related laws still being proposed or uncovered.[4]

Notably, these activists include Scott McDonald and his allies in Alabama, Linda Muller, Cyndee Parker and the Coalition to Repeal the Fingerprints Law in Georgia, and Jackie Juntti and friends in Washington state.

In Alabama, they even "won" when their state tried to put fingerprints on drivers' licenses through administrative fiat rather than by law. No fingerprints for Alabama — for the moment.

Yet every single anti-ID activist with whom I've spoken admits theirs is a losing battle. They describe the struggle against a national ID system as "a hold-

---

[4] Not all of the laws require state implementation, but the national ID license and all of the database and licensing provisions of the Welfare Reform Act do because they involve state documents and state administration of programs.

ing action," "a duty," "something I have to try before giving up." But not one of them has a shred of hope of stopping the ID juggernaut by working within the system.

Why? Because national ID is a control freak's wet dream. Because the number of people alive and awake to this issue is small and the opponents of national ID are easily demonized. Because the media won't even address this issue, let alone demand that the enslavement must stop.

But above all, it's a practical matter. You have fifty states in which you have to "win." You have to "win" not against one horror, one bill, but against many — driver's license, deadbeat dad database, professional and recreational licenses, and more databases and ID documents yet unknown. And governments just keep coming up with more, often introducing the same bill four or five times until they can sneak it through or break down the resistance. In Washington state in 1997, activists knocked down that state's proposed ID license. But before the 1998 legislative session began, the proposal was back, pushed by powerful Democrats and alleged conservative Republicans alike. Now Washington has its Big Brother license. This will also happen with federal bills such as the Voter ID or the Gun Registration bill. This will happen with every bill designed to increase the government's power over your life. Those who want to rule are relentless in their will.

And the ultimate loser... Even if your state legislature showed the small degree of spine and principle necessary to turn aside this federal onslaught (and the money that goes with it), your fellow state citizens would soon be crying for the chains of their ID. Because without the national ID license, there will be no federal "services" for people in your state — no passports, no Social Security, no Medicare. If your state refuses to sign up for the New Hires spy system there will be no federal welfare dollars. The federal government has taken your own money and is using it as a bludgeon to beat you into submission. It is using that money as a fruit to tempt your state legislature into selling its soul.

It works. Your legislature has already been bought and sold — and so have the majority of people who once were free American citizens.

Win your freedom through fighting *this* kind of government, using *its own* rules? No way.

The web of laws described above constitutes nothing but a slave system...or something like the computerized methods farmers use to track their livestock — which amounts to the same thing. It *is* a slave system — *and slaves do not win freedom by politely asking their masters for it.* Or by voting themselves out of it. Or by any other genteel and gentle method.

If you want to try to fight it within the system, I sincerely wish you well. This book is, after all, dedicated to the people who are doing just that. I don't believe they have a chance of succeeding — and they don't either. But I admire them for following some inner voice. Something tells them there was once a free America and that free citizens had a role to play in its governance. That America is gone, but I admire their sense of dedication to it.

The activists may not like this analogy, but I see them as being something like the dog that sleeps each night on its dead master's grave. They are loyal and hopeful beyond reason, but loyal and hopeful to a degree that evokes sad admiration.

Above all, I believe these persistent activists bear watching as a kind of weather gauge of the freedom movement. They may be the ones to tell us when a crucial moment in our history has come. For on the day when these most tenacious, patient, hopeful souls finally say, "No more!" the tyrants truly had better tremble.

I wish the activists well, but I believe it's time to move on to other methods.

We now live in ID State America — a system in which human cattle are catalogued with Beast Numbers. Let's call these things what they are. Let's not honor tyrants and their tyrannies with civil euphemisms.

Update 2002
What's New
Since Chapter One

The SSN-based driver's license was implemented on schedule in forty-nine of the fifty states. (Some states, of course, had already had such a license, even before the federal government mandated it.) Only

Michigan fought it, bringing suit in early 2001 against the federal government on the very correct grounds that the license violated citizens' privacy.[5]

This sweeping nationwide adoption happened despite the fact that the few freedom lovers in Congress (led by Ron Paul (R-TX) in the House and Richard Shelby (R-AL) in the Senate) actually thought they'd performed a miracle and *repealed* that provision of HR 3610 in 1999.

How could a law that was repealed end up being implemented anyway? More on that shortly.

By now most people are so used to this de facto national ID card that some might wonder what all the thunder was about. "Gee, we've been living with it now for X years and we're not slaves yet." Please don't ever take that attitude. Getting used to the loss of freedom, just like the frog gets used to a little higher temperature in the pot, is the most foolish thing we can do.

For a faithfully updated tally of which intrusive features states are currently requiring on their licenses, and for other news about the status of the ID driver's license, check the Fight the Fingerprint Web site, listed in the Appendix.

IDs for the Unnumbered

Although the legislation creating an SSN-based driver's license made no provision for people who don't have Social Security numbers and refused to get them, many states do enable the Unnumbered to sign affidavits stating that they have no Slave Number.

Language on the government-supplied affidavits is different from state to state. Some affidavits require you to declare that you have never had an SSN, while other states make the language so vague that you could swear to an SSN-less state even if you'd had a Number for most of your life. (It seems a lot of licensing bureaucrats really don't like the SSN requirements and are more than willing to save themselves the pain of dealing with angry protesters, especially the few angry protesters who might have good lawyers.)

I know of at least one person who lives in a state that requires SSN-objectors to swear they've never had a Number, who customized his own affidavit, stating that he had given up the Beastly thing. He was given a license with no hassle.

The repealed law that wasn't

It's important to remember the process by which HR 3610 — the legislation that first gave us the national ID driver's license — was ultimately passed. Remember the kitchen-sink provisions, the gigantic unread bill passed in a rush, unread by those who imposed it upon us. This has become standard operating procedure, with many bills dwarfing this one in size. What ghastly police-state content lies undiscovered in these bills, perhaps for years, before storming out to destroy our freedom?

Remember that the national ID license was actually repealed? If that's the case, why did the states go ahead with implementation of an SSN-based license by the original date of October 2000?

They did it in part because of the *other* national ID driver's license trickery mentioned in this chapter — the removal in 1997 of the word "commercial" from the driver's license provisions in the Deadbeat Dads act. Unprincipled congresscritters (or is that redundant?) knew that one of their hidden national ID plans might be discovered and shot down. So, as they habitually do now, they created and hid another one. Amid the cheers of repeal, these serpents of hell were hissing with glee at our foolishness. The only thing we can be thankful for is that the national ID license that remained is the milder one — requiring SS but no biometrics. (States, however, are free to impose biometric requirements of their own, and many have.)

But don't go getting optimistic about the temporary absence of biometrics.

The American Association of Motor Vehicle Administrators (AAMVA) — the order-minded, control-

---

[5] Some other states apparently found the requirement cumbersome. They found that it resulted in a huge number of unlicensed drivers on their roads. In early 2001, Tennessee removed its mandatory SSN requirement. A news release of June 22 of that year from Governor Don Sundquist reports that applications for licenses doubled in the month after the new law went into effect.
(http://www.state.tn.us/governor/jun2001/driverslicense.htm.
However, after September 11, the Tennessee state legislature had second thoughts and began debating whether to issue only drivers' "certificates," not useable as ID, to people without SSNs.

minded bureaucrats who were the (pardon the expression) driving factor behind the national ID driver's license in the first place, continue to push for further development of this license into a true national ID card, complete with biometric identifiers. And the media — those few outlets that even bother to report this — all seem blissfully unaware that this is part of a long ongoing effort on AAMVA's part. With virtually no exceptions, they're all treating it as a new development, a patriotic response to terrorism.

(By the way, has anybody figured out yet why we even have government-issued driver's licenses? Why aren't certifications of our competency to drive issued by driving schools or insurance companies, for instance? The only reason for the government to be in it: money and control. As Carl Watner (editor of *The Voluntaryist*) pointed out, the first state drivers' licenses were just money-raising schemes, having nothing to do with one's ability to drive. Several states didn't even require road tests until well into the 1950s — though they had been issuing licenses for thirty or forty years before that. From early twentieth-century "revenue enhancement" to early twenty-first-century de facto national ID, the driver's license has always served the government's purpose, not the claimed purpose of public safety.)

• • • • • • •

It gets worse.

In July 2002, when President Bush announced his formal plan for homeland security, the plan included a provision that no foreign visitors would be allowed into the U.S. without biometric ID. It also contained a promise to work with international governments on developing and implementing biometric travel documents worldwide. At the same time, the administration piously mouthed its conviction that drivers' licenses were the province of the states, not the federal government.

In other words, without coming out and saying the politically suicidal words "national ID," the Bush administration pledged to help foreign governments develop *global* biometric ID. And lied about it. Biometric travel documents certainly means biometric passports for Americans and everyone else. But the administration has also continued to work quietly with the AAMVA on its plans for full biometric licenses and Ellison-like databases.

Under these plans, you won't be "allowed" to travel anywhere in the world without governments recording your movements via your Number or your digitized biometric ID. Eventually, those of us who fall out of governments' graces may not be allowed to travel at all, just like dissidents in the old Soviet Union.

Since both drivers' licenses and passports are also used as general ID documents — increasingly so — gradually the lifeline of free and independent people is being choked off.

The good news

Along the way, there's still good news.

On having to give an SSN to get a hunting or fishing license: This requirement still applies and isn't it nauseating standing in a sporting goods store, listening to the good little serfs publicly recite their very private Social Security numbers in exchange for the privilege of being allowed to catch game on the master's estates? But in practice not many store clerks, or even fish and game bureaucrats will force you to comply with this requirement if you politely refuse. I also know people who always give a scrambled or false SSN to get sporting licenses; they've never yet paid any consequences.

Professional licenses are another matter. Because of the databases these are tied into and all the opportunities for cross-referencing, it's much more difficult to get away with refusing or lying. Refuse and you won't get the license. Lie and the databases may tell on you.

Why the hell do we need government permits to practice professions, anyway? It's not as if these permits protect the public by eliminating bad doctors, crooked contractors, or snaky attorneys. Another money-making and petty control scheme gone awry. By all means, if you're in a profession that requires a government license, consider whether it's feasible to practice your profession in freedom, underground.

Easy? No. Risk free? No. But freedom-producing? Yes. What if we build a society in which independent boards, schools, insurance companies, and other bodies issued certificates of professional competency — with no temptation to use such certifications to run our lives or break us on the wheel of politics?

The health-care identifier

The provisions for a "unique health-care identifier" in the Kennedy-Kassebaum health-care bill have had perhaps the most interesting history of all.

The good news is that the handful of diligent Congresspeople, led (as nearly always) by Ron Paul (R-TX) have managed to get the identifying number defunded every time it's come up for authorization. So as of now you aren't required by federal law to give a number to your doctor.

Some doctors will still refuse to treat you or will put you though all kinds of hell if you won't give them your slave number. That's unfortunate, but at this point it's still their private decision and their business. You can walk out of their offices and go elsewhere.

The law mandating the health-care number still exists, unfortunately. It just hasn't been implemented yet.

I was wrong to state flatly that your SSN will eventually be used as your "unique health-care identifier." It may be. But there's been talk of making this a more sophisticated type of number with built-in devices against fakery — for instance, a portion of the number that, unknown to you, is a code indicating your birthdate, place of birth, blood type, or is a "check digit" that can be matched with the rest of the number to detect a lie or an error.

And although the "unique health-care identifier" is — for now — not required to receive medical care, when the U.S. Department of Health and Human Services promulgated its standards for electronic transmission of your private data, they put in a database field for the number. So they're ready, whether or not we are.

Finally, if you don't believe yet that Republicans are just Democrats who smoke their cigars instead of using them as sex toys: The G.W. Bush administration, in its first weeks in office, got the chance to kill (or at least seriously mutilate) the anti-freedom provisions of the Kennedy-Kassebaum law — and they chose not to do it.

Although the law was passed in 1996, it took the Clinton Health and Human Services bureaucrats nearly four years to produce the implementing regulations for it. These regs were rushed out in the final weeks of Clinton's presidency.

They were rushed out too fast, as it turns out. The Clintonistas goofed and forgot to leap through all the bureaucratic hoops needed to put the regs into effect. The incoming Bush people had the chance to send the regs back where they belonged — into oblivion or at least into rewrite. But no, the Bushy-tailed statists decided to let the Clinton regs go through, anyway, with only the most minor alterations. The freedom-loving G.W. Bush overruled his own secretary of Health and Human Services, Tommy Thompson, to make sure this extra bit of tyranny was imposed on schedule.

Although the regs don't contain the numbering provisions, they are full of ghastly antiprivacy clauses, which are called, of course, "privacy protection" measures. These allow data about you to be sold to marketers, used for research, turned over to law enforcement without a warrant, and so on. There are indeed huge penalties for medical professionals who violate your privacy without the government's authorization, but the *permitted* violations are so broad (and the language about them so fuzzy) that any pretense of protection is a joke. One of the most egregious omissions is something that ought to be the first line in any defense of privacy; there's no provision requiring that you must give your consent before the selling and trading of your data can begin.

Voter registration and firearms

In the struggle for ownership of identity, individuals have lost a lot of freedom since 1996. But because of rising protest and a few Congressional heroes, the erosion hasn't been as precipitous as it might have been.

The SSN requirement is gradually moving into voter registration, as this chapter hinted, but it's not totally there yet. A 1993 federal appeals court case, *Greidinger v Davis*, temporarily put a damper on states' use of SSNs to ID voters, but as ID-mania takes hold at all levels of government, and as people sheepishly tolerate it, bills to require SSNs of all voters are repeatedly introduced. One of the latest was the glowingly named "Martin Luther King, Jr. Equal Protection of Voting Rights Act of 2002," HR 3295, hotly debated but not quite passed by Congress in 2001 and 2002.

You can't buy a firearm from a dealer without giving an SSN (although no law requires it; it's simply a fiat act on the part of the FBI). You can, however, still own firearms or buy from private purchasers without giving the Beastly Number — until John McCain and his other anti-gun pals in Washington succeed in "closing the gun-show loophole." The "gun-show loophole" has nothing to do with gun shows (where all licensed dealers have to comply with all the Brady Law tracking requirements, including asking for your SSN). It's simply aimed at regulating and tracking *all* firearms sales, including those between private parties. And your purchases will be tracked by your SSN.

Don't forget: As Aaron Zelman and his compatriots at Jews for the Preservation of Firearms Ownership have documented (most notably in Aaron's and Richard Stevens' *Death by "Gun Control"* and in the video documentary *Innocents Betrayed*), governments disarm citizens before committing genocide. And registration, licensing, and tracking of firearms purchases and ownership makes it easy to do that. When a government gets ready to move against a group of people, it uses national ID records (including census records listing race and religion) and centralized firearms records to find the group targeted for genocide and to know which of its members might be armed. Then it bans and confiscates the weapons from the target group (and from all other political opponents, as well).

Final Word on Chapter One

All is not lost — yet. We can be glad that public anger has forced the pace to be slower than it was planned to be. But in a way, that's unfortunate, too, since it just gives us more opportunity to become passive froggies in a more slowly and comfortably heating pot. And that pot is still inexorably heating.

I Am Not a Number!

Chapter Two
Life in ID State America

When the Hutu militias... began their genocidal massacres of Tutsis in April, they needed only to ask for identity cards to decide who lived and who were chopped or speared to death. Like Protais Gahigi, a 38-year-old Tutsi man with five children who were all murdered in the church at a Spanish mission at Musha in eastern Rwanda. The card was picked up recently by Carlos Mavrolean, a cameraman for the American Broadcasting Corporation. He said it was lying on the floor, not far from the altar. Among the splintered pews and scraps of clothing on the floor were three unexploded grenades and a discarded machete. The blood on the card was still sticky.
— *Richard Dowden, "Identity card was passport to death",* The Independent, *London, 7th July 1994*

"Papiere, bitte."
"Your papers, comrade."

Is it really going to get that bad in America? Checkpoints? Travel papers? Internal passports?

No, it's not going to get that bad.

It's going to get worse. Because this U.S. government has something neither the Nazis nor the Soviets possessed. Powerful, fast computer systems capable of handling many terabytes of data, accessible in a moment.

Don't get me wrong. This is not an antitechnology rant. Computers have tremendous power to increase our freedom, as well as to damage it.

They are, like guns, a tool that can be used for protection or coercion.

The way they are about to be used against us by the compulsive control freaks in government, how-

ever, makes death by machine gun look like the more humane alternative.

The worst problem with the national ID card isn't the card itself — though every member of Congress who voted for it should be given a fair trial, then hanged as a traitor. (And while we're at it, let's drive stakes through their hearts to make sure they don't come back some midnight to vote for something worse.) The card is an outrage, an injustice, an abomination against freedom. It is precisely analogous to the plastic tag in a cow's ear or the tattoo upon the arm of a concentration camp inmate.

But as bad as the card is, it is merely a key to far greater domains of evil.

How bad is life going to get in the ID Society?

The short answer is: Worse than Orwell ever imagined.

The slightly longer answer is that three different, but related, forms of invasion will be hitting us at the same time. They are:

1. The ID card or other ID device;
2. Databases that can be accessed using your Beast Number; and,
3. Sophisticated surveillance and biometric measurement techniques now being developed and implemented.

These three will work together to change your life, rapidly, into something most people couldn't even have imagined a few decades ago.

Let's take a look at the impact of each, then make some projections about the impact of them all together over the next few years.

The ID card or device

This is a done thing. This is what Congress passed upon us and what your state may now be in the process of implementing. Although Congress is currently considering refinements upon it and new variations of it, it is part of our present reality.[1]

You must have a Beast Number before you'll be awarded the "privilege" of traveling on the nation's streets and highways.

In some cases, your Beast Number and "insecurity" features may be encoded on a magnetic strip or barcode. In other cases, your state may have already moved ahead to the next level of technology, the smart card, which contains a microchip. The microchip can contain much more information than the mag strip, and can enable your card to be used in a variety of applications.

According to a British government report on smart cards:

> In the European public sector, smart cards are increasingly being used as portable personal files — for health records, for example, or to store and update details of eligibility for benefits.
>
> A smart card can authenticate the holder, authenticate the card and authorize transactions, carrying out all these tasks off-line. It is much more secure than a magnetic stripe card; it has the processing capabilities of a small microcomputer and can store large amounts of information....
> — A report from CCTA: The Government Centre for Information Systems

Although you can expect the uses of your new federalized ID card to grow like Godzilla over time, even the card's initial impact will be pretty damned monstrous.

As soon as the Beast Card is in place in your state, it will be either impossible or increasingly difficult to do any of the following without it:[2]

- Get a passport
- Receive Social Security
- Get Medicare or Medicaid
- Get private insurance
- Apply for a fishing license
- Get Supplemental Security Income
- Drive
- Apply for welfare or food stamps
- Board an airplane
- Apply for a hunting license
- Rent government housing or receive housing vouchers
- Receive *any* form of federal service for which ID is required. This could include such things as getting care at a government hospital
- Attend college
- Practice your trade as a plumber or electrician
- Win a government contract
- Enroll your child in public school
- Cash a check
- Work as a truck driver
- Get any medical care covered by insurance
- Buy liquor (if you are young)
- Buy cigarettes (if you are 27 or younger)

---

[1] The 104th Congress also passed not one, but two, laws requiring production of scannable social security cards. One of these was in HR 3610 (Public Law 104-208, Division C, Title VI, Subtitle D, Section 657), the other in HR 3734 (Title I, Section 111 of the bill).

[2] Some of the items on this list may require you to have the state-issued national ID card. Others may simply require your SS number. Throughout this book you might catch me fuzzing the distinction between things for which—at the moment — you'll need an ID card and things for which — at the moment — you'll merely need to write down a Beast Number. I apologize for any such fuzzing. There may be readers of this book who expect to keep and use their SS numbers for some purposes (getting a job; paying taxes), but who want to keep that number from otherwise becoming a universal identifier. However, I may continue to meld the two aspects of the ID issue for two reasons: 1) because ID and SS themselves are merging so totally that there will soon be no real distinction between them and 2) because I believe the entire SS/ID/citizen-tracking database system *as a whole* should be rejected and done away with. If you want to have an SS number without ID or to have state ID without your SS number, fingerprints or other intrusions, good luck to you. But I think it is time to say good riddance to the entire package.

Also, keep in mind that while the *federal* law does not require state or local governments to use only the federally designed ID, the states themselves are almost certain to pass such requirements on state agencies. Local governments — particularly in major cities or border areas — will certainly follow suit.

- Practice your trade as a hairdresser
- Work legally as a licensed nurse
- Apply for a scholarship or student loan
- Work as a taxi or bus driver, both of which require licenses
- Buy or sell real estate (licensed)
- Practice medicine legally (licensed)
- Practice law (licensed)
- Enter a courtroom; possibly enter other public offices, depending on the level of "security" currently in vogue
- Get a document notarized
- Get utilities hooked up to your new home
- Rent a motel or hotel room
- Buy a car
- Adopt a pet
- Apply for a library card (in some places)
- Withdraw money from an ATM
- And a lot more.

So what's new?

As you're probably observing, some of these are things you'd *already* have difficulty doing without a driver's license or state non-driver ID. Today, however, other forms of ID are acceptable for most purposes. You can use a birth certificate, credit cards, personalized checks, in some cases even envelopes with your name and address on them, to satisfy others of your identity.

None of these currently available alternate methods require a Universal Citizen Identification Number. And none of them key into databases as extensive as those the federal government is creating (a vital matter, as we'll see in a minute).[3]

The list above also contains quite a few things principled freedom lovers ought not be doing anyhow. Applying for welfare or food stamps? If you're the kind who wants to protest the wrongs of government while sucking up government's benefits, you don't belong here. On the other hand, if you're de-

pendent on government's benefits because you honestly can't survive without a government disability check or food stamps, then you won't be able to escape the ID State even if you want to.

Nevertheless, maybe all of the above sounds like no big deal. Maybe the National Slave Card seems like nothing more than one more extension of what you're already putting up with. Just one more degree of heat under the pot. You can take it... sure you can...

But the next level of danger lies in the databases that are increasingly being put under your Citizen ID Number, and that can be accessed by snoops in government bureaus, enforcement agencies, industry, research facilities, or by private hackers.

Step two: tying into databases

Remember the mention of cigarette buying a while back? As I was working on the second draft of this chapter, the following *Los Angeles Times* news story came across my desk. It concerns 7-Eleven stores in California, a state that already has "advanced" features on its IDs:

> The next time you walk into a 7-Eleven to buy cigarettes or beer and you look underage, a clerk will probably ask to scan your driver's license. A small electronic device will allow clerks to quickly determine whether you're old enough to make the purchase. The scanner reads information coded onto a magnetic strip on the back of a driver's license or state-issued ID, which includes a person's name, birth date, address, height and weight....
>
> [A 7-Eleven spokesperson] added that the box does not access motor vehicle records; nor does it create a buying profile of the customer.... The scanners could save store owners from federal penalties of up to $1,000 per violation.
>
> "If this is an additional way to verify someone's identity, then great. But if clerks are scanning the ID without checking, then the machine doesn't help," said John Banzhaf, executive director of Action on Smoking and Health, an anti-smoking group. Jerry Hook, a 7-Eleven marketing manager based in the San

---

[3] Most birth certificates don't *presently* enable easy access to data. However, the same section of Public Law 104-208 that redefined your driver's license also mandates new, federal birth-certificate standards. Once again the fedgov is offering "grants" to states to bow to its wishes, and state legislators and bureaucrats are happy to comply. Look for all birth certificates soon to contain the newborn's SS number.

Francisco Bay Area, said the company is aware the technology is not foolproof. "The VeriFone equipment alone cannot guarantee that illegal sales will never be made."

A message from a friend

Just a brief note on the topic of your newest book project: I'm beginning to feel like we already have a national ID system, even though it may be a patchwork one.

Consider this.

I received a recall letter from my car manufacturer at my new address. No big deal — except that I never informed the manufacturer I had changed my address. Obviously they got it from the VIN number of my car, which links my mailing address through the state DMV computers. I suppose the IRS has access to these computers if a car manufacturer does.

This kind of thing is the reason I took up the Republic of Texas tags. But that landed me in jail.

Tried to rent a video the other day.

The store demands a phone number (they even ask for SS number!) in order to open a rental account. I thought about making up a number which probably would have done the trick, but instead decided to be honest and see what I'd learn about the system. As soon as the supervisor realized I didn't have a "permanent address" or phone and didn't want either of them — she looked at me like a nigger of sorts. I called her attention to the fact that nobody has a "permanent" address, since we are a very mobile society. I politely told her I was in sympathy with their concern about videos not being returned and offered to give her $100 cash deposit. I also explained how easy it would be for anyone to make up a phone number if they wanted to steal videos. She said they weren't "set up" to take cash deposits and rejected my application.

Phone numbers or bills establishing "residency" are often asked for as forms of "secondary ID," I am learning. Now I need to decide whether to take up petty forgery or not.

— Pat

If, by the way, you believe both the state of California and the giant Southland Corporation (owner of 7-Eleven) are serious about not "creating databases on customers" or accessing existing databases, I'd like a little of whatever you've been smoking.

Southland Corporation *will* create databases on customers, if not now, then soon, *simply because it has the ability to do so*. It *will* begin scanning all customers, not just alcohol and cigarette buyers *because it's "easier" and less confrontation-provoking to scan everyone*. Also because the corporation wants the data.

And the state of California *will* one day — mark this — get the bright idea of using 7-Eleven scanning systems to "help catch criminals." The state will then not only *allow* Southland to access state databases; it will *require* the convenience store chain to do so. In the name of "public safety."

The systems *will* be altered to access not only DMV records, but other police records, the New Hires database and other state and federal data. Then, when someone with an outstanding warrant, a past-due child-support bill or an unpaid parking ticket attempts to make a purchase at a 7-Eleven, the system will automatically alert the cops. The cops will take a break from their donuts long enough to catch a "criminal" they were too lazy to find through their own investigative efforts.

Paranoid? But this is exactly the type of lazy, yet intrusive, "law enforcement" governments are coming to prefer. When technology allows it, governments will do it.

Now let's look at what happens in a system with those same capabilities when you, Joe or Josie Innocent, make a purchase at the 7-Eleven.

Into some database goes a record of both your purchase and your chemical habits. Actually, once the technology has reached this level of sophistication, the data will include more than your chemical habits. At this point, the databases will be collecting information on everything you purchase, so stores can tailor promotions to local and even individual buying habits. Perhaps even so they can mail you discount coupons customized to your habits. And Southland's database, of course, will be available to the state government. And the state shares all data widely with other states, localities, universities, and the federal government.

"But I don't care. I've got nothing to hide. I'm not a deadbeat dad or a criminal. And anyway, I think it's pretty cool that stores will be sending me coupons for the things they know I like to buy."

Okay, so look at a scenario concocted for me by syndicated columnist Vin Suprynowicz:

> I don't think we've even *started* to paint a vision of what life would be like under the *full* electronic ID they now propose. You go into the bank to cash a check, and your account has insufficient funds — maybe something as innocent as your spouse failing to note a withdrawal on the joint account, or maybe the IRS seized your entire $10,000 account to get your attention. This means you're asked to produce your "ID card" and wait while some assistant-manager twerp with a nose stud "checks your records."

> You watch the expression on his pimply face as he calls you up on his screen, noting that you're almost finished with a course of ampicillin for an infection of the urethra (wonder how she got *that),* that you have permits to own THREE handguns (he pushes a buzzer, and you notice that the armed security guard comes over and stands directly behind you). The IRS, of course, has planted a "red flag" code which sounds a buzzer in their nearby office whenever anyone accesses your account history, since they're a bit concerned that you haven't called their office to "voluntarily" schedule that audit appointment.

> Now, the wet-behind-the-ears bank "assistant manager" receives a real-time e-mail message to "delay suspect there until our agents can arrive."

> Knowing you've left a child in your hot car in the sun, you snatch the card from his hand, say "This is ridiculous," and try to leave. Afraid of being asked why he let you go, the trainee banker panics and shouts to the security guard, "Watch out, she's armed and the G-men want her held!" The rest of the customers dive for the floor as the fat old man draws his gun, trying to remember whether the thumb safety goes up or down ...

> I'm sure with a little thought we can develop some even more Kafkaesque (but thoroughly likely) scenarios. What, for instance, would happen to someone who *LOST* her ID card, or who had her ID card stolen by some criminal who knew how to defeat the "personal security" code, and who vindictively or purely for profit used the ID card to get into places where the thief then stole arms, plutonium, or sensitive government documents?

> What might happen if someone entered some WRONG data on your card?

...or in your database?

Farfetched?

Believe me, this is farfetched only because the databases aren't quite that complete yet. The technology exists to do all of the above. All that's necessary is to get the data into the computers — and to get it in there under one "unique identifying number." Then the world is open to anyone with the authorization or the talent to retrieve your records.

Don't believe that a bank could — accidentally or on purpose — access your health records? Do you believe the government when it talks about the "security" of data?

Then I suggest you visit the web page of "The Stalker," Glen L. Roberts, who has made a personal crusade out of exposing the government's "mistakes" with confidential information. Visit The Stalker's site (See Appendix). On any day, you're likely to find pointers to web sites where government agencies, schools, and other institutions have *publicly* posted dozens, even hundreds, of Social Security numbers, complete with additional identifying information about the numbers' owners.

Universities have put the Social Security numbers of all their students on the Internet. The BATF has published the numbers of its agents. The Securities and Exchange Commission regularly publishes confidential data on business executives — all available for anyone who wants to snag it.

The Stalker, being an honorable sort, posts pointers to this information, then immediately informs the institutions that he has done so. After Roberts exposed the fact that the University of Indiana had published confidential Social Security numbers on its employees, a university rep wrote Roberts a rather snippy letter. The university, the spokescreature said, truly valued the privacy of employees. It assured Roberts that the university had removed the information from public access, and that it had all been a horrifying "mistake."

Roberts then wrote back to point out that, if the university really, truly had such undying respect for the privacy of its employees it wouldn't — *Oops!* — still have *other* web sites up — containing yet more SS numbers!

Spend a few minutes thinking about the ways this information could be used to violate lives, ruin reputations, steal funds, and otherwise harm the poor suckers who trustingly gave their SS numbers. There have *already* been cases of employers getting confidential health data on their employees. Banks, phone companies, and other institutions have turned customers' records over to government officials without even asking for a warrant or a subpoena. There have been cases of politicians ruining their opponents' reputations with "confidential" data from psychologists or state agencies.

Think about the potential impact of this when everything from your health records to your liquor-buying habits are stored under a single number. Think about the impact when the drive to make information fully sharable between governments, social service agencies, universities, and other members of the statist in-crowd has reached fruition. Think about the impact when banks, utility companies and other institutions may be required by law to open all their data indiscriminately. (Illegal? Well, so what? Half of what we're living with now was forbidden to governments a few years ago. Most of the laws those Republicans passed in 1996 violated Congress' own Privacy Act. Don't imagine mere illegality would stop a power lover for a minute. They'll just pass a law that makes anything they want "legal.") Think about what could happen if some bureaucrat or freelance villain got hold of your personal number and went database hopping.[4]

You could spend a lifetime learning how much greater that harm will be when there is vastly more

data available — and all of it stored under the Beast Number. I'm positive that I'm missing a thousand other horrors as I write about these few.

But still… stupid database tricks don't even begin to cover the chicanery various governments are up to. And in the final of our three areas of danger — surveillance — governments are aided dramatically by industries that are pursuing technology without forethought and by a media that turns a blind eye (or a lying tongue) to disaster.

Before we move on to surveillance technologies, a pair of quick warnings about things you might not want so thoroughly databased…

Databases and your children

In mid-1997, Bill Clinton proposed a national database in which to record the complete vaccination records of all children in the U.S. He claimed that "most people" can't track their children's medical records, even when it may have "something to do with whether their children live or die." Are you that stupid and careless, do you suppose? Are "most people" that careless and stupid?

Whether you are or not, the federal government thinks the country needs yet another database.

Also, according to British researcher Sean Gabb:[5]

In the United States… the education system is fast acquiring a national network of electronic student records. Its purpose is to allow the exchange of information between various agencies, both public and private, and the continuous tracking of individuals through school and higher education, through the armed forces, through the criminal justice system, through their civilian careers, and through their use of the medical services. At the moment, these databases are being fed "only" the following information:

- An "electronic portfolio" for every student, containing personal essays and other completed work that has been submitted on computer disk;
- Assessments by teachers of every student's work and work-related behavior;

---

[4] Here's a cute database trick for you. In November of 1997, as I was speaking to an activist group on the subject of national ID, one young woman in the audience pulled out her South Dakota driver's license. Her Beast Number was clearly visible on the face of the card. She reported, however, that she had *neither been asked to give her SS number, nor told that the number would be used.* She had simply given her name, birthdate and address — and the state of South Dakota had found and used her SS number without permission.

---

[5] "A Libertarian Conservative Case Against Identity Cards," by Sean Gabb. First published by the Libertarian Alliance, London, 1994, as Political Notes 98, ISBN 1-85637-268-5.

- Every student's Social Security Number, to allow later additions from other databases.
  - The National Education Goals Panel, a Federal committee set up under the Goals 2000 Act 1993 to coordinate the national reform of education, has recommended as "essential" the adding of further information to these portfolios, this to include:
- Month and extent of first prenatal care;
- Birth weight;
- Name, type, and number of years in a pre-school program;
- Poverty status;
- Physical, emotional, and other development at ages five and six;
- Date of last routine health and dental care;
- Activities away from school;
- Type and hours per week of community service;
- Name of post-secondary institution attended;
- Post-secondary degree or credential;
- Employment status;
- Type of employment and employer's name;
- Whether registered to vote.
  - It also notes other "data elements useful for research and school management purposes":
- Names of persons living in student household;
- Relationship of those persons to student;
- Highest level of education for "primary care-givers";
- Total family income;
- Public assistance status and years of benefits;
- Number of moves in the last five years;
- Nature and ownership of dwelling.

Though intended mainly for the authorities, access to these records is available also to private agencies. This is intended. In *Together We Can*, a book published jointly by the U.S. Department of Education and the U.S. Department of Health and Human Services, there is talk of "overcoming the confidentiality barrier." The purpose of the new databases is to give all agencies "ready access to each other's data."

Is there anything they *aren't* tracking, these days?

The following news item on the Unabomber investigation was sent to me by correspondent Eric Gray. Emphasis is mine:

They worked elbow to elbow inside the aging San Francisco federal building, agents from the FBI and the Bureau of Alcohol, Tobacco and Firearms and U.S. postal inspectors. They crunched and recrunched scraps of data through a massive parallel-processing computer borrowed from the Pentagon, sifting through school lists, driver's-license registries, *lists of people who had checked certain books out of libraries in California and the Middle West.* "It was just an incredibly complicated jigsaw puzzle," says a former FBI agent who worked on the case....

Sherry Wood, the Lincoln librarian, is equally tight-lipped, though one of the library's unpaid volunteers has described [Kaczynski's] reading habits to the press.

This is not simply a matter of the *federales* accessing routine library records — though that in itself would be invasive enough. The article doesn't say so, but the mentioned lists are almost certainly a compilation from the FBI's Library Assistance Program. The feds have convinced libraries to keep records on patrons who check out "suspicious" books. ("Suspicious" being defined by the professional paranoids of the FBI.) Although, in most cases, the library records simply "lie fallow" until needed for an investigation, you could also be directly reported to the feds if your librarian gets huffy enough at your reading habits. And guess what? Libraries are increasingly requiring patrons' Social Security numbers.

Surveillance technologies: The future is closer than they want you to know

A correspondent, who prefers to be known as Bad-sheep, sent me this the other day from Columbus, Ohio:

On the bus to the movies, this paddy wagon passed us. This girl in front of me said to her friend, "You see what they got in there? They got that thing where you put your hand on it and they can tell who you are."

OTHER GIRL: "No way."

"I'm serious! They say, 'put your hand right here' and they know who you are. This one cop, I was talking to him and he showed me. They got ME in there; I said DANG! They been having that about two months now."

On the bus back I was going for the last empty seat and I banged my head on something projecting down from the ceiling, which I didn't expect because there's never been anything projecting down from bus ceilings before. Once I had seated myself and massaged my poor noggin I looked up. It was CAMERAS. Two of them, positioned in-line along the axis of the bus, back to back. You're thinking now what I saw immediately: namely, that dumb-ass Big Brother failed to overlap the view, and the seats directly below the cameras would be invisible to them. Well, I know where I'm sitting from now on. I asked the driver and he said for sure the bus has a VCR but he didn't think they transmit back to the base. I'm sure they will soon.

Perhaps for some of you, this is no big news. You may be used to schools with metal detectors, sniff-searches of lockers, cameras on street corners, airport searches, unmanned radar installations that snap photos of your speeding car, DUI roadblocks, seatbelt roadblocks, and more.

I haven't personally seen a handprint ID system like the one Badsheep mentions, but I do know that a digital fingerprint ID system very much like it is being manufactured and sold by Digital Biometrics of Minnetonka, Minnesota. And in January 1997 (according to *CJ Technology News*) a company called Printrak International Inc. sold the Romanian National Police (those champions of freedom) a $2.3 million fingerprint scanning system with "latent and ten-print capture station," and a 600,000 record database. If Romania's got that, just think what rich U.S. jurisdictions are getting.

The cameras, of course, have become old hat. Ho hum.

The fact that you *are* used to such things is a sign of how far off-track this country has come — and how late we are to kick off such Big Brotherish burdens.

That's the past, however. The future is rushing toward us at an incredible pace. The following technologies are just a few of the many that either have been introduced in the last few years, are going online as I write, or are being prepared for near-future release:

- Facial recognition software for driver's license photos capable of recognizing you from your photo, or of finding your photo, SS number, and other information from viewing your face. West Virginia and Polaroid have already agreed to put the first such system online.

- Facial recognition video. Walk into a courthouse or police station and have the cameras and computers recognize you, record and report your presence. Reportedly, both these facial recognition technologies are capable of defeating such disguises as wigs, beards, mustaches and eyeglasses because they work off the basic measurements of your facial features.

- Nets that can be shot by police from special guns to ensnare fleeing suspects.

- Similar devices to entrap "suspects" from a distance in wads of goo shot from a gun.

- "Crowd control" or siege-breaking devices that work by inducing nausea via sound waves.

- Pinheadsized cameras that can observe you in your home (also used in sieges).

- Infrared devices that can follow your motion within the walls of your own home. In use now. Used on the Branch Davidians and Shirley Allen (the middle-aged Illinois woman besieged in 1997 because relatives alleged that she was mentally ill).

- Microphones that can pick up every sound you make within your home.

- Electronic snooping devices that can recognize what you're typing into your computer — for instance, your PGP password.

- Satellite tracking of "felons" using Global-Positioning Satellite technology.

- Systems to enable police to halt moving cars remotely.

- Systems to allow computer users to be identified by fingerprints.

- Finger scanning systems to identify the holders of credit and ATM cards.
- Systems to allow computer users to be identified via retinal pattern.
- Transponders that can locate any properly equipped auto, rail car, truck, or boat in the world.
- The military is now routinely collecting DNA on recruits. "For the soldiers' own good," of course. And now police are beginning to collect DNA from "suspects." A suspect is anyone they arrest, whether guilty or not, whether arrested for a serious crime or not.
- And yes — The Chip. The long-rumored implantable bio-chip is here and in use. How extensive is its use? In animals, use is becoming more common all the time, primarily to inventory livestock and identify lost pets. In humans? There are only rumors, so far. By the time you read this, that may have changed. When governments *can* implant chips in us, they will. It's that simple.

How surveillance technologies tie into the national ID system

What do surveillance technologies have to do with national ID cards and databases? They all tie into one big package.

Walk into a public building whose video cameras are equipped with facial recognition technology, and automated systems check a police or DMV database. Do you have outstanding parking tickets? The system can immediately alert a security guard or nearby police officer. What else is in that database? Above all, your Beast Number — the key to every other government database in the world.

Let's say it's not an outstanding parking ticket you have. You're one of those "Deadbeat Dads." One of those rotters the politicians use to justify tracking the rest of us every day. What happens to you when you unknowingly walk into an advanced surveillance system that can not only detect your presence — but recognize your identity?

Maybe you've been unemployed for a while and unable to make those support payments. Your professional licenses have been pulled by the state because you failed to pay child support, so you can't get a job in your own field. But you're trying to get back on your feet. You've been working at an underground

job to get the money you need to take care of your kids. But now you're caught on an ID system you didn't know was there. In a public building. On your job. Walking down a public street. Some surveillance technology catches you and automatically checks information about you in a database.

It really doesn't matter whether you've walked past cameras, been forced to press your hand onto a fingerprint reader, or whether you've been caught by some other technology yet unknown. You're caught. And dragged off to jail.

Mr. or Ms. Deadbeat, you could also be caught as a camera snaps your license plate as you drive five mph over the speed limit. The DMV records also contain your SS number. And your license, of course, has also been pulled because of your nonpayment of support. So it's off to jail for you, too, on both the child support problem and the lack of a license the state won't let you have even if you beg.

Good luck paying your child support payments then, friend.

And what about DNA collection?

The law enforcement community's latest masturbation fantasy is to have a record of the DNA of every person on the planet. New DNA-reading technology enables someone to be identified from *a single cell*. The media tells us what a miracle this will be for solving crimes. If a criminal leaves just one detectable cell at the scene of a crime, bingo, check the database and they've got him!

But again, that's not the way it's going to work. This admittedly helpful technology has stunning potential for abuse. What, after all, constitutes a "suspect" or a "criminal" in the eyes of a data-mad state?

As British researcher Sean Gabb notes in his brilliant essay, "A Libertarian Conservative Case Against Identity Cards":[6]

Note the adjective "suspected". Note also what is really meant by "criminal". It is an offense to smoke in an empty railway carriage, to import spirits above a certain potency, to have a screwdriver in one's car "without reasonable cause or lawful authority," for one man to kiss another in public, and for having one's name

---

[6] *Ibid.*

left off the Electoral Register. On present trends, we shall soon live in a country like old Germany, where everything that is not compulsory is prohibited. Already, millions of people in this country have criminal records for acts that by no stretch of the imagination might be described as attacks on life or property. I have no idea how many people have been arrested for such acts, only to be released later without charge. But all will have their individual genetic codes fed into [the new British DNA] database.

Gabb is speaking of British laws and a British database, but the principle is the same everywhere.

Think about how this could be used by lazy or overzealous police agencies. As Gabb also notes, in one German murder case, police got warrants to investigate hundreds of men, simply because they'd been registered guests in the hotel/casino where a dead woman was last seen. In England, hundreds of men were forced to undergo police scrutiny merely because they lived in the same area as a murdered woman. European countries are increasingly demanding "voluntary" DNA "contributions" from hundreds, or even thousands of people for no other reason than that they lived or worked near a crime scene.

Every soldier who now enters the service becomes an entrant into that DNA "criminal-detection" system. How soon before people being booked for the most minor crimes are forced to submit to DNA gathering, just as they are now fingerprinted?

Worse. New evidence shows that every living thing routinely and constantly sheds DNA. If you sign a policeman's ticket book, your DNA sloughs off onto the pad. Drop a letter in the mail protesting the income tax or a local political abuse? Your DNA is on the letter. How do you prevent that "evidence" being gathered and entered into a database without your consent — or even your knowledge?

And you, Mr. Deadbeat Dad or Ms. Deadbeat Mom? That good old Welfare Reform Law also mandates collection of *your* DNA without your permission in order to verify parentage of a child. Now, while most of us agree that parents have an obligation to their children, this business of snatching evidence right off your body — without warrant, consent or

any form of due process...well, it just isn't exactly what you could call a good precedent.

And here is some more news from Britain that came in as this book was about to go to the publisher. It was forwarded from the online news service, WorldNet Daily:

SMART cards with a personal identification code, which will allow people to pay taxes, claim benefits, and apply for a passport without filling in a form or speaking to an official, are being developed by the Government....

Although the code will initially be a PIN number, researchers are hoping to allow an individual to be identified by a fingerprint, an iris scan, or even a DNA sample.

A small number of cards giving access to certain government services are to be piloted in the New Year [1998] to test how practical and popular they are.

Mark Gladwin, Deputy Director of the Central IT Unit, said: "You can identify somebody by something they have — such as a card — and something you know — such as a number.

"But the best identification is something that you are."

People will be able to use the cards in "information kiosks" or through the black box installed in homes for accessing digital television. There will also be smart card slots in banks and Post Offices across the country.

In an absolutely pricelessly typical statement, a conservative spokesperson, John Redwood, was quoted as saying, "The Conservatives would need reassuring that any reduction in civil liberty was more than made up for by increased convenience and the control of crime."

Oh, yeah. The ringing conservative cry the world over: "Give me Liberty, as long as it's convenient!"

The article — naturally — also quoted government officials as proclaiming: "huge potential savings," and saying that "the cards would not be compulsory," "but... it could become difficult to operate in the future without one," and that, of course, those silly, misguided opponents might "...see it as the potential for an ID card."

Now there's the understatement of the year!

You are the criminal

The ease of gathering, storing, and analyzing data, — coupled with the state's recent assumption that all people are potential criminals, is enabling this sort of thing to happen.

Is the real intention to "catch criminals"? Yes. But only because the governments of the world now see five billion living humans as criminals-in-waiting, if not criminals in fact.

Entire books could be written about the impact of surveillance technologies when coupled with databases and universal ID numbers. I am barely touching on the subject here. "Barely touching" is also what the media does. But the mainstream media makes this chapter look like in-depth analysis.

Here's one that could hurt or help us

December 30, 1997, *The Guardian* (London) — A pen which can identify who is using it by the way it is held was heralded Tuesday as an important step in combating fraud.

The LCI Smartpen, which contains tiny pressure pads, a spirit level, and a computer processor, paves the way for making secure financial transactions without proof of identity. It could have a huge impact on buying by credit card over the Internet, where security fears are highest....

A computer inside the pen records the pressure applied and the degree of the pen's tilt. This information is then encrypted and passed, via a battery-powered transmitter at the top of the pen, to a nearby computer.

If the database were a *private* one, and not SS-based, fingerprint-based, DNA-based or otherwise keyed to our "real world" identity, this could indeed be a boon for privacy. Used by banks and governments, however, in conjunction with centralized databases, it becomes just one more means of tracking every purchase we make and (possibly) every place we go.

Neither this article nor any other information I've seen on the Smartpen answers such questions as: What if you injure your hand? Or what if you're sitting at a different angle? Or even how reliable is it?

(Gasp!) Could the media actually be manipulating us?

You'll notice, as you read media articles on the new technology, that the reporters will *always* mention two things: 1) the huge money savings these systems will allegedly produce and 2) the enormous number of criminals *already caught* by some newly introduced technology.

Often, the numbers will be staggering. For instance, in one case, where a technology was used to help police stop 414 vehicles (on the grounds of air emissions violations), a radio report gushed that the police had also found that 83 — *eighty three!* — of the drivers stopped were wanted for anything from outstanding parking tickets to major, but unnamed, felonies. The report went on to rejoice over the number of criminal vehicles impounded and the potential fines to pour into the city treasury.

Another report trumpeted, "New technology catches *three felons* on first use." The "use" had involved about 15 people.

After seeing these sort of stats again and again, a reasonably skeptical person begins to doubt.

Are there *really* that many criminals running around loose?

Well, yes. But only because nearly everything is a crime. (I've got a parking light on my car that's been out for months...) These stats are as absurd as the ones Handgun Control, Inc. keeps putting out about the hundreds of thousands of "felons" kept from buying guns by the Brady Law.[7]

Of course, "catching criminals" and "saving money on welfare cheating" isn't what any of this is about. By now, you know what it's about.

You will also notice that very few articles about these gee-whiz new technologies will mention any fears of privacy violations, excess police power or constitutional violations. If they mention such things at all, as often as not it's in the form of a one-paragraph quote from someone who sounds more than a little paranoid, or a quote from one of the standard

---

[7] As of this writing, fewer than a dozen "felons" have been arrested for attempting to buy guns, four years after the Brady Law went into effect. Most refusals have turned out to be for such "crimes" as outstanding parking tickets or errors in the police record. Handgun Control regularly ups its estimates of "dangerous felons prevented from buying guns," however. *Their* figure is now over a quarter of a million.

I Am Not a Number!

official privacy guardians, such as the ACLU, that somehow seems off the point or difficult to understand.

In its August 25, 1997 issue, *Time* magazine did an allegedly in-depth cover story called "The Death of Privacy" in which it focused almost exclusively on the way *private companies* or freelance bad guys could abuse technology. While there was certainly good, cautionary information in the story, it failed entirely to mention the government's role in fostering and abusing surveillance technology.

In one notable lapse, *Time* clucked its editorial tongue at "private satellites... eagle-eyed enough to spot you — and maybe a companion — in a hot tub." No mention of the *military* and *government spy agency* satellites that have had that capability for years.

Gather 100 mainstream media articles on surveillance and ID technology and the message you will have is, "Ooooh, government uses technology for goooood things. Ohhhhh, only criminals and private businesses use technology to hurt you. We'd better ask the government to use more of its woooooonderful technology and legislation so those baaaad people won't hurt us."

I know — I know darned well — that there are people reading this book who are still saying, "But we *need* to catch welfare cheats," and, "The police *should* be able to stop criminals' cars," and, "People who defy the police in standoffs *deserve* to be reduced to helpless nausea."

And if we were dealing with a government otherwise "bound by the chains of law" that *might* be true. But we are dealing with a government whose driving interest is the preservation and growth of its own power. Welfare cheating won't cease because of the new citizen-tracking methods. Real criminals will still go unpunished. Nothing will change in the world of real crime because of these new technologies.

The welfare cheat being "caught" in the news articles will, tomorrow, be the free-market business person being caught for the crime of making a living.

The cars being halted in mid-drive won't belong to fleeing bank robbers, but to "polluters" (who are already being roadblocked and immediately removed from the road in New Jersey and California). They will be people without insurance or "tax protestors."

How will the police *know* the vehicles belong to the uninsured or the untaxed? Check those databases.

The people reduced to nausea by sound waves won't be gunmen holed up in empty houses, but innocent men and women going about their business, but living unapproved lives. Or other innocent people pursuing unsanctioned activities (like handing out FIJA leaflets outside a courtroom or picketing an IRS office).

No buying or selling without the Mark

I am not Christian. Yet the new, sudden, and secretly passed SS number requirements evoke thoughts of *Revelation 13:16-17* even in a devout unbeliever like me:

"And he causeth all, both small and great, rich and poor, free and bond, to receive a mark in their right hand or in their foreheads: And that no man might buy or sell, save he that had the mark, or the name of the beast, or the number of his name." Revelation 13:16-17

We have already seen in this chapter how many services and "rights" will be denied you from the outset, if you refuse to use The Card or take the government's Mark.

Banks will not deal with you. (Banks were, in fact, one of the prime movers behind this slave law.) Health insurance companies will not cover you. Stores will not cash your checks. Employers will not hire you. Eventually, doctors will not treat you without The Card.

Gradually (sometimes by their own choice and sometimes under threat of law), businesses of all types will cease serving those without The Card. You can expect this to happen over the course of the next ten-fifteen years.

Revelation says that in the end times you will be able neither to buy nor sell without the mark of the beast. Those who refuse may die of starvation, cast out from the security of an all-pervasive provider. But those who accept lose their souls.

Our situation is identical. Whether you believe in the literal existence of the soul or merely the metaphoric human spirit, the depth of the loss we face is devastating.

Whether you believe in a literal antichrist or merely see a tyrannical, but mundane human power overshadowing the world, its impact — if we grant it what it wishes — is the same.

In America, we still maintain the illusion of freedom. We like to pretend that cooperation with such schemes is "voluntary."

But, as with "voluntary" tax filing, penalties await those who refuse to "volunteer" to accept the government's Mark. We've already seen in this chapter some of the implications of any refusal to "volunteer."

And when the government controls (or "mandates") the distribution of food, general medical care, housing, and on and on…When, later, it has decreed a cashless society, with buying and selling done only with a card of its specifications (based, of course, on your Number)…

It will have made itself entirely analogous to *Revelation's* beast. If we don't stop it now, it will go that far. And then it will begin to consume its cattle. And cull its herds.

We must either be its possessions or its enemies.

We will outsmart the bastards. We must.

Anyone can state a problem. Anyone can exclaim in horror. Anyone can moan in despair or declaim in rage. What you have just seen in the preceding pages is the last you shall see of that in this book. No more damn whining!

It is not my job — and ultimately it is not *our* job — to piss about the terrible things would-be dictators have dictated.

No matter what we do, they will go on passing laws, and those laws will get worse even than they are now. We could shoot the bastards, and shoot the next crop of bastards, and the crop of bastards that rises up after them — and all it would do is make the next crop of bastards even nastier.

Shooting them isn't smart right now. But neither is doing nothing.

Our task is not to sit in one spot and weep over our fate. Our job is to make our own fate, within the limitations presented us.

All the preceding negativism was strictly in the name of stating the problem. This is what power-cravers have attempted to do to us. And this is what millions of new slaves have *let* the power-cravers do to them, in the name of Holy Security.

Now let them all go to hell together.

It is up to us — not to fix *them*, not to undo what *they* have created for themselves, or what *they* consented to by closing their eyes — but to live our own lives. It is up to us to work and trade in freedom with others who also refuse to be slaves.

We are the people of freedom. We are the people who will live, despite all that is done to curtail our lives. We are the people who will die rather than submit. We are the people who will go to prison, yet still not be imprisoned. We are the people who will be tortured, yet still not suffer inner torment — because we know what true, human freedom is — because we have a goal that transcends our momentary pain.

We are smart, determined, adept, educable, skilled, experienced, principled, and fierce. We are fierce with a fierceness born of desperation. We *cannot* give up because the defeat of compliance is worse than the defeat of death or prison.

We are of every race and creed and color and size. We are rich and poor, male and female, educated and unschooled. We are fearless and frightened, experienced and naïve, iron-hard and soft as velvet. We come from many sides of the political spectrum. We are the camo-clad militiaman in the woods *and* the aging New Leftist in the university who sadly recalls that "liberal" once signified a love of liberty. The only thing we have in common is a passion for freedom. But that is a passion that has driven the human race on an ever-upward climb throughout all its history. Those who seek to suppress our passion have no conception of what a huge, potent, angry genie they are trying to stuff into their tiny little bottle.

Ultimately, we are stronger than they. We may die. But what we love will live, because we loved it, because we lived it.

And now it is time to get on living. That's what this book is really about — living and how to do it — successfully and in freedom — under the nose of the government of ID State America.

And speaking of The Mark...

News and rumors flood across my computer screen all day long. To stay sane, I have to ignore a large percentage of this verbiage, and I've developed some very thick "bullshit filters" to help me do that.

If something sounds just too-too "conspiracy theorist," I'll tune it out until someone else sends confirmation. That's what happened when I first heard that the U.S. Department of Defense was issuing (or planning to issue) its soldiers a card known as the Multi-Technology Automated Reader Card — The MARC. This card can be used for a variety of functions — including serving as pay vehicle (just charge the card with "money" instead of issuing a check), credit card, meal ticket, etc.

Oh, get real! I protested. *Surely if they were planning such a thing they wouldn't have the brass to actually call it "The Marc"!*

And I filed the rumor away. Then, later, in the fall of 1997, while I was investigating some very real (government and industry) sites pertaining to high technology ID and surveillance, I stumbled across the MARC entirely by accident. But by golly, there the MARC was, front and back images, write-up and all, at this site:

http://www.dtic.mil/c3i/marcard.html

DTIC stands for the Defense Technology Information Center. When I went back in December to get photographs of the card off the page for inclusion in this book, I got nothing but a message saying:

Access Forbidden.

However, if you select "quick search" on their home page (http://www.dtic.dla.mil/), then type in "MARC," you'll find several other cheery, PR-type articles about soldiers "getting smart with smart cards." Turns out they've been using them since the Haiti operation in 1994.

And now they're introducing a plan to plant a microchip under the skin of all U.S. soldiers.

Update 2002
What's New
Since Chapter Two

The main difference between now and the year I wrote this chapter is that what was prediction then is reality now. What was just getting underway is the established order now.

The vast public protest against privacy loss has forced many corporations to back off from their worst (or at least, their most visible) abuses of personal data, including overt overuse of Social Security numbers. It's pushed the government into at least mouthing respect for privacy. So in some areas, privacy hasn't eroded as quickly as it appeared to be doing in 1998. Despite all the pious rhetoric, however, things are steadily getting worse —and as usual may be made worse yet by some of the proposed "solutions."

The new technologies

Many new technologies have come to light and many new means of surveillance have been implemented by law or regulatory fiat. They are too many to cover in detail here and many are already well known to the informed public. But to give a non-comprehensive sampling, they include:

- The FBI's Carnivore system, which mass-surveils e-mail and Internet activity, no warrant needed, thank you very much.[8] This sort of thing, too, is global. In the UK, the Regulation of In-

---

[8] Internet service providers are now required to enable this surveillance, just as telecommunications equipment manufacturers are required by the 1994 Communication Assistance to Law Enforcement Agencies (CALEA) law to produce telephones and phone systems that can be wiretapped at will. In fact, a couple of months after September 11, the Justice Department simply *decreed* that CALEA applied to Internet service providers and — by golly — had applied all along, without a single change needed in legislation or regulation. This is a perfect example of police-state governance and the type of governance we increasingly have in America today. The rules are whatever those with guns and badges *say* they are. And if the gun-toting feds tell us the rules are completely different tomorrow, then we'd better just shut up and obey. Against this, alone, if nothing else, we should rebel if we believe we deserve to be free.

vestigatory Powers Act (RIP), requires ISPs to be prepared to intercept and store all electronic communications, including e-mails, faxes, and web surfing data.

- The FBI's Magic Lantern key-logger, which can grab your encryption passwords or anything else off your computer. (The FBI is currently denying that any such program exists, but key loggers have been around for years and it's hard to tell what all the fuss is about.)
- Obnoxious "red-light" traffic cameras that snap your vehicle, its license plate, and sometimes even your face as you drive along the highway. Courts have dealt a blow to these systems, recognizing them for exactly what they are — sleazy schemes to raise money via Big Brother technology, with no connection whatsoever to public safety. But many of them still exist and they're too good a deal for local police and municipalities to give up without a fight.
- Cameras, cameras, and more cameras. Despite the laughable failures of facial-recognition camera systems (see the Foreword), various types of surveillance cameras continue to proliferate in public places. Britain, overwhelmingly the most heavily surveilled nation on the globe, now has more than two million of them.
- Smart dust. What? Smart dust? Yes. This one's still futuristic, but the technology is under development to let police and the military spy on you via small "camera particles" (for want of a better word) floating in the air.

Perhaps most ominously of all ...the Digital Angel and VeriChip have been introduced to the market. The VeriChip is an implantable chip, injected under the skin, that can identify you to a scanner. It resembles the ID chip now commonly implanted in pet cats and dogs. It will eventually contain all kinds of data about you, like your medical, criminal, and financial records. Digital Angel, made by the same company (Applied Digital Solutions), is a wearable tracking device (so far not implantable, but DSA has constantly "misstated" its intentions for further development of its products — for instance, claiming it had absolutely no plan to make an implantable chip almost up to the day it started selling one).

This year, the first American family, the Jacobs family of Florida, was implanted with the VeriChip. And the two products are now being marketed together in South America. Perhaps there would be no problem (and some benefit) to either of these products if they were to remain voluntary. They really do have useful implications for locating kidnapped children, identifying and treating accident victims, or finding wandering Alzheimer's patients. But all evidence says that they won't be voluntary for long. First, governments will require government schoolchildren and dementia victims to be chipped ("for their own safety," of course). Then prisoners and parolees ("for public safety"). Then it will be all newborns …and eventually, through decree or attrition, all of us.

The VeriChip is the tiny acorn that will grow into the poisonous tree of the Biblical Number, planted in the head or the hand, without which we won't be allowed to buy or sell. Taken together with the Digital Angel tracking device, which can ultimately locate us everywhere we go and give the government a record of everywhere we've been, it's simply every tyrant's ultimate wet dream.

(To keep up with developing new technologies, check some of the resources listed under this chapter's heading in the Appendix.)

TIPS informers

We may get so busy fearing high-tech surveillance that we forget good-old (bad-old) human spies and snoops. Let's not. Aside from the obnoxiously obvious (like airport security screeners making sure that eighty-year-old Medal of Honor winners can't commit mayhem with their metal hip joints while young Moslem men are allowed to rampage unmolested), there are the less Big Brotherish but equally creepy expansions of the security state in the aftermath of 9-11.

One of these is the TIPS program, run by the Office of Homeland Security. TIPS — which stands for Terrorism Information and Prevention System and enlists truck drivers, taxi drivers, mail carriers, utility workers, and others with access to your home or business as spies. Next time you call in a phone repair technician, make sure all that subversive literature (like this book) is out of sight. Next time the mail lady knocks to leave an express package, be sure you're not cleaning your rifle on the kitchen table. And you'd sure better hope you never have a midnight emergency that requires the Roto-Rooter man and doesn't give you time to cover your gas masks and survival foods. Oh, and don't forget that neighbor down the street who's got a grudge against you or doesn't approve of your lifestyle. He, too, can report you as a potential terrorist. All "evidence" reported by these freelance, warrantless government agents goes into — guess what? — another giant database.

As I write this, Congress is considering killing the TIPS program before it fully gets underway. As I write this, the Justice Department swears, absolutely swears, that it's changed its mind about enlisting all those folks who visit your home. (It's only going to use truck drivers, bus drivers, dock workers, and the like.) The U.S. Postal Service first said it would participate, and then that it wouldn't. The program called TIPS could disappear and is obviously mutating faster than a virus. But the practice of secret informers will never disappear and will only get much worse — unless the U.S. returns to a system of freedom. Informers are one of the keystones of every police state.

How the government really feels about your privacy

Just a few more quick notes on changes in privacy policy and technology.

Please don't fall into the trap of thinking government — certainly not the federal government — will ever protect your privacy, despite all the highly publicized rhetoric to the contrary.

If a government really wanted to protect you against privacy abuses, it could pass a single, one-paragraph law not much more complicated than this: "No private company may disseminate any data about an identifiable individual without that individual's express written consent. No government agency may gather or disseminate any data about an identifiable individual without either the individual's express written consent or strict compliance with Fourth

Amendment protections of the privacy of persons, possessions, and papers."[9]

That it chooses instead to come up with various and complex schemes like "privacy czars" and voluminous, complex privacy regulations for different industries, is both typical and a sure sign of government's ineptitude and bad intentions.

Take the above-mentioned "privacy czar," for instance. This office, which already exists in some countries, basically transfers authority over your private information from corporations and scattered government agencies (which shouldn't have control of it, anyway) to a centralized government information office. You don't gain one bit of control over your own data or your own life when a government institutes such an office, although you usually do gain a government ombudsman you can approach with your most serious privacy complaints. The government does gain control — and also enlarges the size of its own fiefdoms.

We'll see a few more examples later in this book of what happens when government takes it unto itself to "protect" your privacy.

The FBI rises again

Finally, in the wake of 9-11, the Department of Justice revised FBI policies, restoring to that agency powers it had had back in the 1960s before the dreadful political abuses of the J. Edgar Hoover era were revealed. Most notably, the DOJ restored the authority to go on fishing expeditions — attending church services, political meetings, and other public gatherings *with the sole hope of stumbling upon something incriminating*. (FBI agents, like anybody else, have and always have had the right to go to church or political meetings for private reasons, but this move means that, once again, we all have to fear to speak about controversial subjects for fear that

---

[9] A constitutional government, of course, wouldn't have that sort of direct authority over businesses — not even under the catch-all Interstate Commerce clause. But state governments could pass such a law. And a right to individual privacy is implicit in the Bill of Rights, in the Ninth and Tenth Amendments. In any case, with the fedgov already having seized so much power, they could pass a law like this one a lot more easily and a lot more honestly than they pass all the industry-specific "privacy laws" that allow their biggest campaign contributors to rape us little folks.

some federal spy will be recording it as "suspicious.")

One of the powers supposedly being restored to the FBI was the authority to access library records to see who's been checking out controversial books. However, it's very obvious from the reference on page 27 in this chapter that the government has never ceased tracking controversial reading habits and the FBI has never ceased to have access to those records.

What else are they up to that we simply don't know?

● ● ● ● ● ● ●

For a fascinating account of how an evil government used national ID and databases to commit the ultimate horror on a targeted group, read *IBM and the Holocaust* by Edwin Black (Crown Publishers, 2001).

Chapter Three
The Undocumented Citizen

"I have some sad news for you — the Big Boys will have contempt for you whether you rebel or submit. Better, then, to rebel. I say it's TIME the rabble were roused."   — Jim Goad, *The Redneck Manifesto*

This book is for people who commit themselves to noncooperation with the National ID State, Slave State America. The information in the following chapters is written from the viewpoint of, "Okay, we've refused to take The Card and refused to use The Number. Now what?" It's about plans, alternatives, solutions, creations, risk-taking — in short, it is about *action*.

From Chapter Four onward, it's primarily about what we can do as members of a vast, free, ad hoc community of UnNumbered Citizens. But before we reach that point, we have to decide, one by one, whether we want to become Undocumented Citizens at all, and how we might want to do it.

For some of us, it was easy...

Some of us made up our minds the moment we heard Congress had passed the Slave Card. We would never take it and never cooperate with the system imposing it. Period. Action is all that matters to us now.

Others, no doubt, are reading this book while trying to come to a decision.

- Maybe you want to refuse The Card, or give up The Number entirely, but need to know more about the risks and opportunities you'll face.

- Maybe you believe you can't give up The Number or The Card because your life is dependent on the system for reasons beyond your control.

- Maybe you have no objection to some part of the citizen numbering and tracking system, but simply want to keep things from getting "out of hand" in your own life.

- Maybe you hate the whole business, but just can't imagine how you could do without an SS number or a government ID card.

- Maybe you just don't think The Number, The Card, and all their attendant surveillance and tracking technologies are any big deal and you're reading this just to see why anyone thinks they are.

- Maybe you already place your hopes in the use of fake IDs and fake SS numbers and wonder how the new laws and technologies will affect what you're doing now.

- Maybe you *want* to use false IDs and SS numbers and wonder if it's possible to fake the new systems.

You will, as always, have to make your own decisions. Once again, the information in this chapter makes no pretense of being comprehensive, and it isn't intended to give "advice." It is just a beginning — what one woman knows and believes.

You will have to analyze your own situation and find your own resources. I've given some sources in the Appendix that might help you do that.

But let's look now at some factors in the decision to withdraw cooperation from the Slave State, and a few methods you as an individual might use to help you survive after making a decision to say no.

Noncooperation — not resistance

The original title for this chapter was "Individual resistance: a beginning." But resistance isn't what we really need to do.

This chapter is still about individual decisions, and about beginnings. But "noncooperation" now strikes me as a better term for what we need to do. The word "resistance" creates, or reinforces, an unproductive mindset.

Resistance implies having a force against which we must push. Resistance implies a belief that the tyrant government of the U.S. is a worthy opponent for our efforts — and that our efforts should focus on throwing ourselves against that government in hopes of winning our freedom back.

It may come to that, someday.

However, we will have far more success if we *creatively disregard* the usurper government's laws and goals. That isn't to say we should *ignore* what that government does; we need our awareness. The U.S. surveillance government is like a poisonous snake that's almost within striking distance. We need to know where it is and what it's doing — but it would be really, incredibly dumb to hurl ourselves upon it and start wrestling.

Let us observe and be wary of it.

But while doing that out of the corner of our eye, let us emphasize a mindset of self-ownership and free thinking. Let's put *freedom* — not fighting — into its premiere place. If we focus on, and practice, freedom, then government ceases to be such a force in our minds. If it ceases to dominate our minds, its role in our lives subtly, but importantly, shifts.

Leaving the abuser

Let's put government into perspective. A *good* government, if such a thing could exist, would be a small and secure government, practicing respect for individual rights. It would operate within severe restrictions, and within those restrictions, it would reflect the will and needs of its citizens, not of its own desire for power.

Think of it in terms of relationships. A person who is genuinely strong and secure doesn't try to control your life. Strong, secure people don't feel threatened by your independence or opinions. They don't follow you around and spy on you. They don't have to resort to threats and punishments when your behavior doesn't match their notions of propriety.

What kind of person feels compelled to know where you are every minute of the day, to snoop into your affairs, to beat you if you disobey arbitrary rules, to constantly try to make you feel inadequate and insecure, to change the "rules" of the relationship all the time, to order you around? A real insecure jerk, that's what kind of person. An inadequate person. In the words of Judge Reinhold (ordered to peddle worthlessly oversized stereo speakers in the movie, *Ruthless People*) a person "…who is worried about the size of his… um… equipment."

Control freaks are small, scared people.

Despite its apparent size and power, the current U.S. government — and all would-be tyrants — behave like weak, insecure entities. That's reflected in the behavior of individual politicians, who make careers out of forcing other people to obey their will, and individual bureaucrats, who may enter their fields out of a fear of failing in the marketplace, but who stay because regulation enables some of the world's smallest, most petty people to control some of the world's brightest and most innovative. It's reflected in the enforcers, who no longer show up at your door with a polite manner and a clipboard, but who come in gangs, wearing disguises, and kick your door down in the middle of the night.

Government is dangerous. And government is presumptuous — both of which traits give us every reason to fear and, yes, to hate it in its current manifestation. The Hitlers, Stalins, Nixons, and Clintons are dangerous people, as are the institutions over which they preside. But they are also, we should never forget, sick, desperate, even pathetic little people leading miserable lives. They are people who must surround themselves with unreality (in the form of fawning flappers and carefully tailored reports) in order to face their days without falling apart.

Every government's attempt at total control is doomed to failure. So, like any freelance abuser, governments escalate the violence, the threats, the arbitrary rule-making. Their failures to impose order become more pronounced and more frustrating. Then people begin to rebel. So governments crack down even harder, creating more rebellion.

This is exactly the pattern of any one-on-one abusive relationship.

And what's the best attitude for the abused party *in any relationship* to take? Not to placate; that only escalates the hostility; the abuser senses weakness and vulnerability. Not to fight; that only enables the abuser to justify its behavior and become worse. Not to negotiate; negotiating is possible only between equal parties. When one party can crush the other — and knows it, and is willing to do it — no negotiation is possible.

The best course is simply — *to leave*.

It isn't easy to leave a country. Besides, sadly, few countries are any better than this one. And, after all, this is our America. Some of us will never leave it, no matter what.

So don't leave the land. But do leave its *government*.

We can leave the government intellectually and emotionally, while staying right here. We can cease giving a usurper state our credence, our allegiance or our respect. We cannot ignore it. But we can live despite it.

To a certain extent, even we who remain bound to this land can also, literally remove a part of ourselves from the reach of this government (by getting our assets out of its way, by encrypting our electronic transmissions, and by other methods). And we can, by thinking and acting free, remove a great deal more of the government's power from our lives than most of us imagine.

To contend
without contending

A lot of us — me emphatically included — have a mindset of struggle. We have a drive to oppose injustice and fight for rights. In a way, that's all well and good. Given how much there is to oppose in this world, we'll never get bored and might be of some use to the cause of freedom.

Still, we fighters remind me of Marlon Brando in *The Wild One:*

"What are you rebelling against?"
"Whaddaya got?"

I sometimes fear that, if all unjust authority were swept magically from the world, we wouldn't know what to do. We wouldn't know how to just ease our minds and live free.

There was a time when I thought that wouldn't matter, anyway. Unjust authority isn't going to be swept from the world, and even if it were, there will be plenty of freelance injustice left to oppose.

Still…

If we make the decision to simply *depart*, mentally, emotionally, philosophically and (as much as possible) physically from an unjust system, we will be staring straight into the awesome task of living free.

There will be a lot for us to do: adjust our mindsets, create new lifestyles, prepare for new hazards, among other things. Still, some of us crotchets are inevitably going to focus a lot of energy on that Big Bad Government out there.

I picked up a phrase in high school that I find useful in that circumstance. It came from some text of eastern philosophy, long forgotten now. But the concept is attractive:

To contend without contending.

Possibly, we may best defeat an unjust government not by "wrestling" with it, but by living so well, thinking so freely, laughing so heartfully, and loving freedom so much that our moral force just topples that idol right over.

On the other hand, we may not topple it. But the attitude may help us live more freely inside and out, even with that government still there. And our ideas and examples may inspire others to stop throwing themselves uselessly against obstacles and join us in freedom.

It's worth a try, anyway.

What noncooperation *isn't*,
part I.

As mentioned in Chapter One, there are good people out there who have been resisting their states' attempts to impose ID laws by writing letters, educating people, circulating petitions, lobbying the legislature, testifying at legislative hearings, and urging others to contact state legislators and governors.

But they're not going to win in the long run unless the entire mental and philosophical climate of this country changes in some major way.

Influential people want this ID legislation. The federal government wants it. Banks want it. Motor vehicle bureaucrats and "public safety" enforcers want it. Corporations obsessed with "security" want it. People and politicians who hate immigrants want it. Given that Slave ID cards are rapidly being introduced all over the world, there's strong evidence to indicate that the UN and its backers who crave global control want it. And they *will* get it, by hook, crook, land-mine legislation, or fiat. Don't kid yourself that citizens can win victory in the legislature or in the courts. Not in the long run. Not unless millions more wake up, turn off the TV, and refuse to condone this business here and now.

There is absolutely not a flicker of a sign of a hint of a hope that any widespread, national, citizen outrage is developing to oppose Slave ID. And that's the only way ID State America will ever be stopped through conventional citizen action. If enough people get mad and refuse to put up with it. But that's not happening.

What the anti-ID activists are doing is being the "loyal opposition." But the loyal opposition is emphatically still part of the system. They are resisting. But at the same time, their resistance is a form of cooperation. They're fighting on their opponents' turf, using their opponents' rules — never a winning thing to do!

Noncooperation is not "working within the system."

Noncooperation means withdrawing all support from those who would unjustly rule you.

What noncooperation *isn't*, part II.

It's early in the battle against national ID, but already there are signs that some states are accommodating (or being forced to accommodate) conscientious objections to the Slave ID. The federal legislation makes no mention of the rights of religious or other objectors; nevertheless, objectors are a force to be reckoned with.

On October 25, 1997, UPI reported that a Los Angeles County Superior Court judge had ruled in favor of five men who objected on religious grounds to having their Social Security numbers used as part of their drivers' licenses. For the moment, those men don't personally have to use a Beast Number for their ID.

But the article continued:

> Prosecutors say they'll appeal the ruling on the grounds that a universal driver's license application is needed because it [the license] is used to track parents who are delinquent in child support payments.

Can't coordinate those databases without The Number, you know. And that's what this is really all about.

Nevertheless, because of the nascent resistance, several states are now "allowing" religious objectors to fill out "affidavits" if they don't want their Beast Number associated with their state ID. As my correspondent Mike Kemp points out, people who try to use the affidavit are often harassed unmercifully.

And of course, they'll simply end up in another sort of database — that of suspected "anti-government radicals."

But frankly and bluntly, I don't much care what happens to people who politely ask to be given a personal exception to an evil system.

If you are content to find some polite, legal little finagle, some personal breathing space, some tiny, private exemption *within* the soul-destroying system being imposed upon millions of your fellow Americans and billions of your fellow human beings, then you are practicing another form of evil yourself.

Oh, I know you may be doing it with the best of motives. You don't want to be some noisy, impolite, high-risk protester. You *do* want to be a good, obedient citizen. You have a family to provide for and you don't want to do anything that might damage their economic well-being. You believe with all your heart and soul that one should always work within the system.

Perhaps your church tells you to "render unto Caesar," no matter what Caesar demands of you. Finding a private loophole is the nicest way you can follow the church's dictates while still living with your own conscience. Maybe you even feel that it's a test of your Christian free will to refuse the Beast Number while millions of others ignorantly or eagerly sell their souls. Maybe it even makes you feel superior that these lost souls aren't as principled as you.

It also makes you a collaborator.

It's people like that — who'll tolerate any evil as long as they can find their personal little exemption from it — that ultimately enable all oppression. People who will tacitly approve any evil, as long as some legal loophole minimizes evil's effects in their own lives are as dangerous to freedom as the Hitlers and Stalins and Big Brothers they help make possible.

There were even Jews in Hitler's Germany who held positions of leadership in their communities, with the approval of the Nazis. These, the members of the *Judenrat*, worked hard to placate young Jewish rebels, counseling against rebellion, assuring their fellows that they could make "the system" work on their behalf. They kept things calm. They squeezed the last hopes out of a hopeless system. Ultimately, they helped the Nazis decide which of their fellow Jews should go to the camps, and which could remain merely ghettoized…for the moment. No doubt they thought that "working within the system" and "being civilized" was the right thing. They, of course, received special status for their compromises. And they helped make the slaughter of millions possible.

If that's all you want — your own personal "out" — then you're not resisting, either. You are helping impose the system on the rest of us by making it more "acceptable" to people with polite objections to it.

Noncooperation is not hunting for loopholes!
Noncooperation means refusal to cooperate in any way with evil.

Noncooperation is living by your principles. It is taking that stand, regardless of what the law says, regardless of the practical consequences. It is doing what you know to be right *because you know it to be right*. It is following the logical consequences of your beliefs to the bitter end. It is being true to yourself. It is nothing less.

Understand, I have no objection to anyone refusing the national ID or participation in databases *on religious grounds*. On the contrary, if you have religious, philosophical, moral or any other reasons at all to

oppose the ID — go for it! That's what this book is about.

But when the very system is evil, and you recognize that, how can you live with yourself while you seek *favors* from it?

Fortunately, if you do choose to cease cooperation, there are a lot of methods by which you, as an individual, can refuse to cooperate with the Slave Card and the Beast Number System. Methods to suit all kinds of styles.

Some are more effective or more dangerous than others. And — let's lay all prejudices on the table — I believe that total noncooperation, without even a pretense of using the state's documents, numbering and processes is the one that is more effective and more principled than any other. (I'll give my reasons toward the end of this chapter.) With that in mind, let's take a look at some possible methods of individual noncooperation.

Methods of individual noncooperation (and some consequences)

There are many ways to resist the Slave System without working within it or seeking personal exemptions from it. Some are:

- Cooperating in part
- Using one or more forms of fake ID
- Using fake "real" ID
- Doing the above, while using bribes to make that method more effective
- Using sovereign citizenship methods
- Using offshore identity documents and privacy protection
- Cooperating on the surface while dedicating yourself to sabotaging the system from within; in other words, being a mole

This book is not about alternate ID or citizenship. There are lots of other books and web sites for that. But since these are techniques that The Undocumented might use, let's take a quick look at how the above methods might work, won't work, or could be made to work in ID State America.

Cooperating in part

It's possible that you are willing to use the SS number in some cases while refusing to give it for others. For instance, faced with the daunting task of trying to get a job without one, you might give in to using it on the job. Having a regular job, rather than being self-employed, means your employer takes money out of your paycheck, which means if you want anything back, you've got to use the number to file your tax return.

Or maybe you want to file your tax return, even when you "owe" money, either because you believe it's a responsibility or because you're scared silly about what the IRS will do to you if you fail to file. So for work and taxes, you use your Number.

But for other purposes, you balk. Perhaps you refuse to get a driver's license tied to the SS system because you take seriously the words "not to be used for identification" that once appeared on SS cards. Perhaps you won't give your SS to the phone company, a credit card issuer, or the Department of Fish and Game (when you apply for a hunting license).

Personally, I think this is harder than "going cold turkey" and refusing the Beast Number altogether. It leaves you in a perpetual quandary. *When do I refuse? On what grounds? In which situation might giving my Number be dangerous? In which situations is it "okay"?*

Using your SS in one circumstance automatically leads you into using it in others where you might consider the use objectionable.

Giving your SS to an employer so you can have the "benefits" of work and a government retirement plan also means you've got to insert yourself into the national database of workers.

If you're a family person and you want to file taxes, the decision to give in and use *your* SS also means you've got to get Beast Numbers for your children. It's required now, if you want to deduct the kids. Until the late 1990s, the government "allowed" you alternative methods of "proving" your children exist — but no more.

So partial cooperation will result in constant compromises and constant temptations to give in.

However, I also realize not everybody is a born radical, and everyone has different levels of acceptable risk and acceptable levels of government intrusion. If you cooperate partially, you should try to think out, in advance, the circumstances in which you'll use the number and the reasons for which you'll refuse to use it.

You might also be able to use a few of the following methods to *partially* fake out the system — to preserve at least some portion of your privacy.

Keep in mind that we're talking about illegal things, here. Always weigh carefully any decision to use illegal methods. Know the consequences, and remember that you are responsible for your own decisions.

Using fake ID

This is a classic, of course. Today, undocumented aliens can acquire full packages of fake U.S. ID for as little as $200. In parts of the country where demand is high, you can literally buy this sort of documentation on the street corner.

Even if you can't buy it on the street, you can acquire fake ID in a variety of ways, from purchasing it via mail order to making it yourself using your computer and following directions in books.

Look for books on ID and privacy from Loompanics, Paladin Press, Lysias Press, and Eden Press. Reliable authors include Sheldon Charrett, John Q. Newman, Ragnar Benson, and Barry Reid.

With the changes in federal law, however, it's going to get a lot harder to make and use fake ID.

Will it become impossible? Never. Where there's a market demand, which there clearly is, and where there's a buck to be made by supplying fake ID, there will be fake ID. Where people want or need to slip between the cracks of the system, there will *always* be ways to make fake ID work.

What's going to make it harder isn't the insecurity features, themselves — the digitized photos, the facial recognition software, the mag strips, fingerprints, retinal scans, and microchips. What's going to make it harder is the way these things will be tied into the databases, and the way the databases will be so easy for officials, corporate types, researchers, and other Friends of Government to access.

Even today you may be able to use fake ID in a drug store or show it to a prospective employer. But if a cop stops you when you're driving with a fake ID, you're in deep yogurt, because the cop can access a computerized record that will reveal your fake in seconds.

In the future, ID will be scannable, and you can expect nearly everyone you deal with to have, and use scanners. The scanners will transmit data to computers, where the data on your card will be checked against the data in the system. If it matches, you'll be okayed. If it doesn't match, you'll be rejected for whatever service you're trying to get, your card might be confiscated, and you could, depending on the circumstances, be arrested on the spot.

Don't forget those pilot programs to *require* employers to scan Social Security cards *before* they can hire anyone. And don't forget those scannable Social Security cards being developed, along with the national ID driver's license.

One interestingly ironic thing, of course, is that while the scanning technology and other forms of instant database access are going to be terribly hazardous to holders of false ID, they're also going to be catastrophic for the fools who place their faith in Slave ID.

And they might help make your conventional fake ID more useable than it appears at the moment. How? Ask yourself a simple question:

How many databases do you know that contain perfect information?

Have you ever seen a credit report that didn't have at least one mistake on it? How many direct mailers get your name or address wrong in their files? How many cases have you heard about of John R. Smith being arrested because there's a warrant out for John B. Smith? How many people have you heard of who've had their credit ruined because someone else fraudulently used their SS number, name, or address? How accurate are the IRS's records, do you suppose, given that agency's record of accuracy overall? How accurate can the Social Security Administration be?

How accurate is that famous Deadbeat Dads Database going to be — the one they're so interested in tying your driver's license records into?

Reportedly, as many as thirty-five percent of all database entries, everywhere, have some error in them. And even if more sophisticated systems reduce the number or rate of errors, Garbage In/Garbage Out is still a fundamental truth of the universe.

In the long run, this gives you, as a holder of fake ID, an excuse and an advantage. "Oh, it didn't scan? I can't imagine what's wrong!" You're just one of many whose ID didn't work today. But you're ahead of the game; you're already prepared with a reaction.

And another issue: How responsive are all these government computers going to be, anyway? How often do you try to carry out some sort of transaction, only to be told, "Oh, sorry, the system's down agaaaiiinnn"?

The long and the short of this is that, while fake ID will get chancier and chancier for the holders, there are also going to be millions of poor suckers holding *genuine* Slave ID who aren't going to be able to get jobs or have their phone service turned on or whatever, all because of computer screw-ups! And I must say, it serves them absolutely, completely right for knuckling under to this sort of nonsense without a fight or even an objection.

Once a screw-up occurs, given the known responsiveness of government agencies, some of these "good citizens" may not be able to get jobs for months or may have their government checks tied up for years while they try to cut through the red tape to find that one-digit error causing their records to go crazy on them.

Ha!

In short, although banks, employers, and government agencies can be expected to take this scanning stuff very seriously in the short run, eventually, anyone who deals with these systems is going to become used to frequent screw-ups and downtime and will develop a cavalier attitude toward the technology. Even the control freaking federal government will eventually have to "allow" some alternative — and more time consuming — methods of checking the validity of your ID.

With luck, you'll have gotten what you want and be long gone before they discover you're a free human being. So, yes, there's still hope for fake ID.

Fake "real" ID

Okay, it sounds like a contradiction in terms. But the good old free market always finds ways to circumvent restrictions, and that's already happening here. The market has found ways to put "real" ID into the hands of people who need it. And will be finding more ways.

In two states that implemented new, high-tech, "uncounterfeitable" IDs, thieves quickly broke into driver's license bureaus and snatched the equipment for making the stuff. It happened within weeks, and I haven't heard about anyone being caught. It will certainly happen again and again, no matter how many hopeful security precautions states take and no matter how many penalties the states or the feds impose.

Another method: In California, DMV employees have been arrested for selling "real" ID on the side to people who didn't go through the nice, polite application process. (Don't worry, just because *they* got arrested doesn't mean you won't be able to get ID from the next black market entrepreneurs who move into the territory.)

Possibly, this second form of "real" fake ID could even be made to scan successfully in some circumstances. It might not get through the Social Security Administration's database, but it might get you approved by many state databases. For example, if the fakery was performed at the DMV itself, you might have a nice, little fake database entry to go along with your fake card.

Employees have also been caught selling "blanks" of the new ID cards, which hackers can use to make their own "real" ID.

No doubt, too, free market computer experts will learn to duplicate DMV equipment. Or they'll hack into state ID systems and insert new records or delete old ones. Or they'll find ways of buying hardware or software identical to that of the state and turn out identical, though nonscannable, models. The best moment will come when someone figures out how to give you a real, scannable ID on your fake card. And they will. It will happen.

And if California government employees aren't beyond selling their services for a buck, is there any reason to think federal employees are any less approachable? Would an SSA employee create a false database entry for you? Who knows? Is it possible the underpaid HR data entry serf at your company could be persuaded to jigger your Deadbeat Dads database entry so that it said what you wanted it to, rather than what the feds want to hear? What about employees of the companies who manufacture the license-producing equipment?

The possibilities are endless. At this point, there are only three certainties: 1. Every system designed to give total centralized control will create more chaos than it eliminates; 2. The more government power, the more corruption; and 3. The resulting chaos and corruption will cause a few million trusting fools to lose the last of their respect for law and government.

Hope for the fakers — and a wake-up call for ID believers

From an AP story December 29, 1997:

Durango, Colorado — Burns National Bank is canceling its debit card program after discovering that someone in California was manufacturing counterfeit cards to gain access to customer accounts....

[After initially learning of the counterfeiting] the bank canceled its existing debit card accounts and issued new cards with an extra security feature. But within four weeks, hackers had gained access to customer accounts again....

Counterfeiters manufactured plastic cards and then took account number sequences off software that resides on the Internet before encoding them in the magnetic strip on the back of the card.

It's the same mag-strip technology now being used on many drivers' licenses. Federal and state databases are accessible through the Internet. Hackers are clever and determined. "Secure" identity systems? How secure do you feel?

Using fake or "real" ID along with bribes

It isn't necessary to say a lot about this. It's simply self-evident that in a corrupt and controlling system, bribes will play an increasing part in getting things done. The more power government arrogates to itself, the more opportunities there are for bribery.

In everyday America, at the end of the 20th century, bribes aren't a common thing. Oh, yes, there's that East-Coasty, slip-a-twenty-to-the-maitre-d' mentality that most Western types, like me, have seen only in the movies. And of course, everywhere in the world that you find governments, you also find big scale bribery: Give a few thousand to get a contract, a few hundred thousand to get a couple of meetings with the president, give a job to the mayor's nephew in return for favors granted.

But we don't live in a culture of *baksheesh* or *mordita* as much of the rest of the world does. Most ordinary people don't think in terms of having to slip a twenty, or a hundred, to the store clerk, the secretary of the prospective employer, the policeman, or the telephone company rep to earn ourselves a little better service.

That will change. When people are regularly getting bounced by corrupted, inaccurate databases and come to realize that "legitimate" solutions could take months, everyone will gradually get used to the idea of greasing the wheels with bribery to get the system rolling again.

This is going to be a tricky one, at first. Whom do you bribe? How much? How do you feel out the situation to know whether you'll get a good reception or an arrest? Frankly, I wouldn't have a clue.

But eventually, it will become common. Second nature. Corrupt systems always evoke bribery. Impossible situations can't remain impossible; money will eventually open doors. If you want to know how much to bribe an employer for a job or a passport agent for a permit to travel, you'll probably be able to call up a list of average prices on the Internet.

It will be difficult in the first few years. It will be difficult to the extent that anyone takes the new ID systems seriously. But once people develop experience and cynicism, fake ID and *baksheesh* will probably get you anywhere.

Using sovereign citizenship

Warning: I'm *really* cynical and negative about this option.

Sovereign citizenship is the act of declaring oneself to be not subject to certain levels or functions of government. It is not merely a philosophical declaration, but is done through recourse to legal, (sometimes quasi-legal) means. Sovereigns turn to common law or to documents and statutes that predate many corrupted and unconstitutional government functions.

Where they've been successful, sovereigns have been able to drive without licenses or state auto registration tags, and have otherwise escaped some of the onerous impositions of the control state, such as income taxation. They may use alternate forms of ID and substitutes for other government "requirements." Or they may stand on their rights and use none.

There's a lot of appeal in that. More all the time as the ID State seizes control.

I like the *idea* of sovereign citizenship. So far, though, I've never seen much I like about it in practice.

There's definite historic, intellectual, and emotional merit in the concept of sovereignty. However, to my mind, the process is incredibly tedious and often legally dubious. It involves constant research, fighting, and citing in Legalese that's every bit as tedious as what lawyers do. (And I personally think what lawyers do is more tedious than garbage collection.) It's also meeting increased retaliation from legiscreatures and bureaucrats as one aspect of what they call "paper terrorism."

(Isn't it interesting? *They* can send agents out to commit murder, make bombs, or confiscate our homes and bank accounts without trial, and that's just fine. But when some of *us* start demanding answers to questions about the tax code, filing liens, or doing pro se court pleadings... oh, boo hoo, the poor put-upon gov-o-crats are victims of "paper terrorism"! Dontcha feel sorry for the poor dears?)

But I digress...

Success of sovereignty methods has been limited and local. More often, I've seen friends singled out, even jailed, for having the "wrong" tags on their car, making the "wrong" sort of legal filings, or being unable to produce the "correct" citizen ID papers on demand. One friend, stopped for a minor traffic infraction — but with unapproved plates on his vehicle — ended up spending three days in jail without even being allowed to call an attorney. When he tried to assert his constitutional rights, the cops jeered, "Rights? You think we give a shit about your rights? You've been watching too much TV."

As sovereign techniques become better known (as is happening now), they're more likely to provoke similar hostility and stern counter-measures.

Sovereigns also seem to spend their lives in legal research and legal wrangles of one sort or another. That's fine for them what likes it. But it's my definition of hell. And as with voting, lobbying, etc., I simply can't see that carrying on a constant legal battle with "the system" is any way to get free *of* the system. You're just giving your life to it in a slightly different form.

Some of my friends swear by sovereignty, though. And even some who aren't sold on it still use selected sovereignty techniques. So remember that I'm speaking as a born arty type and a made outlaw — neither of which has the proper personality for poring over old law books or doing battle with lawyers. If your inclinations lie elsewhere, go for it.

There are plenty of sovereignty resources on the Web. Just type the words "sovereign citizenship" into any Internet search engine.

Some sovereigns also take advantage of another technique I find more promising — the use of offshore documents.

Using offshore ID documents and privacy protection

I have in the past been cynical about this option, as well. Not because it doesn't work; it does. But because I've perceived it as a method available only to the rich.

However, I — and a lot of other former doubters — are taking a new look. There are still many pitfalls and false promises awaiting people of modest means who seek offshore havens, either as ID sources or places to stash assets. But there is tremendous hope here, as well — both for we who remain in America and the souls who venture outward, taking themselves physically out of the grasp of the BATF and the EPA.

One nice thing about going offshore is that it includes lots of options — from remaining in the U.S. while establishing trusts, corporations, bank accounts, citizenships, and other legal fictions overseas, to literally packing up and spreading your life over five or six sunny little islands somewhere.

Offshore "legal fictions" can serve, in many cases, as your identity. A corporation and/or trust based in a foreign country can own your property, bank accounts, and so on without your SS number being used as a tracking device.

I know only a few people of ordinary means who actually live as expatriates, rather than simply moving their paperwork, not themselves, out of the country. But most of them are making great success of offshore living as a freedom tactic while, bless 'em, having wonderful lives. Expatriate living is not without risk. (But then, what worthwhile thing is risk free?) But we can expect many more fed-up people to explore it.

Many people who remain in the U.S. are using International Motorist Qualifications in place of

drivers' licenses, and have had this nongovernmental document stand up in court in lieu of government ID. (The IMQ is a photo-ID document, requiring no driver's test and no citizen tracking, issued from a foreign country and available over the Internet.)

Increasingly, established offshore bank and investment firms are offering their services over the Internet. Countries (both real and imaginary) are even advertising their citizenships for sale via the net. A variety of other foreign ID is available. Encryption is making international transactions darned near impossible for governments to analyze (even if they can trace their routes). And a lot of good things are happening to attract a lot of freedom-seeking people.

The bad news: that certainly means offshore ID-and-privacy protection methods are going to be cracked down upon. The U.S. will eventually refuse to recognize any foreign documents that don't meet some arbitrary "security" standards. Smaller countries will be bullied into changing their own forms of documentation to make them as odious and onerous as U.S. documentation. And, alas, governments all over the world are tightening up ID requirements… just because they're governments and enjoy doing that sort of thing.

The good news: It's just too big a job for any government to handle… and there will always be little island or mountain nations that make huge portions of their revenues by offering offshore services — and they just ain't gonna be bullied for nothin'.

So here's an opportunity for people who want to be "legal" while avoiding the Beastly burden of SS-based, data-clogged U.S. ID documents.

Let's look at two major strategies for using offshore ID documents.

One is to remain in the U.S. while adopting foreign documents as a formality.

The other is the PT life (Perpetual Traveler, Previous Taxpayer, Passing Through, etc.), developed by Harry Schultz and Bill Hill.

You might notice some of my old cynicism creeping in here. As a basically poor person, I still find a lot of this out of reach, despite promoters' claims to the contrary. But the reality is changing, and so might my eye-rolling disbelief.

Staying here while having citizenship there: Are you as poor as I am? Well, for just $75 His Majesty, King Murjel Hermios, Distinguished Monarch of

EnenKio Atoll, Paramount Chief (Iroijlaplap) of the Northern Atolls of the Ratak Archipelago of Pacific Ocean Islands and his Honorable Ministers will sell you a passport.

It's a great place for freedom, this EnenKio Atoll. Individual liberty. Private banking. International free-trade zone. Good grief, they're even planning a free-market spaceport! The fact that the place is… well… not to be too blunt about it… but the fact that the place is *underwater* part of the time is merely a small drawback. (Libertarians who recall the ill-fated island utopia of Minerva are used to that sort of thing; and anyway, you aren't going to live there, are you?)

The really somewhat more serious problem is that EnenKio Atoll is also known as Wake Island, and it's been in the possession of the U.S. military since 1899. No actual EnenKioans, including King Murjel, inhabit the land.

Never mind His Majesty's claims — quite possibly valid — that the U.S. holds his kingdom illegally. (Has that ever stopped a government before?)

The plain fact is this passport entitles you to nothing but a dream. A sweet dream, indeed. But nothing more.

I dare you to try to enter the U.S. or any other nation using your EnenKio passport. I dare you to use it as an ID document anywhere in the U.S. You might get away with it now and then. How much do you want to count on it? How effectively do you suppose His Majesty's Honorable Ministers will protect you, their honored $75 citizen, if you get in trouble with U.S. goons? How effectively will they protect you if the INS decides to take your claim seriously and deport you as an undesirable alien, or something along those lines?

Nevertheless, the correspondent who originally pointed me toward King Murjel's web site, points out that you might nevertheless be able to use your EnenKio passport as ID in some circumstances. For instance, let's say you're opening an offshore bank account and the bank requires a photocopy of your passport as identification. Possibly, the bank won't know EnenKio doesn't legally exist. Also, quite possibly, the bank (which makes its living serving foreigners of sometimes dubious reputation), may not care. Having a bad Xerox of an unknown passport in their files might be all they need to protect them-

selves from harsh judgments from the rather laissez-faire banking authorities in their little kingdom.

It could be worth a try — in circumstances that aren't likely to get you arrested.

The cost of a "serious" passport runs just a tad bit higher.

For "a minimum $75,000 contribution to our economy" you can purchase second-citizenship in the very real nation of Belize.

The Republic of Ireland had a program (now suspended) that would grant your entire family citizenship for a "mere" $250,000 plus an investment of one million and purchase of a home. Other countries are advertised on the net as selling passports for as "little" as $35,000.

You must be extremely careful, however. According to Nicholas Pullen, writing in the August 1998 issue of *Access*, a publication of the Sovereign Society, only three nations — Belize, Dominica, and St. Kitts/Nevis — currently offer legitimate "economic citizenship." With any other program, you may be dealing either with corrupt government agencies or independent scam artists.

These citizenships really do grant a variety of benefits, including some degree of escape from America's onerous new identity documents. So. Got your checkbook ready?

While you're writing out that check, though, keep in mind that the U.S. recognizes dual citizenship only under rare and specific circumstances. If you manage to beg or buy citizenship and a passport elsewhere in the world, don't expect to be able to make easy leaps back and forth between your two "nationalities" — unless, of course, you're rich enough for the government to indulge you.

In second passports, I see hope. But I don't personally see it through rose-colored glasses.

To my mind, the far more hopeful aspects of offshore privacy protection involve doing banking and business offshore. There are some truly great opportunities there, and you can take advantage of some of them for only a few thousand (perhaps even a few hundred) dollars. These will be covered in the chapters on finance and work.

PT: The more advanced variety of the multiple nationality idea, PT, is an interesting theory. PT involves having separate countries for domicile, citizenship, banking, business, and "playgrounds" (where you actually live).

The philosophy behind being a PT is, according to Dr. Hill:

> In a nutshell, a PT merely arranges his or her paperwork in such a way that all governments consider him a tourist — a person who is just Passing Through. Government officials look at PTs and consider them to be people who are merely Parked Temporarily. Unlike most citizens or subjects, PTs are not then subject to taxes, military service, or lawsuits. Nor are they persecuted for holding outlandish beliefs or pursuing exotic activities.

I suspect that, with work, it could make interesting practice, as well. But I still can't agree with those who brightly tout it as a hope for the middle and working class. This is a high-cost game.

First, there's that passport. A real one is *expensive*, as we just saw. Furthermore, it's still hard (though not impossible) to find a banking haven that doesn't want big bucks.

Open your business in a country other than the one you live in? Well, yes, you can actually do that cheaply, as long as your business is Internet-based. It's pretty cool.

But separate your "domicile" from your "residence"? Doable — but not usually cheap! To stay even remotely legal with this plan, you have to move from place to place, as well, to avoid overstaying specified time limits for visits. (Because legally, you are just visiting the country in which you prefer to live.)

PT enthusiasts point out, rightly, that more and more working people are able to live where they wish now, thanks to telecommuting. But they often ignore the enormous costs of a mobile lifestyle. Or their idea of reasonable cost is somewhat different than mine.

For instance, one sincere and brilliantly living advocate of PT pointed out recently that you could cut down on the costs of traveling from country to country by buying a certain type of sailboat for only $149,000.

Now, I'm sure $149,000 is petty cash to some of you fine readers. If you currently live in an "ordinary" $400,000 home in California or Hawaii, the idea of selling it, buying a $149,000 boat, and having a quarter of a million left over for living expenses probably sounds great. (Even with all those boaty maintenance costs, mooring fees and so on.) But anyone who uses the word "only" and the figure "$149,000" in the same sentence has lost me. That's three times the cost of the little rural house I live in.

In short, I don't mean to be negative, but for most working people, I don't see these plans as being practical yet.

Nevertheless, of all plans for evading Big Brother, PT is most appealing. It's footloose, fancy free, anarchistic, modern, exciting, jaunty, original, adventurous, and it's in the true libertarian spirit of allegiance to principles and freedom, rather than to nation-states.

I also know of people who are living one variation of it, quietly, unofficially, probably even illegally — but very well. These people (not an organized group, but just a bunch who've wandered toward freedom in the same location) do live full-time in one country. It's a Caribbean island with a rather laid-back attitude. They have no "official" status in the country, but because they have needed skills — mainly in computer technology and archeology — the local government welcomes their presence and quietly disregards their unofficial status.

This kind of arrangement is found in small, developing countries all over the world.

Whether you wish to remain in the U.S. or find your future elsewhere, there's an interesting new organization called the Sovereign Society that might help you. You'll find more information about it in Chapter Seven and the Appendix.

This book is for those who stay in America. You could live part-time in the U.S. and practice PT by having citizenship and business arrangements elsewhere. But America isn't so laid back about its "illegal immigrants." In fact, fear of immigrants is what started this whole Big Brother ID thing. So onward to the worst-case, bravest-case method of noncooperation with Slave State America...

Being a mole

We will have a few rare, precious, dangerous brothers and sisters in spirit who will, on the surface, submit placidly to Slave State America. They will take their Number and their Card and plod quietly through their cattle-like lives — while screwing over the system from within. And screwing it to such depth, with such power, and with such vengeance that they might bring it to its knees.

I'm thinking especially of the software engineers who will build system-destroying databombs while working on the computers of the IRS, SSA, or Department of Health and Human Services (where the central connection for the Deadbeat Dads Database resides).

I'm thinking of the administrative cog-in-the-wheel who one day walks out of work carrying the blueprint of the FBI building housing the fingerprint files.[1]

I'm thinking of the computer hardware mavens constantly trying to "fix" government computers that, darn it, just never seem to function right despite their most diligent efforts.

I'm thinking of the clerks who smuggle out data that expose cover-ups and secret government plans… and smuggle it not only past the guards, but past the uncaring media to put it into the hands of a growing Internet community, a growing underground community.

And yes, if it comes down to war between free people and an oppressive government, I'm thinking about the martyrs who'll carry explosives into "secure" government institutions and blow the buildings and their systems sky high. I hope with all my heart that such actions never become necessary. I hope if freedom fighters ever perceive them as necessary, they'll be executed only at effective moments, and only — *only, only* — against the guilty. Never harm the innocent!

Some of these moles, these saboteurs from within, will truly be with us, philosophically. Others may not have a political conviction in the world. One day, they just may reach some point of personal desperation and fury — with their boss, with the system, with life — that they'll strike out. Intelligent folks, they won't have to pick up a gun or a baseball bat. They can be far more dangerous than that.

They can destroy the physical systems that enslave us. Or at least send them crashing into momentary chaos.

And no security measures in the world can stop them all. Hell, the security guardians, the security system designers, the security system maintenance people are likely even to *be* the moles.

But this alternative, of course, is for the very unusual, the very well-placed or the very desperate. It's not a choice that's even available to most of us, or wise for most of us — even if we had the patience, and the rather schizoid nature, necessary to survive it.

There is also potential (depending on the mental climate of the country and the means by which the sabotage is accomplished) for this to backfire horribly and bring opprobrium and even more crushing legislation down upon the freedom movement. Violence is *not* an option, except in the most total desperation.

Why I believe total noncooperation is most effective

Our aim is to live free. The above methods (and others unmentioned here) can help toward that end. Every bit of noncooperation is healthy. And many of the offshore options can otherwise help guard your privacy *regardless* of what you do, or don't do, about American government ID and numbering systems.

Some methods are more high risk than others. Some, like false ID, are "quiet" methods; while others, like claiming sovereignty, are inherently "noisy" and more public. Some give their largest benefit to the individual practicing them; others, like the method of the mole, offer nothing but misery and loneliness to the doer, yet have great potential to harm "the system."

To each his own.

I believe, however, that total, principled, non-cooperation with the dictates of the ID state is the most effective of all methods. Whatever *else* you may do, I believe it's best if you don't even make a pretense of participating in state or federal ID and database schemes — unless your purpose is explicitly to monkeywrench them.

To use fake ID to get a job or pay your taxes, for instance, gives legitimacy to the concept behind the system, even as you try, understandably, to evade the consequences of the system.

I think we need to declare — quietly or loudly, but always on principle — that the national ID state is

---

[1] Already done. It became part of a fedsting, though, and nothing came of it. But what if there's another copy out there? Or what if our brave little mole tunnels out with a future one?

wrong and not deserving of even a pretense of our cooperation.

Why?

Because it's all gotta stop somewhere. Things have gone too far. Cooperation, collaboration, and compromise have gotten us where we are now — with a government taking the final steps to exert ownership over us.

We don't need a government that "grows more slowly" or takes smaller steps in the direction of tyranny. We need to turn government around, point it in the other direction, and give it a hard kick in the butt so that it moves out of our way *fast* and *now*.

Compromise, cooperation, and polite disagreement won't accomplish that.

Using time-tested appearance-of-cooperation methods such as fake ID won't accomplish that.

We must refuse all cooperation because government no longer recognizes any limit — except whatever limit we impose upon it by withdrawing our support from it.

We need to cease cooperation because if we let this ID-and-database business rule us, we're no better than cattle. Because if we just find our own private loopholes, then all we are is cattle that haven't been tagged yet, but are still part of the herd.

Because our souls are at stake, literally or metaphorically.

Because enough is enough is enough! Because it is time. Time to say flat-out NO. Time to take back our own lives.

Can I say it any more clearly?

My choice

For good or ill, noncooperation is the course I've chosen and will live by.

I have rescinded my Social Security number. Regardless of whether the SS bureaucrats choose to accept my decision, it's a done thing. What they think of that, or anything else, is immaterial to me. I own my own life.

I will not apply for the Slave ID license.

I will never give a universal ID number to anyone.

I will do whatever it takes to remain out of government databases. Where I cannot remain out of a database, I will do my best to obfuscate and sabotage the information being collected.

I may state that my objections are religious or philosophical, but I will never fill out any government's forms begging for a personal exception on those grounds. I will simply refuse to cooperate on those grounds.

Smart or stupid, this is my personal choice.

This is what I believe to be the most effective, and most principled choice. But I acknowledge that it's not for everybody. And I'm also aware that there will be situations, over the years, that will make me want to fudge these choices for the sake of "getting along." Will I have the courage *never* to deviate from this Big, Tough Stand? I don't know. I hope so.

And I gotta admit, I wouldn't mind some play with alternate ID and privacy protection — with dual goals of getting out of the government system and monkeywrenching the system to make it ineffective.

And if all those high falutin' principles don't move you…

…There's one practical reason to prefer no ID to fake ID. As a lady named Mary pointed out while I was speaking to a group she belongs to, the penalties are generally much more harsh for having fake ID than for having none.

That was brought home by a piece of legislation introduced in the 105th Congress by Arizona Senator Jon Kyl. The Identity Theft and Assumption Deterrence Act (S 512) purports to protect those unfortunates who've had their identities stolen by credit card scammers and such.

However, if passed, S 512 would make *any* use of fake ID "with intent to deceive or defraud" a federal crime. The punishment? Fines, fifteen years in prison, and forfeiture of assets.

Of course, *any* use of fake ID could be construed as being intended to "deceive," so this law could be applied to you if you simply happened to be carrying a fake ID card in your pocket — and some law enforcer or persecutor decided he didn't like your attitude. But don't worry, the law hasn't passed — yet.

Being noisy about this choice, as I am being here, may not be the most effective strategy; that's just the position I've put myself in by writing about this subject. It could turn out to be a really dumb choice, as far as my immediate, personal interests are concerned. If so, *c'est la vie*. The kind of life I want to live will be impossible if ID State America triumphs. So if I can't thwart that ghastly system, I might as well die or go to prison trying.

But there it is; I believe the best course for freedom is the most total resistance possible. To walk away from a corrupt system and build a life independent of it.

Your choice

Those of you who know me know that, although I have pretty strong opinions, I don't like to tell anybody, "You *must* do this or that." I have no power to get away with such a stunt, anyway. I can't *make* you do anything. But above all, I believe we're all best at determining which decisions we "must" make for ourselves.

So while I may storm and emote, I have to step back from my passions to say, "It's your choice." I believe that if you don't make a choice for non-cooperation, you aren't fully making a choice for freedom. But it's still your choice.

As we've already mentioned, there are people who feel they can't cease cooperating because their health or age leaves them vulnerable and dependent on government services.

But I will also congratulate the few brave souls who *will* take a stand, even at the gravest risk, even unto death. And I hope that when my day comes for old age, poverty, or ill health, I will either have found alternatives to government systems or will have the courage to die rather than submit to evil. We just can't know until we reach that moment of reckoning.

If you're a healthy, able person hesitating on the cusp of withdrawing your cooperation, then be aware of this: Noncooperation equals hardship.

Harkening back to the analogy of the abuser, we should never forget that the moment at which an abuser is most likely to kill you is *the moment at which you leave.* Because that is the moment at which you publicly declare that the abuser has no right to control you. Nothing infuriates a control freak more than that.

The government is the same. It will tolerate, to some extent, people who try to "fake" its systems (e.g., it regards the standard "tax cheat" in an entirely different and kinder light than it regards the principled tax resister). But those who question the government's fundamental "right" to perform certain functions are intolerable to tyrants.

So there may be terrible dangers.

And even aside from the dangers of attack and persecution, there are the everyday inconveniences. Once you say no to Slave State America, life isn't going to be as easy as it was.

If you want an easy life, you don't want the life of noncooperation. If you want an easy life, though, you're not going to have a free life. Your choice.

But also remember that people who succeed in leaving abusers, who succeed in overcoming the abuse and the mindset of abuse, find a glowing revelation on the other side of their travails. Life *can* be different. You don't have to "take it." You don't "deserve" arbitrary rules and punishments your government metes out to you. You don't deserve to be watched, tracked, and forced to account for your every movement.

And once you understand that you don't *have* to put up with it anymore, you have a world of new opportunities — even though that world still contains very real dangers.

Us and a few million others

Many of us have for years sought and found individual ways to escape the tightening net of legislation, regulation and police power.

But although many of us have freed ourselves, at least in part, our quiet methods haven't increased the amount of freedom in our surroundings. Therefore, because the country has become steadily less free, it becomes harder for us, personally, to remain free.

Although it isn't our responsibility to free anyone else, I believe we owe it to *ourselves* to try to increase the amount of freedom in our surroundings. We *don't* accomplish it through covert, halfway methods.

In using false ID, for instance, you are still *acting* as if the government had a right to force you to carry Slave documents.

On the other hand, simply saying NO to the whole idea of universal government ID calls into question the validity and authority of the law and the law spewers.

Will we be treated as freaks in some cases? Yep. Will we be denied many services? Sure. Will some of us get arrested, or at least royally hassled by cops and bureaucrats? Yes. Killed? Yeah, some of us.

Help is available. But we're all feeling our way as we go here.

We already know that refusing the Slave Card will bring us hardships. But opportunity also begins at the moment we put the whole dirty system of government "benefits" and government ownership behind us and move onto the next stage of our development — when we move on to freedom. By forcing us to look at alternatives for living free and guarding our privacy, the government has also inspired an explosion of creative thinking and alternative strategies.

We already have many more privacy options than we had a few years ago — and we're at the bare beginning of this time of "creative escape."

Our greatest hope and opportunity lies in the fact that there are going to be so many of us that we'll not only have the *ability* to build alternatives to government systems — but we'll have that mother of a necessity to do so.

Although some of us feel very alone at the moment, in a world unaware of, and utterly unconcerned about, the slave system being imposed, the fact is we are *not* alone. There are millions of us out here, angry and principled, refusing to be pushed any further. We will be driven to find each other, work with each other, and support each other. Widespread though we may be, geographically and philosophically, we are closer to each other than we are to the silent and unknowing people around us.

We are becoming, whether we intend it or not, a *community* of freedom seekers. Might as well take advantage of that.

Update 2002
What's New Since Chapter Three

Boy, I was mad when I wrote this book. And rightly so. But one of the things that's changed since its original publication is my attitude. Never today would I compare Clinton or Nixon to Hitler or Stalin, having studied the works of them all. (Would Clinton have been Stalin in his dreams? Yes, he might have. Do-gooders like the Clintons are the most dangerous

people when unleashed, because they believe their ideals are more important than the individuals on whom the ideals are imposed. Stalin, Mao, Pol Pot, and Hitler were idealists all. But regardless of how police-statish the U.S. has already gotten, we do still have both cultural and political leashes on our politicians.) If I were writing this book from scratch today, I'd tone down my rhetoric. Well, just a tad.

At the time I wrote *I Am Not a Number!*, I was still stunned and furious that the politicians of the 1994 "Republican Revolution" would not only fail to get government off our backs (which would have been no surprise), but would prove to be such utter betrayers. I was relatively new to such phenomena as laws sneakily passed at midnight, bills no representative had actually read before voting for, and the catastrophic paragraph deliberately sneaked into the foot-high stack of legalese. I was horrified (and still am) at how much harm had been done to my country, secretly, and in such a short time. I'm horrified at how much more has been done since, and how few people know, understand, or care.

But now it's also all old hat. Today, if I learned that John Ashcroft or Tom Daschle had made a deal to sell America's soul to the devil, I'd probably yawn, "So what else is new?"

That said, however, I wouldn't change a thing in this chapter but some of the harsher rhetoric. Resistance may be futile, as they say. But resistance to evil is utterly necessary to a principled man or woman.

I still — 100 percent, more than ever — endorse "leaving the government" even if you can't or don't want to leave the country.

However, in the meantime, one other nation has arisen as a beacon of hope for those who want to leave both country and government in search of freedom. And one group has been founded that might help people leave the federal government (at least partially) while still remaining within America's borders. I'll talk about both of those after Chapter Four.

Affidavits reviewed

Earlier, I mentioned that states were accommodating non-SSN holders by allowing them to file affidavits of their status, rather than be forced to get and give a Slave Number to get a driver's license or nondriver ID. In this chapter, I virtually called such affidavits a form of collaboration with the enemy. I still have serious moral doubts about these personal exceptions to the law. Nice, cooperative little affidavits won't bring down an evil system.

I was greatly impressed by Scott McDonald, the anti-numbering activist. When weary bureaucrats, tired of his obstinate refusal to give an SSN, offered to create such an affidavit for him so he could get drivers' licenses for his teenaged twin boys, he refused on those very grounds. He wasn't looking for a personal exception to an evil, dangerous, unconstitutional system; he was working to end the evil.

Nevertheless, on this, too, I've mellowed. I understand that few people have what it takes to stand up as Scott and his sons have. Better to get a personal exemption from an evil law than to submit an SSN. It's not the highest thing you can do and it doesn't advance the cause of freedom, but it's better than giving total cooperation.

A clarification

Recall this passage from Chapter Three: "If you're a family person and you want to file taxes, the decision to give in and use *your* SS also means you've got to get Beast Numbers for your children. It's required now, if you want to deduct the kids."

I didn't make myself really clear. I think its obscene to deliver your helpless children into the control of the state by tacking Slave Numbers on them. It's especially obscene to do it only so that you can save money on your taxes — what a crappy thing to sacrifice your children for. Far, far better morally to keep the children free and resist taxes if your own life, heart, and conscience will allow you to do so. What I meant by this example is that if you use an SSN for one thing, you'll always be drawn to use it for another — and they'll all seem like perfectly plausible reasons, and they'll go on seeming plausible until you've reached the gates of hell.

Fake ID revisited

Fake ID, of course, has become a lot more controversial since 9-11. (Especially since the media and the proponents of "infallible" ID don't bother to tell us that all of the hijackers had Social Security num-

bers and many had perfectly legal, nonfake, government-issued ID. In what way did any of these things hinder them from committing the worst single act of murder in U.S. history?)

Good fake ID is harder to get than I implied, and harder now than it was then. A really good package of false ID goes for several thousand dollars. And without a doubt biometrics will make fake ID harder to pass off as real. Your best bet for seriously good-looking, but nonofficial ID is to get it from a compromised clerk at the DMV or from a thief who's stolen the DMV equipment and templates. Illegal aliens do it every day. And will continue to do so no matter how many laws are passed against it.

No matter how stringent ID requirements become, and no matter how technologically sophisticated IDs eventually are, a person with the means (and Osama bin Laden's minions have means up the ying yang) will always be able to get "real" fake ID. That is, people will always be able to bribe the licensing bureaucrats to create the genuine item under a false name, complete with database entries. They'll always be able to get passports issued by cooperative governments. And terrorists will always be able to get genuine, legal, perfectly legitimate ID from their own governments or other governments that foster their causes — then murder people anyway.

And even an ordinary malcontent with a "legitimate" government ID could set off a bomb or release some nasty chemical into a crowded subway.

On sovereign citizenship

This has always been a dubious cause in a practical sense (even when it's a morally valid or legally correct one). Where it worked at all it often worked simply because small-time court officials weren't familiar with it or simply got weary of fighting the cranky people who pursued sovereign arguments and so gave in.

For instance, the International Motorist Qualification I mentioned is a real and valid thing, but it's only supposed to be used in conjunction with your original state driver's license. But I had an acquaintance who simply beat the courts down every time he got busted (which was often; he must have been a rotten driver) and won case after case on his right to drive with the IMQ as his only document.

Some sovereigns are 100 percent correct in their interpretations of law and justice. But tell it to a judge who doesn't give a damn. Others twist law and court cases to mean what they want them to mean, and this can get innocent followers into hot water. This is dangerous territory — but that's also just one woman's rather prejudiced opinion. If you want to explore individual sovereignty, pro se litigation, and such things further, check the resources in the Appendix. But be sure also to read attorney Larry Becraft's page of invalid legal arguments and don't make the mistakes others have made.

Second passports

The question of second passports becomes ever more difficult. Many programs that sell them are scams, and it's hard to tell the genuine from the bogus unless you have the resources to investigate the laws of each offering nation and the reliability of the agency claiming to broker such documents.

If President Bush has his way and all international ID and travel documents become biometric, then legitimate second passports will become much less useful to someone who wants to keep numbering and biometrics out of his life in any case. But they may still be helpful for escaping oppressive taxes or claiming the protection of a freer country if you get caught breaking a law.

In the Appendix, I've listed the best sources I could find for second-citizenship information.

The PT life

Once worldwide travel documents do become biometric, and eventually become linked to One Big Database, the PT life will also become less useful as a means of avoiding numbering and biometrics — unless you carefully confine yourself to countries that are, shall we say, laid back about checking the data. The PT life might still help you in other ways, though, just as a second passport could.

And of course, if you're connected enough, you may even be able to persuade one of your adopted governments to give you a "cover" ID so you can still travel under another name even as your genuine biometric data goes into the scanners.

For the best and most up-to-date information on offshore options, you get what you pay for. You must subscribe to a good newsletter or belong to an organization specializing in privacy and wealth protection. Only from such sources — who have people on the ground all over the world, testing various methods and watching for all new laws, regulations, and enforcement policies — can you hope to get the straight goods. (This is also an area where a lot of charlatans operate and you must be very, very careful about whom you trust.) Some long-established and/or known reliable sources are listed in the Appendix.

Part II
Free Nation America

Chapter Four
The Free American Community

"I'm not opposed to civilization. I just don't want to live there." — K. Parker Stoops

There are a lot of books about how you, as an individual, can get around the system. Some of these books are good. All of them are going to need to be updated — real soon — to cover the new laws and tracking systems.

But there aren't many books that talk about the potential for freedom when millions of people (or at the very least, hundreds of thousands) all cease co-operating, drop out, go underground — or whatever you want to call it — at once.

Obviously, each of these freedom seekers has individual goals. But each seeker also shares some goals with others and has something to offer other freedom seekers. Individually, freedom seekers may have little in common and no contact with each other. As a whole, however, they form a separate society. Or multiple societies with common interests.

That's what's beginning to happen in response to the ID State.

There are too many of us who will consider this system our ultimate line in the sand. The line we must never allow ourselves to cross. Hundreds of thousands of us, from all walks of life, will be dropping out at once — within the next few years.[1]

All of us know people, right now, who refuse to get drivers' licenses, don't pay the income tax, have opted out of the banking system, live mobile lives,

carry fake ID, or have otherwise exempted themselves from government control. A lot of you readers may *be* such people. Good for you. The rest can learn from you.

But in excreting the laws that lay the foundations of ID State America, Congress and its regulatory appendages have created a need that goes beyond what we can do for ourselves as individuals.

Let me give you one example (to be amplified later).

The U.S. medical system is rapidly being federalized. Doctors and hospitals get a lot of their money from the government, and the whole industry is increasingly regulated.

The ethics of the profession have long dictated that a suffering person get some degree of medical care, even when unable to pay for it. This system of ethics existed for centuries before the government got into the health care act.

Soon, however, the government will totally control the rules of the health care game. Even where it is not the sole payer, it will be the sole regulator of medical services across the land.

Yes, the alleged poor will still be treated "for free." But *no one* will be treated without their number, their Card, their Mark. After all, the reasoning goes, even the poorest of the poor have Social Security numbers. And our record-keeping requires the number, therefore…

Listen up and believe this if you don't believe anything else I say. Within ten years of the moment I write this, *you will not be able to get care at a hospital or doctor's office unless you present your Card*

---

[1] We shouldn't forget that our numbers might be swelled by people seeking freedom or surcease for other reasons as well — chaos or catastrophe among them.

I Am Not a Number!

for scanning. Even if the doctors want to help you, it will be *illegal* for them to do so.

Tough luck, kiddo. Suffer.

Now you, as an individual, should be able to get a fake Card. As we've already seen, the black market for them is revving into action and, to the extent that it works, you'll be able to wangle some medical care before the central database finds out you're using an invalid number. To the extent that your chosen method of fakery doesn't work, you and you alone are out of luck. Or you may be able to find a black-market doctor somewhere who'll treat you despite the law.

But think on a broader scale. Nationwide, there will be thousands of doctors, nurses, nurse-practitioners, dentists, chiropractors, physical therapists, and other medical professionals *who also will have refused to submit to The Card*.

You might have noticed there are *a lot* of medical professionals in the freedom movement and some of them are just about pissed postal already. They've seen government control at its worst, coming at them for years, and they've *had* it. Some have probably "had it" long and hard enough to risk everything on resistance.

Like you, these people need to survive. They have a service to offer. You and they need to find each other. You and they need to arrange terms on which to trade services and fees. You need to know how to find them. They need to know how or whether to trust you (since you could turn them in to the feds for bandaging your little finger — and the cost might be a long prison sentence, as well as confiscation of everything they own). We need a kind of underground Yellow Pages. An underground Rotary Club. A medical directory of the resistance. It needs to be as open to you as it is invisible to the fedsnoops.

We need to be establishing these networks *now*. All over the country. And in all kinds of professions.

We need to be establishing communities of free people all across this land, and all around the world. That's what this book is really about.

Recreating the dreams of freedom

Our task, as I envision it, is to create a Free America within the burgeoning Slave State America. That is, we must ultimately build an entirely new society living within the borders of this now-conquered land.

In truth, there may be many separate societies within America's borders. There might be Christian patriot communities, pagan patriot communities, anarcho-libertarian communities, minarchist-libertarian communities, ideologically mixed communities, communities made up of a religious and cultural rainbow of people, and communities that are all-white, all-black, all-one-form-of-homogeneity-or-another.

Some may be literal, physical communities, hidden in desert or mountain valleys like little Galt's Gulches. Some may be existing small towns which simply happen to have within their borders an unusually large and cohesive population of freedom-seekers. Hard as it is for me to conceive of it, there will certainly be mini-communities of freedom-lovers within the concrete-and-blood canyons of major cities.

Commonly, our Free American Communities will have no fixed, physical existence at all, but will consist of like-minded individuals with computers, or like-minded individuals traveling the roads of the country and perhaps meeting occasionally, like members of the Rainbow Family.

Nevertheless, America will be fundamentally divided into two: one America a fixed, rigid, legally defined nation of the unfree, the other a fluid, dynamic nation of the free, existing under the surface of the other.

"Nation" may not be the best word for what we are about to create; the nation-state as we know it is dying. It is being abolished by a joyful, boundaryless blossoming of communication technology. But nation is a good, useful word for the moment, to the extent that the word implies some degree of shared heritage and belief.

Those of us who hark back to constitutional roots may see themselves as literally rebuilding the old American nation. Even those who look forward to a different world may still find the concept of nation helpful in keeping a sense of community with far-flung fellow freedom lovers. Ours will be a nation of ideas and of creative ways of living.

So that's our mission, in my more-or-less humble opinion: to build an America within an America. It's not only our mission; it's a blood-red necessity if we are to survive as free people without leaving this land.

Living right under their noses

Let me make an important distinction. When I talk about creating a Free America, I'm not talking about new constitutions or old ones, laws, amendments, conventions, continental congresses, or anything else that seeks to impose order and the rule of law on our present chaos.

As the old tagline goes, the Constitution is better than what we have now. No doubt about it. And there have been many sincere proposals for "refounding" the country through law and reform of government. Such efforts may be noble, and the aims of some of them may be desirable.

But they *ain't gonna work*. They're futile. Until more people are ready to take the risks of living free, any government that gets *imposed* upon the country by any means is going to be worse than the one we've got.

Our best hope lies in living quietly, independently, right under the nose of the tyrant. (At least until the present usurper government weakens and we strengthen; then, perhaps, other methods will be useful. But by then they may also not be necessary.)

Let those who crave their "security," their welfare checks, and their subsidies go on living under the federal government. Let them make the choice to sign their lives over to the state in return for ephemeral "protection."

We will live in a parallel universe, so to speak, governing and taking care of ourselves.

Whether or not the usurper falls in our lifetimes, we will be more free than if we had submitted to its whims.

These things that are driving us toward this outlaw freedom are scary. But the opportunity is exciting.

We'll never recreate the old America of the Revolution. And even if we could, we'd find we didn't like it. Because, despite its noble Enlightenment ideals, it isn't for us. We are Twentieth Century people, and soon to be Twenty-first Century people. We have the chance to create something new out of the combination of ancient values, new technologies, and the experiences of our own lives.

We can reinvent concepts of commerce, protection, medicine, work, and a raft of other social functions. We can build new homes in new places, if we wish. We can try out the types of social organization we've fantasized and philosophized about. And if they don't work, we can try something else. If we have the passion and the persistence, and if we're sneaky or patient enough, we can build a rocket and colonize space.

We can do it all because we've quit hanging around waiting for freedom and decided to make freedom happen, instead.

We will do it as free individuals, operating within Free Communities.

Why community?

Communities have always been (at best) a mixed blessing for individualists. Sometimes they've been a downright curse. They're a curse when they consist of masses of people pressuring us into conformity, legislating us into obedience, or taxing us into slavery.

But now, for the first time in more than a century, we have an excellent opportunity — and a pressing need — to create communities of our own, to our specifications.

But why do we need community at all? We may need community to:

- Provide basic survival services, such as food, water, sanitation, heat, and light
- Care for us when we are sick or in need
- Maintain services for convenience and comfort
- Maintain lines of communication (e.g., telephone services, mail delivery, Internet services)
- Offer means of travel (e.g., roads, buses, trains, etc.)
- Provide entertainment and recreation
- Sell us goods we can't produce for ourselves
- Trade and barter with us
- Help us build our homes
- Help us defend ourselves
- We need the individuals within communities to intellectually challenge us, comfort us, love us, inspire us, worship with us, share ideas with us, and otherwise feed our mental and spiritual selves

• And much more

Not every community — especially not every underground community — will offer all these benefits. But every community, even the sparsest, can offer some life-sustaining something if we want to take advantage of it.

And we, even those of us who more easily picture ourselves as hermits in the woods, have some skill or trait that we can offer to others. Again, if we choose to.

Never mind that some of us would rather see ourselves as the lone wolf, the cave-dweller, the rugged individualist, the trapper, the hearty pioneer.

The lone wolf occasionally needs a thorn extracted from its paw. The cave-dweller needs a mate. The hermit needs clothing. The rugged individualist needs supplies to build his house. The trapper needs a loan to buy new traps. The hearty pioneer would like to sit and talk with other pioneers now and then.

Community.

Types of communities we can create underground

It's interesting, the different ideas people have of "community."

One net acquaintance, when I told him about the concept of this book, immediately assumed I had to be talking about a built-from-scratch haven in the desert or mountains, and immediately began lecturing on the need for everything from sanitation to religion in such an undertaking.

Others see "community" as simply, "the place where you live."

Another acquaintance, a member of the family-and-community oriented Latter-Day Saints, spoke of community more as a sharing of common beliefs and goals.

It can be all these things.

When I talk about community, I too think of people bound by shared goals and values. But in many cases, I see no need for physical contact between the group's members.

Like a growing number of people (especially those who "hang out" on the Internet), I envision a community tied together by technology. My closest friends and allies are, in many cases, people I've

never even seen in person. But we have chosen each other, across states and across oceans, because of beliefs we share and personalities that mesh.

Although the means of doing this is new, technology has simply enabled us to expand older concepts such as "communities of faith" or "communities of interest."

Of course, there are times when you do need services that can only be delivered face-to-face. Or you simply want friends you can touch. For that you need community, also — physical community — even when it's only a community of two.

To a large extent, "community" can be what you make it, whatever you need and want it to be. Let's look at four types of communities and how they might operate in post-ID America.

They are:

• Created physical communities
• "Found" physical communities
• Virtual communities
• Mobile communities

Created physical communities

In the early nineteenth century the wilderness edges of the country teemed with groups of people following utopian visions. They established communities and lived according to a variety of quirky, idealistic lifestyles.

Most of these groups practiced some form of communalism and most failed rapidly. But they had the opportunity to make their choices and to experiment with unusual beliefs — something that has, in recent years, been more likely to earn you Death by Government.

The Appendix contains a list of books and articles about these people and their efforts.

For libertarians, the modern model for a fully independent utopian community exists mainly in another book, Ayn Rand's magnum opus, *Atlas Shrugged*.

"Galt's Gulch" was the haven in the Rockies built by millionaire Midas Mulligan and named after the novel's hero John Galt. It was totally self-sufficient, hidden by a mysterious "ray screen," and populated with freedom lovers retreating from a society that exploited and abused them.

Ayn Rand gave precious little explanation of how her crew of millionaires, artists, and dreamers got their plumbing built or repaired. She gave no explanation as to how a whole townful of building materials got up in the Rockies with no outsiders noticing, or how food, medicines, and other goods continued to make their daily way in unnoticed. And darnit, Ayn, it sure would be nice if a working diagram of that ray-screen thingie turned up in your papers someday. Even better if the thingie had the ability to defeat modern satellite imaging and infrared detection equipment.

Nevertheless, Rand created a vivid image. Most people in the freedom movement understand vividly what it means to "build a Galt's Gulch." And many of us, desperate for freedom, dream of building our Gulch right now.

Is it doable? Can such a place be built, and if so, can it fulfill its purpose of giving freedom lovers a safe haven?

I expect that, over the next few decades, a lot of people will try.

There are, in fact, many modern utopian communities operating, and leads to some of these are in the Appendix as well.

Many of the existing and semi-successful ones are New Age communities or interesting experiments in lifestyle, like Arizona's well-known Arcosanti, not the dream homes of freedom seekers.

Arcosanti is interesting, and we can learn from it. (SF writers Larry Niven and Jerry Pournelle also drew on the ideas of Arcosanti's founding spirit, Paolo Soleri, in writing the novel *Oath of Fealty.*) But it isn't for most of us. As described on its web page:

> 27 years ago, the Cosanti Foundation began building Arcosanti, an experimental town in the high desert of Arizona. When complete, Arcosanti will house 7,000 people, demonstrating ways to improve urban conditions and lessen our destructive impact on the earth. Its large, compact structures and large-scale solar green-houses will occupy only 25 acres of a 4,060 acre land preserve, keeping the natural countryside in close proximity to urban dwellers.
>
> Why: Suburban sprawl, spreading across the landscape, causes enormous waste, frustration and long-term costs by depleting land and resources. Dependency on the automobile in-

tensifies these problems, while increasing pollution, congestion, and social isolation. Arcosanti hopes to address these issues by building a three-dimensional, pedestrian-oriented city. Because this plan eliminates suburban sprawl, both the urban and natural environments should keep their integrity and thrive.

> Arcosanti is a prototype: if successful, it will become a model for how the world builds its cities.

> How: Arcosanti is designed according to the concept of arcology (architecture + ecology), developed by Italian architect Paolo Soleri. In an arcology, the built and the living interact as organs would in a highly evolved being. This means many systems work together, with efficient circulation of people and resources, multi-use buildings, and solar orientation for lighting, heating and cooling.

> In this complex, creative environment, apartments, businesses, production, technology, open space, studios, and educational and cultural events are all accessible, while privacy is paramount in the overall design. Greenhouses provide gardening space for public and private use, and act as solar collectors for winter heat.

Interesting, but I wouldn't want to live there. Arcosanti is also too visible to be anyone's idea of a "Gulch." And, in practice, it's having a difficult time progressing from mere experiment to viable community.

There are also a growing number of patriot or religious communities, some described by Dr. Paul Clark in the January 1998 issue of *Media Bypass* magazine ("In Defense of Dropouts: Alternative Communities Crop Up").

These include:

- The "covenant communities" established by Bo Gritz in the Idaho Panhandle, To buy into the 1,800-acre development, you must sign an agreement that you agree with the principles of the community.
- Star of the Sea, an Arkansas haven for Catholic traditionalists.

- Twin Oaks, near Richmond, Virginia, where about 100 people lead a largely self-sufficient life.

All three of these exist on different bases. According to Clark, Twin Oaks is a for-profit corporation, with residents not owning their own land and businesses, but shares in the community's land and businesses. Star of the Sea hopes to become an incorporated village, complete with government. Gritz has set up something more like a traditional private land development.

The visibility of these communities creates problems for them. As Clark points out, in America "Freedom of association does not exist." Legally, these communities are forbidden to exclude people who don't share their beliefs. And this alone could give a snooping government an excuse to shut them down — through crushing "civil rights suits," if not through outright violence.

I know of one interesting, more diverse and more libertarian, community operating in the Southwestern U.S. called Greyhaven. Its proponents praised its defensibility and relative invisibility. But on the other hand, they also did much to expose its location by discussing the place openly on Fidonet and the Internet. I don't know whether Greyhaven still exists, or under what conditions it may presently operate.

There has been, however, a sudden explosion of Galt's Gulch projects among libertarians and other freedom seekers. Within the last month, information about at least a half dozen new projects has come into my computer. Some are large-scale development projects. Others, inconspicuous little plans to bring fellow travelers into one rural location.

Perhaps the best hope of all lies in the plans I'll *never* hear about — because their planners have been so successful at creating something both free and invisible.

Doing it yourself: Although the totally self-contained "Gulch-type" community would cost a fortune, an independent community can feasibly be built without a great deal of money. For instance, twenty or thirty families could pool funds, buy a ranch in Wyoming, and move trailers onto the property. With large Wyoming parcels selling for less than $1,000 an acre and occasionally for as little as $100 per acre, it's doable with the right group of people. In some

areas there is no county zoning. Even where building restrictions exist, you may be met with a laissez-faire attitude. Wyoming law enforcement doesn't spend much time pushing Wyoming ranchers around.

Unfortunately, self-sufficiency isn't a likely proposition in most parts of Wyoming — or the rest of the Rocky Mountain region. These inexpensive lands are dry, barren, and good for little except grazing and hunting. Well water is often undrinkable, forcing residents to haul tankloads of water from the nearest town or have water delivered. The land may be far from phone, cable, and other utilities. (Which may, depending on your point of view, be a blessing.) The climate of Wyoming is also something beyond horrible, with short summers, harsh winters, and a wind that fills up the local mental health centers after its been blowing for three or four days straight.

Similar conditions — or different, but equally unfavorable ones — are likely to pertain wherever land is cheap. (Although I hear glowing reports from freedom-seekers in eastern Kentucky and eastern Tennessee.)

Another plan might involve a lot of families and individuals simply buying or renting homes and trailers in a rural area. Such a development could become an informal "Gulch" or it could lead to a different goal altogether…

Taking over a county or town: There is the old idea of simply selecting an isolated, rural area (but one that already has some political structure and "infrastructure") and bringing in enough people to change the political and philosophical climate.

Esmeralda County, Nevada, has been talked about as a possible freedom haven. Other places like Nye County, Nevada, and Catron County, New Mexico, have also been considered. Any place with a population of a few hundred or a few thousand might enable newcomers to assume political power.

That's one of the hopes of Bo Gritz, Jack McLamb, and friends, who have their land developments near the small town of Kamiah, Idaho. I admire what they're doing, but (aside from the fact that I don't personally agree with major parts of their philosophy), I'd worry that any Bo Gritz development, particularly one in the Idaho Panhandle, would serve as a fed magnet.

Until recently, the only serious effort to draw libertarians to a given area was Mary Margaret Glennie's push, about ten years ago, to bring libertarians to Fort Collins, Colorado. Only a few came. And Fort Collins, being a metropolitan city of nearly 100,000 people, is also not a suitable Gulch site or a likely place for any one group to be able to shift the political climate.

The most notable recent "takeover" of a county by an interest group was the Rajneeshis' temporary conquest of Antelope, Oregon. The religious group and their Rolls Royce-cruising founder simply moved in and built a commune so large they were soon able to outvote the natives. They were, however, utterly despised by those natives — and by the media. Even though the other residents were *politically* powerless against the Rajneeshis, the group's obtrusive presence brought investigations and, ultimately, retaliations.

Sri Rajneesh, the founder, was eventually hounded back to India to escape tax charges. He died there not long after. Several of his followers went to prison, charged with violent crimes. The Rajneeshis were probably guilty. But such charges could be brought against any "outsiders." And we have to remember that we *are* going to be "guilty" of many, many crimes under the control freaks' laws.

Unfortunately, any community (Gulch-type or with political aims) built by freedom seekers without the utmost secrecy and discretion will soon be riddled with feds and their informant-spawn. Not to mention those opportunistically infecting local enforcement people. And probably Multi-Jurisdictional Task Forces, to boot. A sad fact of life.

I also have principled objections to the idea of political takeovers, and doubts about whether any hidden Gulch can truly remain hidden.

Still, if somebody wants to ask this poor writer, her dogs, and her loved one to join a promising hideaway Gulch, making a commitment only of time, talent, and her few, poor thousand dollars, hey, I'll sure consider it. In the meantime, I'm investing my hopes in the next alternative.

And I think both human nature and economic realities will make the following option the most important and most widely adopted of all.

"Found" physical communities

This option is less romantic than a true gulch and less dramatic than taking over a county. However, it's also less costly, less risky, and even more invisible (in some ways) than a real-world gulch is likely to be. It's also far more likely to succeed.

Why? Because it doesn't require participants to get up off their butts and follow risky utopian visions — just to stay where they are (or pick a place they'd like to be) and cope like hell.

A "found" physical community, as I picture it, is ideally a small town, isolated from any large metropolitan areas, preferably in a state that has a less-than-usually intrusive government. (Montana, Nevada, Arizona, Wyoming, and possibly some New England states come to mind. Tennessee, Kentucky, and West Virginia are possibilities, not so much because of their governments, but because of their areas of isolation and historic attitudes. There's no such thing as a truly inoffensive state government, though Montana seems to have one of the best — as well as a lot of land to settle in.)

My ideal found community would be large enough to have most of the services needed for survival, and would be surrounded by farms and ranches for self-sufficiency in hard times. It would be large enough not to be one of those rural "glass houses" where everyone knows the color of everyone else's underwear. Yet at the same time, it would be small enough to have an insular, independent attitude.

A nearby river or lake would be an asset as long as it didn't draw too many tourists or eco-bureaucrats.

The town would be defensible without being a fortress. I wouldn't much care about the nature of its government; its my experience that nearly all small-town governments are Congress-in-microcosm — money-sucking, favor-giving, corrupt, unprincipled, and thoroughly disgusting. The aim isn't to involve yourself with local government, and certainly not to take it over, but simply to exist outside of its gaze as much as possible.

The town, like any other, would be populated by folks with a variety of views, and the goal of a libertarian found community isn't necessarily to change that fact. In my scenario, at least, the aim is simply to be able to take advantage of some existing services and to establish a local network of Free Community services as needed, then to live quietly. You are an ordinary neighbor to your ordinary neighbors, but an ally and asset to fellow freedom seekers within the same town and county.

Choosing an established town (even the established town in which you already live, if suitable), means you don't have such expenses as well-drilling and bringing utilities out to a remote site. Most people simply find life easier in town. And in a small town in an independent region, you have a fair chance of finding a utility company that won't insist on Slave ID, a hospital that'll treat you like a human being, or a policeman who doesn't give a hoot that you own and carry guns.

In other words, much of the groundwork for a Free Community is there, even if the community as a whole is anything but free.

You could either attract interested others to a town like this or, since it's hard to get people to pick up and move anywhere — and since small towns offer few real jobs — gradually make connections through gun clubs, church groups, grange organizations, and other sources. If you already live in a town like this, you've probably already done it.

In the small town where I live, I discovered early on that one local restaurant always seemed to be filled with interesting talk of guns, ideas, and freedom. It took a while to identify the players, but eventually my S.O. (Significant Other) and I realized that one man seemed to be at the center of all this — and that he was, of all things, the local Catholic priest! Now, although we have few connections ourselves, *he* has connections near and far, large and small, and he is a passionate and interesting freedom-lover. So connections can and do happen through serendipity.

That our particular connection came through a church is an interesting reflection of history. Though most American churches have sold out to government values, churches have often been defenders of freedom when people were threatened by government power.

What about found communities in big cities?

Although I don't personally like cities and don't consider them havens of freedom, others, I'm sure, will establish freedom circles even in the wilds of Manhattan or Los Angeles. And I'm not talking about libertarian discussion groups, which already exist in mind-bogglingly vast array, but about Free Communities of *doers in the cause of freedom*. Quite possibly, cities, with their greater variety of people and

more open-minded attitudes, might even offer better Free Community possibilities than the small town I envision.

The important thing is to find or attract a large and diverse enough group of people that you can support each other with your skills as well as your philosophies.

But of course, your Free Community isn't limited to your city or town. The Free Community is everywhere…

Virtual communities

The virtual community has *always* existed. But it exists today as it never has before — and bless the Internet for that.

In the pre-Civil War days of the underground railroad, escaping slaves and the families who hid them were more truly a community than their near neighbors who practiced slavery, ignored slavery, or simply chose not to "get involved." Most people in the underground railroad "community" never even knew each other. Yet they shared common goals and values.

But the Internet has made a miracle out of this type of far-flung community.

For instance, I belong to a small "community" of political humorists and satirists who publish their work in cyberspace. We all found each other through roundabout ways, mostly by discovering and admiring each others' work. So far most of us haven't physically met. But we form a community of common interest and also seem to have strikingly similar personalities (as far as that can be discerned via writing and a few phone conversations).

In turn, each of us belongs to other cyber communities. Several of my fellow satirists are members of Christian patriot net communities. I'm not. I'm a member of an informal community of libertarian radical curmudgeons. They aren't.

For us, these informal, invisible, ethereal communities will probably become the basis of underground communities of the future.

If you aren't on the Internet, no real explanation of this kind of community is possible. If you are on it, none is really necessary. Experience it. It's amazing.

Virtual Communities will exist within and between all other types of Free Communities. They will tie together freedom lovers in far-flung locales. But they will also help us talk to that Catholic priest who lives five blocks away. In some cases, they will exist on their own, without tying together any other communities.

They will help us form the basis of transportation networks, communications systems, community security and (I'm sorry to have to say) a modern underground railroad.

And that doesn't even begin to touch on the *other* uses of the Internet to freedom-seekers — uses unconnected to community building and community living.

If you aren't on the Internet, get on it if you can. It's important to the future. (Yes, it has its risks and vulnerabilities, too. But the benefits are enormous.) Have fun and find your little community out there.

Mobile communities

They gather around hot springs in the California desert. They gather around huge flea markets — or flea markets gather around them. They wander up and down highways in vans, trailers, and motorhomes. They follow rock groups. They follow the weather. They follow rodeos and fairs and whims. They may be known as snowbirds, gypsies, homeless people, or pests, depending on their status and their nature.

But many of these people form another sort of community — the mobile community.

You could pass right by one of these communities and not even know it was there. They live under railroad bridges and in parks in Missoula, Montana, in the summer. They camp in state and national parks, or roadside rests. They might gather formally, like the Rainbow Family, or simply show up in the same place, drawn by something in the psychic tom-toms.

You saw them, hilariously, traveling the salt flats in the movie *Independence Day*. You can read about them in Jon Krakauer's touching biography of a young, doomed wanderer, *Into the Wild*. You've probably been among them and never even knew.

Most mobile communities, like most other communities, aren't made up of consciously, politically motivated freedom-seekers. Many might be made up of criminals, deadbeats (actual ones; not the ones the government's tracking) and people who can't get along with anybody for long. But they do have an edge in the freedom-seeking department. A lot of

these people are doing what they are because they want to be left alone. Just plain left alone.

Which could make them good neighbors and good teachers. And which could make a mobile life ideal cover for someone seeking independence.

I have a friend, Pat, who lives this way. He's a highly educated former professional with skills in both software engineering and music. In 1997, he began an experiment in mobile living by purchasing a stripped-down trailer and equipping it as custom living space, then hitting the road.

He immediately ran into more than a few difficulties:

- His innovative shelf systems, made with light ropes, spilled their contents as soon as he hit the road and had to be redesigned.
- The acoustic coupler with which he hoped to connect to the Internet via payphones refused to function in any but the most favorable conditions, leaving him far less connected than he intended to be.
- His car developed $2,000 worth of mechanical troubles (perhaps in part from trailer-hauling), then his portable computer died and went wherever dead computers go.
- Police in the rural area he first explored quickly spotted and hassled him.
- The generator he thought would be an adequate power source didn't function anywhere near to specs.

However, Pat has been on the road more than a year as I write this and he's made a lot of personal discoveries about living free.

- It turns out that, for him, big cities actually ensure greater opportunity for privacy than the small towns he first looked at. (He is still, however, exploring options. And as a mobile dweller he can do that easily.)
- Big cities have also brought him gigs as a musician.
- Just as he gave up on his generator, he walked into a stunning deal on solar panels.
- He foresees that increasingly wide cellphone coverage can help him stay more connected through his new computer.
- But in the meantime, he has adapted and is learning to appreciate long absences from the Internet.

He has also met many other people living similar lives. As he travels and discovers more free and mobile fellows, he establishes his own Free Community, without boundaries.

Some ways communities can work together

Choose the type of community you want — or come up with any other. The world is full of possibilities. And best of all, your possibilities aren't mutually exclusive.

You can move between a gulch and a small town. You can travel and be part of a virtual community at the same time, thanks to increasing teleconnectedness.

You can stay put in a single kind of community, but work with others — similar or dissimilar — anywhere in the world.

Communities of all sorts can — and routinely will — aid each other in many ways.

- Mobile and virtual communities can serve as couriers and news-distributors to gulches and "found" communities.
- All of the land-based communities can serve as stops on an underground railroad — while mobile communities can also transport freedom seekers, and virtual communities can transmit word to potential helpers.
- Communities can trade with each other, both goods and skills.
- Communities can defend each other as needed.
- In event of a major collapse, widespread Free Communities could form a network of self-sufficiency and innovation that would aid recovery of prosperity.
- And in time, when Ozymandias falls of his own weight, Free Communities could serve as the beginning of a new, free *aboveground* America.

As we go along with the rest of this book, talking about work systems, medical care, security, and other aspects of community living, keep in mind how different kinds of communities in different places and with different skill sets can aid each other.

This scary old world is full of interesting possibilities for us to invent and develop.

Where's your own safe haven?

The vast majority of readers of this book will stay right where they are — unless they are driven from their present location by catastrophe or happen to move for some other reason. It's simple human nature. Simple inertia.

A smaller group — probably made up of younger, less settled readers and retirees who are sick of being settled — will seek out small towns, country hideaways and mobile lifestyles. Even then, however, it's a good bet that their ultimate choices will be made only in part on the freedom-haven qualities of the place or the lifestyle they select.

While a handful of freedom seekers will look *only* for the qualities that might make a secret, secure, self-sustainable haven, most people are going to have a lot of other criteria in mind — nearness to family, aesthetics, recreational opportunities, available work, medical facilities, open spaces, and a myriad of other qualities.

If even a few dozen readers of this book successfully create true, independent, hidden Gulches, I'll be very surprised. (Well, no I won't. Because if they do it right, I'll never find out!)

That's one reason why — although whole books could be written on topics like selecting land, finding water, obscuring ownership, etc. — this book is going to focus more on services and strategies useful to *any* freedom community, whether in the heart of Greenwich Village or in the dead center of Esmeralda County, Nevada.

Nevertheless, if you're setting out to Gulch, or if you're choosing an existing location for its haven qualities, here are some factors to consider:

- Suitability for defense
- Concealability — either in the sense of physically hiding or in the sense of misdirecting casual inquirers; for instance, a Gulch that looks like an ordinary farm or ranch, or a house in a small town that is actually "hardened" and well-stocked with emergency goods
- Availability of potable water
- Distance from metropolitan areas
- Difficulty of access from metropolitan areas
- Friendliness of locals

- Willingness of locals to leave you alone
- A state where the legislature is in session less than six weeks per year (an indicator of less love of government)
- Low taxes
- Distance from popular recreational areas; or invisibility to popular recreational areas
- Sparse population or sympathetic population
- Friendly gun laws and/or lax enforcement of gun laws
- Low ratio of police to citizens and/or laid-back attitude on the part of local law enforcement
- Self-sustainability; e.g., nearby small-scale agricultural operations, hunting, fishing, good soil and climate for growing vegetables
- Back roads and trails for alternative emergency travel
- Availability of power; potential for solar, hydro or wind power
- Lack of zoning or lax enforcement of zoning ordinances
- Building materials handy
- Mix of local skills and products for possible trade
- Availability of telecommunications; e.g., Internet service providers for both telecommuting and networking
- And more

Gulchers should also carefully consider options for ownership of land, other property and businesses. This is a complex matter on which the success of the entire venture could depend.

Options for gulch ownership

Ownership options include, but aren't limited to:

- Sole ownership of a gulch by one individual, with residents renting or leasing;
- Sole ownership of a gulch by one individual, with residents earning their positions by working for the owner's company;
- Development of land by one individual or group of investors, with residents purchasing individual parcels;
- Joint ownership of the land by gulch members, with separate ownership of structures or trailers on the land;

- Ownership of all land and facilities in the name of a corporation, with residents holding shares;
- Ownership of all land and facilities in the name of a trust, with residents as grantors;
- Ownership of all land and facilities in the name of a church or other nonprofit organization — as long as you don't end up being burned as heretics by the FBI;
- Individual ownership of adjoining parcels of land, with no formal gulch organization at all;
- Some combination of the above.

Gulchers, whether considering group or individual ownership, should look into using offshore trusts or corporations, which can help place an insulating layer between property and the U.S. government's ability to seize it. Individual homeowners in found communities might do the same.

Under current forfeiture laws, property can be confiscated *regardless of who or what owns it* for certain types of crimes, such as drug dealing or marijuana growing. However, for other "crimes," such as keeping the money you earn, removing property from your ownership can protect it from being seized. I'm not giving tax advice. This is complicated, and there are endless ifs, ands, and buts. Among other things, the IRS *can* seize property, for instance, if they can "prove" you transferred ownership to "evade" taxes.

Keeping ownership offshore and/or obscured is simply a good privacy practice. But the best method for doing so is for you and some advisors with legal savvy, to determine.

The most important thing you need

Above all, of course, we need the right people and the right factors to move them. There are a lot of different ways of going about that.

Mary Lou Seymour, a very active activist from South Carolina, explains that in any planned effort there's a need to "Educate, agitate and organize." In other words, to make people aware of the need for community building, to stir them to want to create communities, then to present a plan on which to act, or build a plan with their assistance.

I don't regard it as our responsibility to educate the general public. In any case, the government is doing a great deal of "educating" through its own brutality and heavy-handedness. However, we can educate ourselves and our allies about options for becoming more free. Community building — of whatever variety — is one of those.

We are just starting. And no matter which options we choose — whether that of being a community-of-one who only occasionally touches base with other freedom lovers, or the option of founding our own physical communities — there is a lot to do. Some of us are going to want to start the agitating and organizing steps of community building now. Some already have. In the last few weeks and months I've received an extraordinary number of proposals or leads to organizations doing just that. And more power to them. I hope this book helps, and I hope more books, pamphlets, and speculative novels come along to fill in the picture.

But while some of us will end up organizing (or being part of) big, planned projects, for others, the task will be different — and driven by that mother, Necessity.

We'll need a doctor one day, but those who accept federal funds may be off-limits to us, by then. Necessity will drive us to find a free market source — and that freedom-loving doctor will become part of our Free community. The law will, on some future day, prevent us from getting electricity or water without a Beast Number. Necessity will drive us to steal or borrow or find alternative independent sources. Those who help us may become part of our Free Community — or we part of theirs.

We will be thrown together with our fellow freedom lovers, discovering new ones along the way — in the electrician who'll connect you privately and indirectly to the grid, the chiropractor who'll treat you without insurance, the grocer who'll sell you goods even when you don't have a card to scan, yes, even the Catholic priest who'll turn out to be the center of a local underground network because his good, brave, free heart will let him do none other.

So, onward...

And now, let's get specific about some of those things we're going to need to find and do and build and make.

As you read, keep in mind that the needs of created communities are going to differ from the needs of

found ones, and the needs of mobile communities will differ yet again. Virtual communities need little that other communities require, yet have urgent needs of their own, such as reliable connectivity.

In a created community, you may have to supply nearly everything — from water to work — for yourselves. In a found community, you may be able to take advantage of many "civilized" services while others may be cut off to you by your lack of The Card — and conditions could change in an instant. It would be impossible to cover all those various needs in one book — even if we could anticipate them all, which we can't.

Building a Free America will take knowledge and skill. But above all, it will take a sinuous adaptability.

In living as we choose to live, we automatically become outlaws. And we will become more serious outlaws — and be pursued more seriously — as federal and state governments make more laws and arm more agents to seek us out. This may cause us to have to go further underground.

With luck, we may be able to live somewhat normally, using our alternate services. In worse-case scenarios, however, we may need to invent our own communications methods, travel in secret, develop alternatives to U.S. money, smuggle goods, provide our own protection services, evade roadblocks, and I fear — to fight back.

The following chapters will look at safe ways of using existing services and facilities, but also examine some of the measures we and our communities might have to adapt for the worst of times.

Be prepared for change...

Update 2002
What's New
Since Chapter Four

This chapter — and indeed, the premise of the entire book — seems very optimistic as I revisit it after three years. The very idea that freedom lovers would do so much work and take so much risk merely to avoid Slave ID now seems almost laughable. With few exceptions, many of us continued to do as we always do — whine about how bad things are getting and make feeble, ineffective protests while passively submitting to every act of enslavement that comes down the pike. More serious freedom lovers have cagily sought ways to maintain personal privacy while doing (understandably) little to stop the dreadful downhill slide of our entire society.

Yet building freedom communities seems no less necessary than it did back then. To remain within everyday America means to sink gradually and passively into acceptance of what should be unacceptable. It means trusting in the benevolence of government, which is something one should never do in the best of times and should certainly not do in the midst of a global push to register, regiment, and control every human being. Even being a lone outlaw, resisting evil laws — something I heartily endorse — isn't enough.

Don't be fooled that all the latest restrictions are imposed upon us in the name of "security"! So were the tyrannies of Nazi Germany. When pressed, no advocate of ID for "security" can say how it would really make America safe.

Nevertheless, citizen-surveillance in the name of security is a fact we've got to live with, just as earlier we learned to live with it in the name of "preventing illegal immigration," "stopping the drug trade," or "preventing money laundering." And if we can't rid ourselves of it "within the system," what are we going to do? The lone outlaw gets weary. We all need support — and communities provide that.

Communities update

Interested to see how the intentional communities mentioned in this chapter are faring several years later, I did some research and came up with this:

- Arcosanti (which was always more of a demonstration of alternative community building, rather than an actual community) still exists. It's a place to take group-motion dance workshops or learn ecologically sound methods of sewage treatment. It gets profiled on National Public Radio now and then. That's about it.
- Land is still being sold (and resold) at the Bo Gritz/Jack McLamb covenant communities (Almost Heaven and Shenandoah) near Kamiah, Idaho, but any real promise of community has failed to materialize. Gritz' life has been ex-

tremely troubled, and the nonappearance of Y2K catastrophe may also have derailed many people's commitment to "head for the hills." Still, Kamiah is a gorgeous place to hide out.
- Star of the Sea, the traditional Catholic community near Hardy, Arkansas, still exists, but I wasn't able to find out more than that.
- Twin Oaks, near Louisa, Virginia, is still going strong with 100 members, no central leadership, no group religion, but communalized living and industries. They proclaim themselves to be self-supporting and largely self-sufficient from work such as making hammocks and casual furniture and indexing books.
- One long-term intentional community I didn't mention in the original *I Am Not a Number!* is the Padanaram settlement near Williams, Indiana. This 30-year-old religious community, whose leader is now past 80, is also still going strong. It supports itself largely via timber-related work and agriculture.

The Free State Project

One of the most interesting community-building efforts to arise since the original release of *I Am Not a Number!* is the Free State Project, created by Yale grad student Jason P. Sorens and growing in strength as I write this. The FSP is different from the types of communities I wrote about in this chapter. It's based on conventional activism, but activism in such an unconventional framework that it deserves an extensive look.

If the FSP succeeds, the residents of one small U.S. state might be able to do such ordinary American things as add a room to a house without a government permit, drive without a national ID license, carry a gun without any registrations, permits or governmental hoops to jump through — and in short, live in ways all free Americans once took for granted. It would be possible because the government of that state would be dedicated solely to protection of life, liberty, and property and would stand as a bulwark between its people and everyday federal bullying.

Here's how the project works. The FSP is currently signing up members and collecting data on eleven states with populations smaller than 1.5 million. Once 5,000 people have joined, they'll vote on the state they think is best for life and liberty. Once 20,000 have joined, all FSP members are pledged to move to the chosen state as rapidly as possible. If the FSP doesn't get the first 5,000 members within three years, they'll simply disband. Similarly, if they never get the needed 20,000, no one will be obligated to move. As of this writing, more than 1,000 have signed on.

What can a mere 20,000 people accomplish? A lot if you're talking about 20,000 freedom activists amid a population of a million or so. That's quite a different thing than 20,000 bodies sitting in front of TV sets guzzling beer and chips or 20,000 people lost in one of America's mega-states like California or New York.

The FSP starts with the realistic assessment that the federal government —the government at which freedom activists futilely throw so many of their efforts and funds — is an immovable obstacle. But one very small state *can* be changed. And it in turn can not only improve its own laws and regulations, but can do such things as keep federal agents from operating within its borders.

To join the FSP, all you have to do is pledge to move to the chosen state (your membership form gives you a place to opt out of certain states, say if you just wouldn't move to Wyoming even if the rest of the U.S. looked like Nazi Germany). You also pledge that once you've arrived there, you'll "exert the fullest practical effort toward the creation of a society in which the sole role of civil government is the protection of citizens' life, liberty, and property." (FSPers are quick to point out that voting and conventional political activism isn't the only way to do that.)

The FSP is not secessionist (though that might remain a last-ditch option) and it's not utopian. These folks aren't hoping to create heaven on earth, just to reduce government interference in our lives by two-thirds or so. And wouldn't that be a relief?

Proposals to move to State X and take over the government are nothing new and I've never supported one in the past; they've struck me as hare-brained schemes without sufficient practical thought behind them. The FSP is different. FSPers are approaching their task intelligently and sensibly, while never losing sight of the prize — liberty. I believe they deserve all the support they can get.

Contact information for the Free State Project can be found in the Appendix, along with the URL of a more extensive article I wrote about these great folks.

News about Costa Rica

For those who might like to get out of the U.S., some interesting developments have recently taken place in Costa Rica. This pleasant, Spanish-speaking Central American country has a lovely coastline, temperate mountains, no army, and an attitude expatriate Americans describe as friendly and laid back. It's the unofficial home base of Laissez Faire City (though the self-described first cyberspace community changed its original plan to establish a physical mini-nation there). And recently the indigenous *Movimiento Libertario* has put some candidates into the national legislature.

Costa Rica is worth a look, and you'll find a few places to begin in the Appendix.

The net

The vast potential of the Internet community — a glowing thing back in 1998 — hasn't yet been fulfilled and may never be. The net encourages all talk and no action. While it certainly has spawned marvelous online cybercommunities (hundreds of thousands of them) and made possible powerful political action that has left politicians stunned and reeling, too little of the net's community-building power has translated into real world action. Let's hope the net doesn't simply turn into a giant corporate entertainment morass and mind-control device like television (which I don't think it will — but not for want of trying on the part of Congress and other Big Money folks).

The Internet is still in its early stages, and quite possibly people in less free countries will eventually make more of the net's community-building power than Americans have. You could still use the power of the net to find members for a nascent freedom community, to make your plans, to locate suppliers, and in a hundred other freedom-enhancing ways.

• • • • • •

The next couple of chapters are heavily slanted toward community activity in very tough times. For individuals on their own, living in days that are still tolerable, some of this information will be irrelevant. Keep it for the future. Take what you can use when you can use it.

Chapter Five
Communications in
the Free Community

With the best of luck, we'll have no need for the information in this chapter. Communications in our underground Free Communities will be no different than communications today. We'll use our phones, our Internet service, the post office, and all our other common methods of information exchange, just as we do now.

But what if the opposite happens? What if you can't get phone service to your house because you refuse to give the phone company your Slave Number? What if the Internet (or just your service provider) goes down, temporarily or long term? What if you learn or suspect that there's a cover on your mail? Or a pen-register or full-scale tap on your phone line? What if an economic collapse or system crash brings down your phone service? What if a long-term truckers' strike halts the mail? What if phone or mail services are cut off to your "Gulch," your ranch, or your town for political reasons?

As an individual, you know how important good, reliable communication methods are. Now compound that importance when thinking of how communications — or their failure — could affect Free Communities.

If the only free community in which you "reside" is a virtual community, then without communications technologies, your entire community has effectively been nuked.

If you live in a found community (whether city or small town), you may need to resort to secret methods of communication if you have reason to believe the local commissars are keeping an ear on your activities.

If you are among the innovative few who manage to achieve a fully self-sufficient gulch community, you may feel relatively invulnerable. But what about your communications with the outside world? With other gulches, with found communities? In other words, what about the one, big "virtual community" of communications that ties a hundred or a thousand physical communities together?

If we are to create underground railroads and free trade routes, as I believe we will, we'll need communications that can sprint ahead of travelers to let far-flung friends know that shipments or fleeing freedom-seekers, are on the way — or to let the travelers themselves know that danger may lie ahead.

It is vital that every form of Free Community, to survive, have reliable methods of communication *now* and backup methods for dangerous times to come. With such technologies as packet radio, we may be able to maintain sophisticated communications even in very hard times. But we may also, unpredictably, be forced to use very primitive, secretive — but effective — methods of the past.

As best we can, we should prepare for these eventualities today.

This chapter gives an overview of communication methods and how they might be used (or abused) if our withdrawal from ID State America, or an economic collapse, affects normal communications.

I've broken them into four levels of technology and security:

- High tech
- Mid-tech

- Low tech, above ground (more or less)
- Low tech, underground

Of necessity, this chapter *is* just an overview. There's no way to cover all the attributes, potentials, advantages, disadvantages, or possible abuses of every technology or method. So, once again, the aim is to give a starting point. If you want more information about anything mentioned here, check the Appendix for organizations, web sites, etc.

High tech

The Internet

The Internet is the best thing going for freedom, and if you aren't already on it, I urge you to beg, borrow, but preferably not steal a computer and a modem, find yourself an Internet service provider (ISP), load some e-mail software and a browser and join the cyber-community of freedom.

This wonderful, decentralized mode of communication is the most inherently anti-authoritarian ever devised. I laugh to think that the U.S. Defense Department invented it for itself in the name of "security." The Defense Department and its contractors created the Internet to survive a nuclear war by swiftly and automatically routing around damaged locations. But in doing so, they also created a technology that routes swiftly and automatically around attempts at centralized control. It's a wonderful joke on them.

The Internet enables us to talk with like-minded people the world over, to transact business in privacy, to use encryption that the government can't break, to bypass the corporate/state media, and generally to raise hell and raise our own consciousness. We can even use it to broadcast, listen to, and watch our own radio and TV programs. It is our modern "Committees of Correspondence."

Nothing could make the federal government feel less "secure" than this — its own child turned rebel.

But having said that, let's acknowledge that the technophobes and pessimists also have valid points. We should heed some caveats and take some precautions.

Elementary precautions for privacy on the Internet

- Be aware that the sites you visit can, and usually do, gather information about you, such as your ISP, the location from which you're calling, and the type of browser you're using. One way to get around this is to use an anonymizer while surfing the net — that is, by visiting a web site designed to disguise your identity as you visit other web sites. Still, the anonymizer site has its own tracking tools, so there's no totally anonymous way of using the Internet. Your best hope lies in obscuring your tracks as much as possible.
- Install cookie-management software to keep the sites you visit from gathering even more unauthorized information about you.
- When you need secure e-mail, use an anonymous forwarding service or a nym server. You can also gain some anonymity by using net-based e-mail, rather than sending and receiving mail directly through your ISP. Several options are listed in the Appendix.
- Encrypt as much personal correspondence as you can with PGP.
- Be aware that Internet browsers may have some ability to read the files on your computer. The Netscape browser, version 3.0, had a feature that would enable someone to do that, provided they knew, or could guess, the exact file name they were looking for and the exact file structure through which to track it. This was supposedly a bug, and supposedly fixed, though I wouldn't trust that. Microsoft's Internet Explorer is designed with the capability to let help-line technicians snoop through your system (in search of pirate software, as well as to diagnose problems). Your best protection lies in encrypting with PGP every file that might reveal anything personal or anything politically incorrect. Also, if you observe suspicious hard-drive activity while browsing, get out of there. Someone on a web site may be snooping in your computer.
- Don't fill out online surveys.
- Transact business over the net only when you're absolutely certain the transmission *and* the storage of your credit card, electronic money data,

and other information about you and your purchase is encrypted and secure.

But what if the Internet goes down?

Even though the Internet was designed to survive nuclear war, it isn't invulnerable. Any disaster that widely affected phone systems throughout the U.S. or the world would cripple the Internet. Even though messages could route around the damaged areas, that wouldn't help you much if you were located *in* the damaged area, or if the damage was so widespread that even the Internet couldn't handle it, or handled it with impossible slowness.

But a greater problem, one that might particularly affect freedom seekers or the otherwise politically incorrect, involves taking down a single ISP or a single user. It is possible, for instance, to cut off access to any given domain name.

Say, for instance, that you and a handful of other rowdies receive your Internet services from Paulrevere.net. Paulrevere.net is a "domain name" licensed to your provider by an allegedly private company. But that company is actually about as "private" as the CIA. So somebody gives the order to kill off, or at least interfere with, that troublesome entity called Paulrevere.net. And bang! Your provider is gone. Or at least, temporarily disabled.

This sort of thing can also happen by accident, and in fact did happen in 1997 to the NASDAQ, the over-the-counter stock exchange. For a few hours, that organization was cut off the Internet by an error that caused its domain name to be unrecognized. The people at NASDAQ were still able to access the net, so it took them quite a while to realize anything was wrong; but no one was able to access NASDAQ on the Web or send e-mail messages to it.

It could just as easily be done on purpose. And it could just as easily be your personal account that could be shut off at your ISP, for a variety of reasons.

Also, the modems at your local access number could be sabotaged or otherwise taken off line. Your ISP could go broke. Or your phone service could be halted.

Even though the Supreme Court recently decided, resoundingly, against Internet censorship, that hasn't stopped the congressional control freaks for a moment. Under censorship bills now before Congress, your provider could also be held liable for any information "damaging to children" it allows to pass through its wires. And of course "damaging to children" could just as easily mean political as pornographic. So, using a variety of flimsy excuses, your provider could be threatened or sued into denying you access. Or, just as your banker is now expected to watch for and report to the feds any transactions it regards as possibly being "terroristic," your ISP could be forced to report, or curtail, any messages suspected of being "anti-government."

This bill hasn't become law — and might never. But be aware that the tactic of pressuring your ISP is a potentially very damaging one for your free speech.

And be aware that, even if the entire net is relatively secure, there are a lot of localized, and very personal, ways your own access could be cut off.

Anything that affects your net access or the access of other freedom-seekers can damage your community.

So use the Internet to your heart's content. Subvert, communicate, and have a blast. But prepare a backup method in the event you lose net access, or that net access becomes temporarily unsafe.

Remember Fidonet?

You netizens out there, do you recall Fidonet from those ancient days of computing — like 1994, or thereabouts?

Fidonet — one of several *private* alternatives to the Internet — sent e-mail messages around the world, just as the Internet does. Instead of centralized service providers, Fidonet relied primarily on computers sitting in people's living rooms and dens. Messages traveled from computer to computer via phone lines, just as Internet communications do, but the process was slower, as each computer fetched or sent its mail a few times a day, and the messages might have to make a lot of hops to get to their destinations.

The operators of the system were unpaid hobbyists or devotees who kept the network going out of personal commitment. The process was a lot slower, and a bit more unreliable than the Internet. It also taxed the energies and finances of its volunteer providers. But it worked. For years.

And it was entirely out of the government's control.

Fidonet still exists, though it's rapidly being dismantled. My correspondent Gene Hahn, who just took down his own Fidonet node after seven years, tells me there are now more Fido nodes in Europe than in America. And I'm speaking of Fido in the past tense because I fear that might be true by the time this book goes to print.

But save those old computers! Keep your spare, even outdated equipment!

While it's unlikely that any *permanent, widespread* harm will befall the Internet, if something does happen, a renewed Fidonet (or similar system) could form an electronic Samizdat, operating under the fedgov's radar screen. (Thanks to Simon Jester, Apostle of Subversion, for the reminder!)

Cellphones

Cellular phones and related emerging technologies could be a useful alternative to regular phone service, particularly for freedom seekers who:

- Are in a rural area that's within a cellular service area but distant enough from land lines to make hookups prohibitively expensive. This is actually a fairly common situation these days.
- Are under siege. In that case, cellular service *registered in someone else's name* so that enforcers didn't know you had access to it might give you a temporary means of alerting friends or media to your plight, until the besieging enforcers discovered it and cut off your service. If it's registered in your name, you're likely to be cut off before you can use the service in a siege.
- Must travel a lot. This one's kind of a no-brainer since travel is already one of the primary justifications for cellphones. However, think how much more useful a cellphone could be to a traveler who needed extra flexibility. Again, try to keep the service out of your own name.

Cellphones are vulnerable to eavesdropping. It's illegal, and modern scanners are blocked from receiving cellular transmissions, but that won't stop anybody, and has certainly never stopped a determined law enforcer. Your conversations could be picked up even by accident. The best way to deal with eavesdroppers may be to use one of the newer, digital services.

Cellphone service is also vulnerable to sabotage (say, by someone who might blow up a relay tower)

and can be cut off by officials as easily as land-line phone service.

It's also expensive — and can be ridiculously so for people who travel from zone to zone and have to pay "roaming charges." That's changing, but still has a ways to go.

Someone also just sent me a rumor that your location can be traced through your possession of a cellphone, even when the phone is turned off. I'm putting that one into the BS file for now. However your location and movements certainly can be traced — easily — through your *use* of a cellphone, as the following article demonstrates.

From a Reuters news report, December 28, 1997:

ZURICH — Swiss police have secretly tracked the whereabouts of mobile phone users via a telephone company computer that records billions of movements going back more than half a year, a Sunday newspaper reported…

Officials from state telephone company Swisscom confirmed the practice, but insisted information about mobile customers was only handed out on court orders.

"Swisscom has stored data on the movements of more than a million mobile phone users. It can call up the location of all its mobile subscribers down to a few hundred meters and going back at least half a year," the paper reported.

"When it has to, it can exactly reconstruct down to the minute who met whom, where and for how long for a confidential tête-à-tête," it said.

Prosecutors called the records a wealth of information that helped track criminals' movements….

SonntagsZeitung said there was no legal basis for storing such information.

"I am unaware of any law that would allow the preventative collection of data for investigative purposes," it quoted Odilo Guntern, the federal ombudsman for protecting individuals' privacy, as saying.

Packet radio

Digital packet radio enables computers to communicate with each other over the airwaves, rather than via phone lines. You can see how this might come in handy if your homestead is beyond the reach of the phone system or if you prefer not to be on the phone grid.

Packet radios are currently used by thousands of hobbyists to communicate with each other, locally and globally, through e-mail messages and online chats. They also help track weather systems, send emergency warnings, and perform other functions traditionally the province of ham operators. (It was, in fact, ham radio hobbyists who turned packet radio from an obscure and expensive technology into an affordable avocation.)

Packet has its own transmission protocols, such as AX.25. However, it also uses some of the same protocols as the Internet (notably TCP/IP, FTP, telnet and SMTP). Therefore, a message that first went out via radio could later reach a recipient with a more conventionally equipped computer.

In the here and now, packet might help you make a transition to an isolated Gulch or farm by enabling you to telecommute. (Never mind that you are actually radiocommuting.) It could also help you work or carry out emergency communications in a future with a broken infrastructure.

Packet has some drawbacks — the primary one being slowness. As of this writing, most packet operations transmit at 1200 bits-per-second, some at 9600 bps. Compared with today's Internet speeds, this is like having a car that won't exceed 20 mph. But according to Keith Justice, Professor Emeritus at the University of California, Irvine, "[The Tucson Amateur Packet Radio Corporation] is working on higher speed user and backbone development now. I expect we will see a leap forward in a couple of years when that effort produces results. Equipment is available to go forward right now, from commercial sources, but economic constraints and lack of technical expertise by most hams will prevent widespread use until TAPR develops cheap plug-n-play solutions."

Packet radio can operate in all frequency ranges used by amateur (ham) radio, but most activity is on two-meter (144–148 MHz) and UHF (440–450 MHz). Packet radio's reach in these ranges is limited to line-of-sight (10–100 miles), so it requires a network of stations to carry messages any great distance. Fortunately, such networks already exist and

have been growing steadily in the fifteen or so years since the technology became practical.

The federal government requires an amateur radio license of Technician class or higher for using this technology (see the following section). Once you have the basic ham gear and a computer, you can add digital packet radio capability for $110 or less.

To learn more about packet radio, check with the Tucson Amateur Packet Radio Corporation, a pioneer of the modern system (listed in the Appendix), or find a local amateur packet radio club in your area.

Mid-tech

Ham radio

Ham radio is so well known it isn't necessary to say much about it. Ham radio operators have helped emergency workers find their way through flood zones, helped rescue the crews of sinking ships, united lost loved ones, sent messages to soldiers at war, and otherwise been a boon to society.

Despite its reputation, most of us still regard ham radio as an esoteric hobby. However, there has been one fairly recent change that might make ham more accessible. You're no longer required to learn Morse code in order to get a ham license.

(Licenses? Do we need esteeeking licenses? Well, that's another subject...)

There are now two beginner's categories for ham operators: Technician Class (the Morseless one), enables you to use all ham frequencies above 30 Megahertz (MHz). This means you can use the little handheld, two-meter units to give you mobility in a crisis. It also makes your transmissions more difficult to trace. A Technician license lets you operate via FM voice, digital packet radio, single-sideband (used, among other things, for ground-to-air communications) and other modes.

Technician Class used to be the second step, after Novice Class, on a five-step ladder of ham classifications. To get a Technician Class license you are still required to take the written exams (though not the Morse proficiency test) for both Novice and Technician.

The Novice Class is similar. It is more limited in some ways, but enables you to use the below-30-MHz range for Morse code communications. These low frequencies have the longest range and are used for around-the-world communications.

Ham radio has the advantage of being useable for both near and long-distance communications (even communications with outer space, if any of us ever manage to make it to an orbiting colony). As my S.O., an old space buff, points out, some astronauts are hams and will send QSL (acknowledgment) cards to folks who contact them on the space shuttle.

There are ham operators and ham clubs all over the world, and licensing exams are commonly given at community colleges, high schools, and other easily accessible places.

It's advantageous to belong to a club because clubs usually own repeaters (the equipment to extend your transmission range). And while they may let non-members use it, you'll be establishing your credibility by helping pay for it.

The American Radio Relay League (Appendix again!) is the place to look for information.

Ham radio with phone patch

Phone patches enable ham operators to work through the phone system.

Again, clubs usually have phone patches, saving you the time and trouble of investing in one.

CB radio

Anybody who was around in the 1970s doesn't have to be told about citizens band radio. CB was so popular there was even a hit song about it. ("We've got a little convoy, rockin' through the night. We've got a little convoy, ain't she a beautiful sight?") CB talk, or pseudo-CB talk, like "Ten-four, little buddy," became, for a mercifully short while, part of the common American language.

CB is, quite simply, a portion of the radio spectrum devoted to free, unlicensed use by anybody who feels like using it. Until the CB craze, the FCC did license citizens band users but — swamped by applications — a fedgov agency did that rarest of government tricks and actually backed away from regulation. Today, in the U.S. CB use is unlicensed. In other countries, it's either unlicensed or at least very lightly regulated.

Personally, I never quite "got" CB. My S.O. has a CB in his truck, and all it ever does is scare the heck out of me. We'll be driving companionably along and the infernal machine will abruptly issue a screech that

sounds like one of the undead opening its coffin for the night. My S.O. will translate, "There's ice on the road up ahead," or "Speed trap on the freeway." But I'll have to take his word for it because all I ever hear is, "Shreesreerhhsuggruurggsghh-sssspt!"

Personal complaints aside, however, if you can abide the things, CB radios still have their uses — and could have even more powerful uses in a less free future.

Though cellphones and other mobile technologies have largely supplanted them for mobile-to-base communications and for calls to emergency services, CBs can still come in handy when you want to communicate with multiple recipients within a given range.

Motorists can use them to put out general warnings of traffic problems or make queries about road conditions. Think about how much more useful they could be in a world in which motorists, having developed a pirate mentality, use CBs to help strangers evade roadblocks and "checkpoints."

Think about how useful they could be to members of multivehicle convoys, transporting forbidden products or escorting undocumented citizens to safety.

Whenever you need short distance, mobile communications among multiple, simultaneous recipients, CB is still a good technology.

But since anyone within range and tuned to the right frequency can hear your transmissions, you will need to develop personal codes if you want privacy.

CB already has several sets of codes. Most common in the U.S. are the "ten codes," such as:

10-1	Receiving poorly
10-4	Message received. (This does not mean "okay," as some people think.)
10-7	Leaving the air
10-9	Repeat message
10-12	Visitors present
10-13	Adverse weather or road conditions
10-20	My location is….
10-25	Can you contact…
10-39	Your message delivered
10-44	I have a message for…
10-65	Awaiting your next order or assignment
10-67	All units comply
10-85	My address is….
10-99	Mission completed, all units secure

There's even a code for "I have to go to the bathroom" (10-100). Actually, most of the ten codes are so obscure that not one in a hundred CB users is likely to recognize any beyond a few basics (like the ubiquitous 10-4). That means you could easily adopt the more obscure ones as is, with little chance of recognition. Or you could change their meanings to suit your purposes. You could, of course, make up entirely different codes of your own. Keep in mind that the two groups of CB users most likely to recognize the codes are truckers and the police.

When I discussed codes with my S.O., he suggested that one of the most useful codes for anyone convoying forbidden goods or on other forms of secret missions would be one that meant "change channel." Having several codes that signaled members of your convoy to switch simultaneously from, say, Channel 13 to Channel 15 and switch again from Channel 15 to Channel 11 could help you avoid detection. You know — for those days you're transporting undocumented citizens or such forbidden goods as cigarettes or high-fat foods.

Outside of the U.S. and in some parts of the U.S., the ten codes may be replaced by similar "Q" codes. There is also an elaborate CB etiquette, which you'll find listed in any book about CB or on any Internet CB list of FAQ.

In the U.S. the citizens band encompasses the frequencies from 26.965 to 27.405 MHz (AM and single-sideband) and is allowed to transmit at a maximum four watts (12 watts for single-sideband). Within the CB frequency range, there are 40 channels, with the first 30 used for AM and the next 10 for single-sideband (SSB).

Some channels are by custom reserved for special purposes. Channel 9, for example, is an emergency channel that is monitored nationwide by a group called REACT. In the west, Channel 17 is an unofficial truckers' channel. Nineteen is also a truckers' channel, but dedicated to traffic advisories and announcements of speed traps.

There is a newer, related, technology, also reserved for individuals, called general mobile radio service, which operates in the 31.0–31.3 GHz frequency range. If you're interested in that or CB, you'll find contacts for more information in You Know Where.

The maximum legal range for CB in the U.S. is 150 miles, but except under the rarest of atmospheric conditions, this can only be achieved with base (not mobile) stations, using antennas that are both high up and highly directional. The realistic range for a mobile CB is more like 3-5 miles and can be even less in crowded areas where noise from multiple transmissions creates interference.

On the other hand, transmissions of up to 1,000 miles are possible if atmospheric conditions are just right and you use the ionosphere to "skip" your signal. But of course, bouncing your signal off the ionosphere *on purpose* is illegal. Guess what? It's legal in Russia, but *verboten* in the good old Land of the Free. Dontcha just love it?

Scanners

Scanners have long been useful for monitoring fire, police, and other emergency frequencies, air traffic, and other government and business operations (e.g., taxi and bus traffic). They could be useful in natural disasters, or in unnatural disasters, like a raid upon someone's home. Perhaps a scanner could even help you monitor a siege upon your own home, if you have a means of powering the equipment after the cops cut your electricity.

However, all this is changing — rapidly. If current trends in technology and political debate continue "…in twenty years, those fighting for scanners would have them but having nothing left to listen to" (David Pinero, "Open Broadcasting FAQ," alt.radio.scanner news-group, October 1997).

Since 1986, all scanners manufactured in the U.S. have been crippled — that is, certain frequencies have been blocked. (Electronic Communications Privacy Act of 1986.) The ostensible purpose was to prevent civilian monitoring of cordless, cellular, and other types of mobile phones. But as with all federal legislation, the actual purpose is more elitist and boils down to control-for-the-sake-of-control. Police agencies were becoming alarmed at the idea of the public monitoring their increasingly arcane enforcement techniques. On the excuse that "cocaine dealers" were using scanners to evade police operations, they began not only to block access via scanners, but to switch to "closed" communications technologies.

Today, an increasing number of local, state and federal enforcement agencies are also using "trunked" communications or digital communications that can't be heard on existing scanners. Many agencies are also encrypting their transmissions.

There are some purely practical reasons for the technology switch. Trunked communications, which enable as many as twenty stations to use one frequency, are simply more efficient than having one station monopolize a frequency. However, in addition to enabling multiple stations using one frequency, trunking also enables single stations to use multiple frequencies. They can seek whichever available frequency isn't in use by another station. Current scanners can't handle the seemingly random jumps from frequency to frequency.

Digital technology is a separate issue, but digital and trunked technologies are often implemented at the same time.

Practical considerations aside, government agencies are clearly enjoying the opportunity to shut citizens out of their communications. Even I will concede that *maybe… some* types of police communications *might* legitimately be kept *temporarily* secret. But the true elitist motives are revealed by the fact that, in many cases, even fire and medical transmissions are now being encrypted to prevent the public from knowing about them.

As David Pinero points out, widespread secrecy has the effect of further isolating citizens from the activities of agencies that allege to "serve and protect" them.

Ironically, enforcement agencies may be cutting their own throats with their us-vs.-them mentality; studies have shown that people actually feel closer to and more confident of — and are more likely to co-operate with — police agencies when they can monitor agencies' transmissions.

You'd imagine that the media would scream over this loss of access to one of the most important leads to news stories, wouldn't you? And they would, if it affected them. However, government agencies are giving receivers to members of the "organized media." It's another unholy alliance between officialdom and the media, creating a sense of clubby loyalty between them, while forcing citizens into greater reliance on an increasingly unreliable source of news.

So what to do about it? Particularly since your personal life, death, or freedom might hinge on what you learn from an emergency frequency transmission?

Well, some legal technology is coming on the market that might help. Uniden, one of the most famous scanner manufacturers, has come out with a "Trunktracker" product that enables monitoring of *some* closed communications.

Pinero calls Trunktracker "significant," but also notes that, "the Trunktracker cannot decipher digital broadcasts, nor can it follow the transmissions of the more complex GE Ericsson system. It is not unforeseeable that GE Ericsson could turn this into a selling point to propagate more of its scanner-hostile systems, while both Motorola and Ericsson could wind up upselling to digital systems."

At the time he wrote his FAQ, Pinero was pessimistic about the chance that vendors and scanner enthusiasts would ever overcome the obstacles of tracking digital technology. But just a month later, he reported "stunning progress" on the part of "several hacks." Once again, free minds and (relatively) free markets triumph over control freaks. He also points out that these modern systems enable agencies to open some of their communications to the public while keeping others closed, a solution that would probably satisfy most mainstream folks.

Nevertheless, the problem of encrypted official transmissions remains. And agencies aren't voluntarily opening their "closed" systems. You can also bet your booties that, where elitist agencies can't outmaneuver free-market technologies, they'll use their friends in the legislature to get new developments declared illegal.

The ability to monitor official communications is crucial to a free society — and will be even more crucial to our free *underground* society, where *we* may be the "criminals" being hunted.

Shortwave

If you are interested in shortwave broadcasting, check into ham radio operations, or see the pirate radio information listed in the Appendix.

Low tech
(and more-or-less
above ground)

Ways to use the telephone

I've covered safe and creative telephone use elsewhere, and plenty of others have also written on the subject. Some of it is kind of a no-brainer, anyhow. So I'll be brief about relatively safe ways for freedom seekers to use telephones.

- Don't conduct confidential calls from home. Remember that, even if your phone isn't tapped, it's relatively easy for law enforcement agencies to put a "pen register" on your line (or your friend's line). The pen register doesn't let them listen to your conversations; it does, however, reveal the number you're calling. (And of course, that same information can also be gotten from phone company records, after the fact.)

- Consider using PGP-Fone or other forms of voice encryption that may become available. Right now, these are still clunky and may cause voices to cut out, etc. But in the long run, they'll offer voice-callers the same security as e-mail users who encrypt their messages with PGP.

- Use pre-paid phone cards for privacy; for extra security, make phone card calls from phone booths. *Then destroy the card and throw the remnants away.* If you're caught with a used card in your possession, every call you've made with it can be traced.

- If you don't have a phone — or if you want to keep in voice contact but don't want people to be able to pin down your location easily — or if you travel a lot and need to be reachable — consider a nationwide paging service with an 800 number. *Do not* use a *local* paging service, even if they offer an 800 number. This makes your location too easy to pinpoint. Contract with a nationwide provider, giving them a distant mail drop as your address. One good service is listed in the Appendix. But keep in mind that new technologies will be rapidly adding options to remote communications.

Using snail

I hate snail mail. Ugh. Slow, expensive, vulnerable to loss, and run by the government! What more needs to be said against it?

However, sometimes ya just gotta break down and use it.

So, if you're concerned about the privacy of your home or community…

- Get yourself a private mailbox (several if possible) in a different city or even a different state. Receive all your mail there. Receive nothing at home. If your mailbox is distant enough that you can't personally pick up your mail, have it sent to a friend, a P.O. box, a business you frequent, etc.

- When you send mail, also send it from another city or place it inside an envelope and send it to the out-of-state or out-of-town business that receives your mail; they'll forward it for a fee.

- Be very careful about the postmarks that appear on your mail; I once moved to a small town and sent a test mailing from there to myself to see what the postmark said. I was happy to find that the postmark was from the nearest "big city," which was almost 100 miles away. Cheerfully imagining my location was undetectable, I went on mailing from my home town. Little did I know that the postmarking procedure was *inconsistent.* Sometimes, the mail went to the big city for marking; sometimes it got marked with the very distinctive name of my tiny town. Don't assume anything!

- Know that "mail covers" can be placed on your (or your friends') snail mail as casually as pen registers can be put on phone lines. "They" can't read your mail legally without a warrant. But they can find out who you're getting mail from and possibly to whom you're sending it. It might be best to receive mail through one location and send mail through another in a different state — or at least a different part of your city. This all gets terribly expensive and complicated. Is it worth it to you? A lot depends on how important it is to you to maintain your privacy, or how likely it is that some official type will be interested in snooping on you.

- Mail covers may be more easily detectable than pen registers, as some goons are inefficient enough to hold your mail for days as they copy the information on the envelopes. Frequent and unaccountable mail delays could be a sign of a cover. On the other hand, how long does it take to photocopy your envelopes? The smart operators may cause no delay at all — and you'll never know if they're keeping notes on how many times Publishers Clearing House writes to you.

- Speaking of which, try to stay off mailing lists. The IRS buys them to find out who might be buying what products. The DEA or other agencies may use them to figure out who's growing marijuana. You can get off most lists by writing to the mail preference service of the Direct Marketing Association, listed in the Appendix. If you want to be on potentially controversial lists — like that of Loompanics Unlimited or NORML — use your mail drop and a false name.

- Tape all four edges of envelopes — all the way out to the edge — and tape the flap and seams as well. This trick, which I learned from one of my faithful snail correspondents, makes it a bear to open letters. But it makes it a bear for anyone else to open them without detection. (Thank you, Woodrow!)

- Always use envelopes designed for privacy — the kind with irregular patterns printed on the inside. That way, even if someone attempts to read your mail by shining a light through the envelope or using a chemical that temporarily renders the paper of the envelope transparent, you'll have an extra layer of protection.

- If you absolutely must communicate by snail, and you have confidential things to communicate, consider: codes, messages hidden under stamps, invisible ink, and that whole host of secret tricks you learned as a kid. All these are detectable — if anyone has good reason to detect them. But for the most part, no one's looking. Even if you don't have anything confidential to say, consider using such tricks just to bug and confuse anyone who might be snooping at you.

Homing pigeons

Seriously, homing pigeons or carrier pigeons, have their potential uses. They can carry small objects as well as messages rolled up in their little leg-carriers.

I don't know a hoot (or is it a coo?) about pigeons. I mention this mainly to make the point that we may have to 1) get creative, 2) do some contingency planning, and 3) have backup communication methods if the systems around us really fail, or if we are cut off from them.

Heaven forfend that that we should ever have to use homing pigeons as a regular means of communication. Today, they are strictly a hobby (see the Appendix). But what if…?

And that brings us back to the past and down to the underground, where we can learn from our ancestors, from hoboes, from petty criminals, from historic resistance movements…from whoever might have useful, low-tech communication methods to impart.

When everything really falls apart…

Low tech (and to hell with all authority)

Comes a day when it's all shut off to you. When thoughts of computers or ham radios are sheer fantasy. When the fedgov has taken everything you have — or denied you the right to earn any more. When you're on the streets, on the run, on the last legs of desperation.

Or comes the day when your whole community, your whole state, the whole world-as-you-know-it is cut off from normal services and twentieth-century technology.

Or maybe the day just comes when you want one more way of outfoxing the bastards, for the sheer ornery hell of it. They're prepared to catch your electronic transmissions or intercept your snailings, and you're going to go right around and under 'em.

What do you do then?

Well, above all, you use your wits. And to whatever extent you can, you use old-fashioned human cooperation.

But for some specifics, the world is full of old tried-and-true methods.

Message drops

In *The Autobiography of Malcolm X*, X told Alex Haley a method he used to use when he was dealing marijuana and the cops were on his case. He'd take a few "sticks" (as he called them), insert them into a crumpled cigarette pack, and discreetly drop them beside a garbage can, in an alley.

Then he'd collect the money from his customer and tell the buyer where to pick up his delivery.

I'm not sure I'd want to buy merchandise that way. But the same technique could serve as a crude (and somewhat iffy) message drop. Instead of "sticks," your package contains paper or film or some other form of information. You could prearrange such drops — Tuesday beside the dumpster at 10:00, Thursday in the dugout at the softball field at 7:00 — or you could notify the intended recipient just before or just after the time of a drop.

Notification might be given directly, but it could also take the form of a signal, about which more in a moment.

Just hope nobody goes into a cleaning frenzy before the pickup, or that no alley-bum goes hunting in your package for cigarettes. (These days it might be better to use, say, a crumpled yogurt carton. Yogurt isn't a big item on the bum diet.)

A slightly more secure and long-term message drop. Here's another message drop that's been used, in some variation, by resistance movements all over the world. (And by drug dealers.)

This one has better long-term potential and can be used by many people. There's also less chance of your message inadvertently being "cleaned up." But because more people know about it, it's also inherently more risky.

It begins with a public business. There are two categories of business that might be good candidates, each with its own advantages and risks.

• One class might be a business where regulars congregate — a bar, a gun store, or a café with a neighborhood clientele.

• The other might be a more anonymous business, like a Laundromat or convenience store, that gets a large amount of traffic from people who don't know each other.

Having a business where numbers of people come and go is the key.

The business operates as a central message drop. Your fellow freedom-workers can go in and get or leave messages, as needed. The business owner or manager could act as a human message drop (either

memorizing brief messages or handling coded paper messages — or possibly delivering objects or instructions that lead the recipient to messages hidden at another location).

In some cases, you might even be able to eliminate the middleman by posting coded messages on a bulletin board, writing them beside a wall phone, or even taping them in a window of the business (looking like advertising flyers). But you'd have to be very certain that they wouldn't be taken down or covered up by other customers or employees.

Again, message recipients could come in on a regular basis or because they've been notified in some way, or they could just come in and check at random.

You can see that a business with a regular clientele has the advantage that no one would think it unusual if the same customers came in frequently. The disadvantage for this type of business (especially a gun shop!) is that it's likely to be suspected, particularly if its regulars or employees are known to have strong political views.

The more anonymous type of business has the advantage of being less inherently suspicious. Depending on the type of business, it might or might not arouse suspicion if the same handful of people were seen there every few days. And in a very public business like a convenience store, it might be difficult to conduct a message exchange in privacy.

Signs and symbols

Signs and symbols have a lot of potential uses in our future.

First, let's look at how they might be used in conjunction with message drops.

You, Boris Badenov, have left a message for your compatriot, Mata Hari. Mata doesn't know to expect a message. But she does know to pass by the kiosk in the University student union every day at three to look for a bright orange flyer advertising an upcoming campus visit by the guru Sri Upchuckaji.

If she sees the flyer, she's to wait three hours, then go to the espresso stand at the corner of Political Avenue and Correctness Drive and order a tall, single-shot latte with banana flavoring and to use the phrase "instant decaff joe" while talking with the clerk on duty.

The clerk doesn't know Mata, but recognizes the order and the phrase (which no serious latte customer would ever use). The clerk slips a message under the napkin that is wrapped around every paper latte cup sold at the stand.

There are an endless number of variations on this same theme. The latte seller might know Mata, in which case no special order or code phrase is needed. The message under the napkin might be the real one, or might simply instruct Mata to another location where she can find the actual message.

The note under the napkin might, in fact, instruct her (in code) to look for a green sticker in the window of the health food store, which would in turn give her a clue to look elsewhere.

As you can see, this sort of thing can get very elaborate. You have to balance your security needs against the human ability to remember and follow instructions. And balance your security needs against being just too-too Secret Agentish.

Some other uses for signs and symbols: Sometimes the signs and symbols are an end in themselves. Ask a tagger. Or better yet, ask a hobo.

Hoboes have been using symbols at least since the Depression (if not before) to let other hoboes know, covertly, what benefits or dangers they might find in a town or at a particular house.

Here are a few of the many traditional hobo signs, with their meanings. While some of the traditional meanings might be perfectly serviceable, freedom-seekers on the run might want to develop a different set of meanings for modern times.

Such signs, if used, should be placed where freedom travelers will know where to look for them, but (especially when placed on homes or businesses) used in such a way as not to draw the attention of authorities. In fact, when identifying specific homes and businesses, it would be better to keep the signs away from the buildings themselves, and let them serve as *pointers to* locations. And think carefully before you use them in that way at all!

Hobo's meaning: Authorities will hassle you in this town
Possible freedom-seeker's meaning: Informant lives here; this organization has a suspected informant; surveillance equipment in use; Big Brother is watching

Hobo's meaning: Water in this location isn't drinkable
Possible freedom-seeker's meaning: Political climate in this town is unfriendly

Hobo's meaning: Barking dog at this house
Possible freedom-seeker's meaning: Expect barbed wire and other barriers; dangerous area — keep out; keep moving

Hobo's meaning: Your can get liquor here
Possible freedom-seeker's meaning: You can get hospitality here

Hobo's meaning: Good road
Possible freedom-seeker's meaning: Don't go this way

Hobo's meaning: Good location for camping
Possible freedom-seeker's meaning: Good location for camping

Hobo's meaning: Someone with a gun lives here
Possible freedom-seeker's meaning: Authorities here will hassle you

Hobo's meaning: You can get food here
Possible freedom-seeker's meaning: You can get food here; you can get work here; patriots live here; telephone here you can use

Hobo's meaning: Not safe
Possible freedom-seeker's meaning: Not safe

I Am Not a Number!

Hobo's meaning: A kind woman lives here
Possible freedom-seeker's meaning: You can get shelter here; you can get medical help here

Don't forget that such symbols can also be drawn on the sides of trains, trucks, buses or farm wagons, on billboards and road signs or on the age-old sides of barns to communicate with travelers or far-away allies. Obviously, this method relies on common knowledge of the symbols, and can't be used to convey very complex information.

But think about the encouragement and or sense of common cause any of the following might give to far away freedom seekers when scrawled on the side of a train:

- A coiled rattlesnake with a raised head
- A U.N. emblem with a slash through it
- An upside-down U.S. flag
- A 13-star Old Glory
- The word "FREEDOM!" (Not exactly a symbol, but who's being particular?)
- The words "John Galt lives!" (ditto)
- A statue of Liberty
- The Liberty Bell
- The profile of an AR-15

Couriers

People who travel as part of their regular job or retirees who travel at whim, can be useful for carrying messages (or contraband) around the country or the world.

Consider these groups of people as possible messengers:

- Truck drivers
- Train crew members
- Bus drivers

- Delivery drivers
- Technicians who service equipment on site
- Traveling sales people
- Pilots
- Musicians
- Any other business travelers
- Large animal veterinarians who travel to farms and ranches
- Trade show reps

In other words, any trustworthy person who frequently or logically travels as part of a job is a potential courier. As you can imagine, some of these people are going to have a great deal of flexibility, while others are only going to be available for limited assignments.

If your need is simply to get messages across town, a bicycling student or cross-town delivery driver might easily be able to make an extra stop on your behalf.

Other people are going to be more useful for spreading the general word, like the vet who might be able to tell half a dozen customers something you might want them to know. Like the delivery driver, the vet may be able to make some unscheduled stops: "Just checking in to see how the abscess on Daisy's hock is healing."

Pilots, bus drivers, or truckers who ply regular routes have a distinct role where messages need to go regularly from Location X to Location Y and back.

Some other business travelers might be useful only for very specialized work. If a company rep is taking a trade show booth to Las Vegas next month, you might be able to get a message to Las Vegas. But it's not likely the rep would be able to detour to Tonopah. And if you have a message that must go to Chicago, you must simply find another way. However, if you have several associates who regularly hit the trade show circuit in a number of cities, you might be able to establish quite a nice little network of communications that way.

You can also use a relay system, with successive couriers picking up the message and carrying it onward from location to location.

I'm not mentioning mail carriers because 1) we may, in some cases, have to become our own mail carriers and 2) while plenty of them may be good people, I also expect them to be increasingly trained and used as spies and snitches, like the way your children are trained by the D.A.R.E. program to spy and snitch.

On the other hand, I'd like to emphasize the value of retirees. Retirees, of course, can go darned near anywhere if they have their health and a little money. And they might be happy to spend their lives doing just that, if you supply them with the messages and the gas for their motorhomes (assuming that option is still available). Some of them are incredibly pissed off at the government — and may take great risks because they feel they have very little left to lose.

Creating creative chaos

The free life is, unfortunately, always something that must be defended. Even if we don't like to think of freedom in terms of "fighting," "resistance," "struggle," the fact remains that we simply can't slip away to some peaceful glade and live forever unmolested and at peace with all mankind.

In all probability you will always have to live around laws and avoid the officious bastards who just can't stand to leave you alone. Whether it's the property taxers, the enviro-fascists, the income taxers, the chemical police, the sales taxers, the medical police, the import taxers, the gun police or some as-yet-undreamed of form of authoritarian — the simple fact is some portion of your life will always be devoted to avoidance and evasion of the people whose greatest desire in life is to control others.

You and the people you work and live with in freedom will need to develop a certain unpredictability — in your communications, as well as in many other aspects of your lives. Unpredictability... well, it's good for the soul. It helps keep you awake and lively. But it also makes it hard to track or guess what you might do next.

And the hidebound, red-tape, securitarian sorts who make up most of government officialdom are the least able to cope with rapid changes and breaks of pattern.

Here's what an Internet correspondent known only as Intel96B had to say:

> Never forget that someone else is trying to penetrate your operation and chaos is a very difficult thing to penetrate. Formally-organized

command structures are what they're trying to identify. So don't have one.

Many people are convinced that the preponderance of civilians who were inducted into the armed services during World War II were probably the most instrumental in confusing the German field command. The Germans could fairly well predict what the British were going to do because of the similarities in battlefield doctrine taught to both of those countries. Similarly, Patton gained some insight into Rommel's way of thinking by reading Rommel's book on the use of armored vehicles in desert warfare. But since the American Army (largely "civilians," not career soldiers) was so unpredictable, mainly because they didn't know themselves what they were going to do until they did it, the enemy certainly couldn't predict with any reasonable degree of confidence what they were going to do, either. And if the platoon leader was killed, a corporal, or anybody with leadership ability, could step in and take command.

Update 2002
What's New
Since Chapter Five

It's odd to look back on Chapter Five now, because I see that almost nothing has changed on the surface — few of these dire things have happened or are even close to happening on any major scale — and yet almost everything has changed underneath and in the background.

What hasn't changed is access to communications. That's remained about the same, with even some technological improvements. Even though the Deadbeat Dad Database law enlisted phone companies (among others) in the endless gathering of Slave Numbers, in practice almost no utility will refuse to serve you if you won't give an SSN (though some may make you pay a hefty deposit). Also, since there's darned little freedom-community building going on out there, many of this book's thoughts on alternative communications for such communities remain futuristic, apocalyptic, paranoid, and fanciful.

(But what the heck; you can't be too cynical or too paranoid. What the government hasn't done today it may be planning to do tomorrow. So the chapter stays as it is, despite the fact that our day for communicating by carrier pigeon might not come for a while.)

But under the surface ...down where the future awaits us, ready to spring forth ...there the world of 2002 is a very different place than the world of 1998. Or at least we know more about government powers to monitor or curb our communications than we knew then.

Here's just a sampling of what's come out or been developed in the last couple of years:

- We've discovered Echelon, the National Security Agencies giant "scoop" that picks up faxes, e-mails, phone transmissions, and all types of electronic communications worldwide. We know — although it's still not officially admitted — that virtually all the English-speaking countries get around their own laws that prevent domestic spying by (oh, this is so viciously ingenious) spying on the communications of *each other's* residents, then sharing the information.

- We know about the FBI's Carnivore Internet monitor (mentioned earlier), as well as key-logging programs like DIRT (Data Interception by Remote Transmission) and the FBI's Magic Lantern. Key loggers can be planted on your computer, either by physically sneaking in and doing it or by transmitting the monitoring program to you covertly via e-mail. They'll record every word you type, including your encryption password and personal data.

- CALEA, the 1994 law requiring all phone equipment to be instantly tappable, has gone into full effect and, as we saw earlier, been imposed upon ISPs as well as phone makers and phone-system operators. So while the Fourth Amendment's quaint little requirement for warrants remains in effect on paper, anyone with the equipment and the know-how can tap into your line virtually at the flip of a switch. This includes not only the feddies and state law enforcers, but freelance crooks who may want to steal credit card numbers and SSNs you transmit over the phone or to listen in on your business plans, love life, or anything else.

- The U.S. Postal Service has also clamped down on users of mail services like Mail Boxes, Etc., succeeding in requiring heavy government ID before you can get service, but failing, so far, in several other control measures.

Perhaps most ominously, it appears that the Internet, which so many of us thought to be beyond the ability of the government to shut down, can indeed be controlled in many ways. Cutting off access to certain domain names (as I mentioned in the original edition of this book) is one, as is surgically slicing certain ISPs or individuals out of the net. A denial-of-service attack could emanate from a covert government operation as easily as from a group of freelance hackers. But the power is broader.

Some have hinted the FBI's Carnivore program, in addition to being able to monitor all net activity at the ISP level, can also be used to cut off net activity at will. If this is true or becomes true in the near future as government exerts more controls over ISP operations, it means that the FBI can, in an "emergency," literally close the Internet to use by Americans.

Another thing to consider: When WorldCom went bankrupt in 2002, Internet service buzzed on uninterrupted. But think about the fact that more than half of all Internet traffic is routed through WorldCom's systems and ask how vulnerable this setup is to major shutdowns or jam-ups, deliberate or otherwise. Clearly the Internet has plenty of ability to spring back or reroute around problems. No one could deny that. It's just not the immortal thing some of us assumed a few years back.

Tracking cellphones

The capability of tracking cellphones and cellphone users is now widely known, and while no doubt this could be a lifesaver for someone whose car has gone over a cliff in a remote area, it's a bitch for freedom lovers. Cellphone transmissions are also notoriously easy to intercept and record. Cellphones are also usually tied to monthly use plans that require you to give the obnoxious and omnipresent Slave Number. But one sign of hope is the increasing number of pre-paid calling plans that enable you to purchase cell service anonymously if you wish. At the moment, the pre-paid plans often have a lot of limitations on calling areas that the monthly plans don't. But if you're a cellphone user, by all means shop for one of these before settling for an SS-based plan.

About voice encryption

PGP-Fone never really did manage to get developed. And unfortunately, neither has any other *affordable* and accessible voice encryption system. Telephone encryption systems do exist, of course. They have for years, and have been in heavy use by government. But they remain out of reach of most people. For a long time, one upcoming system, the Starium 100, was touted as "phone encryption for the masses." Article after article said the little scrambler boxes would cost less than $100 when finally released, meaning you and your privacy-loving friends could have them for less than the cost of a new computer hard drive. But alas, when they finally hit the market, they ran about $900 per unit. As of this writing, the Starium Web site hasn't been updated in well over a year, so promises of dropping prices and advancing technologies from that direction appear to be a fizzle.

Could this be a manufacturing opportunity for some liberty-loving technoid? With CALEA flip-of-a-switch phone bugging, voice encryption will be crucial for freedom and privacy.

Mid-tech changes

Chapter Five contains fairly detailed descriptions of a number of technologies, such as packet radio and ham radio. If you're interested in these, you should contact the organizations listed in the Appendix for the latest technological and licensing updates.

Unfortunately, the many recent attempts to speed up packet radio transmissions have, as of this writing, failed to bring faster packet transmissions within the range of ordinary people. Fortunately, broadband Internet connections via satellite technology have stepped in to bring fast net speeds even to isolated homesteads. Unfortunately, this works only for homesteads with a clear view of the southern sky and it's pretty expensive. Fortunately, high-speed Internet technology is improving and spreading rapidly. Fixed

wireless technology can reach you as far as thirty-five miles from a broadcast tower — or you could set up your own fixed wireless system to serve an entire freedom community.

I Am Not a Number! originally contained an extensive section on pirate radio (unlicensed broadcasts that violate government regulations, designed either for small-scale local communications or for jamming "legal" broadcasts). We've removed that section because, for most practical purposes, pirate radio has been supplanted by Internet broadcasting (which is legal at present and is easier and cheaper to do, as long as you have a computer). You'll find a pointer toward how-to information on both pirate and Internet broadcasting in the Appendix.

I debated whether to remove the section on scanners. Many people believe that the use of mobile data terminals in emergency vehicles has rendered scanners obsolete. And in fact, scanners don't pick up as much routine voice traffic of police, firefighters, and ambulance crews as they did 15 years ago. However, as The Owl tells in his article, "Radio Scanners: Liberty's Ears" (published in the e-zine *Doing Freedom* and listed in the Appendix), scanners may have actually increased in value in this era of cellphone transmissions. With the right equipment, The Owl says, you can even pick up the electronic messages from those nonvoice data terminals.

Many communication enhancements have been introduced or have grown more popular since *I Am Not a Number!* was last printed. These include such things as family radio — the little hand-held gadgets that, within a range of a mile or two, are far superior to CB for communicating with other members of a convoy — and wireless LANS and WANS for computer users. It's beyond the scope of this book to keep up with them all.

Linux

One final — but easy and important — recommendation on communications. You don't have to be in a community to appreciate this one. Most of the key loggers available to law enforcement work with Windows operating systems. These implanted snoop programs exploit some of the same structural weaknesses that make Microsoft software so pathetically vulnerable to viruses and Trojan horses (which is what key loggers are, in a sense). You can give your-self an extra layer of computer protection AND save a lot of money AND have more stable software AND free yourself from Microsoft's corporate arrogance by switching to the Linux operating system.

It used to be just for nerds. And it's still not as much a no-brainer to use as Windows. But this up-date to *I Am Not a Number!* is being typed on the free, Microsoft-compatible OpenOffice program and running under the user-friendly Mandrake Linux OS (free to download or 25 bucks for the boxed set at Wal-Mart). I installed and maintain this system my-self, with occasional advice from helpful Linux gu-rus, and believe me, I'm no computer geek.

Unlike Windows, Linux doesn't just come from one supplier. You can choose your "flavor" of Linux, packaged with various different options, from a vari-ety of vendors. Mandrake Linux, RedHat Linux, and a couple of other Linux "distros" (distributions) are already pretty easy and are being geared more toward ordinary desktop users every day. They come with graphical user interfaces like KDE and Gnome that operate so much like Windows that after a couple of weeks you won't notice the difference.

If you prefer, you can install Linux on your exist-ing Windows machine with a dual-boot setup that gives you access to both operating systems and their software. The more user-friendly distros will walk you through the process of creating a dual-boot sys-tem. They'll even automatically partition your hard drive for you. (They'll "squeeze down" the area of the drive occupied by Windows' file systems and will format the newly cleared portion of the drive to hold Linux — a process you used to have to do yourself with great peril and much hair-tearing.)

Want to have it easier yet? Wal-Mart, through its Web site, sells budget-level computers, some with no operating system installed and others pre-loaded with Linux. If Linux has reached Wal-Mart, surely it's ready for the rest of us.

So even if nobody on the planet ever builds a free-dom community, here's one small, simple thing you can do to enhance your own privacy, freedom, and control of your own technology. Foil the snoops and have a better computer at the same time. Switch to Linux.

Chapter Six
Travel in the Free Community

The riverbank will make a very good road,
The dead trees show you the way,
Left foot, peg foot travelin' on,
Followin' the drinkin' gourd.
— *"Follow the Drinking Gourd" (A song of the Underground Railroad)*

Our rights to travel are first and foremost at risk in the ID State.

- The ID State forbids us to drive without its licenses.
- We can't insure our vehicles if we have no drivers' licenses.
- State and local laws are increasingly being passed or proposed to seize vehicles from anyone driving without a license or insurance.
- As resistance becomes more widespread there will certainly be more checkpoints set up for the express purpose of finding Undocumented Citizens — therefore there will be more seizures, more arrests, more fines, more prosecutions, and more names added to lists of "terrorists, subversives, and troublemakers."
- We must now show government-issued photo ID when boarding commercial airplanes.
- The requirement for ID could be extended at any moment to trains and buses; ID requirements already exist when crossing borders on ground-based mass transit.
- Even walking down the street, we may be required to show state ID if stopped by a policeman and may be arrested if we don't have it. ("De-

tained and released," they may call it, if we're lucky. They say that doesn't mean arrested. Oh, yeah? Check a dictionary!) We are not, theoretically, required to produce drivers' licenses or other state ID on the whim of any enforcer. But in practice, people who don't are often brutalized and arrested. In the future this "requirement of force" will no doubt become a requirement of law.

In addition, we may find our free communities singled out for heavy, selective enforcement. Once police know that a large number of residents in an area lack official ID...or once they learn that traffic on certain roads has a higher-than-usual percentage of Undocumented Citizens...they'll stake out those areas as easy pickins'.

Your driver's license has become your internal passport — just like they had in the Soviet Empire and Nazi Germany.

We will need to develop some travel strategies to help us anticipate and get around restrictions. We may also need to develop special strategies to help convoys, free-market traders (smugglers), and fleeing "criminals" (freedom seekers) make it across country in perilous times.

What follows are a few thoughts on how to travel safely under police state restrictions and without police state documentation. But as with so many other aspects of our new lives, we'll need to be creative, quick-thinking, and adaptable.

On the road

A lot of people refused drivers' licenses even before DLs also became Slave IDs. Until recently, having a license seemed a small matter to most of us. Even those of us who might have opposed state licensing on principle went out and got our cards because it wasn't all that invasive or expensive or unreasonable.

So now we're going out there, licenseless. Or with fake licenses. Or alternatives to licenses, such as the International Motorist Qualification. What can we learn from our pioneering friends?

Barricades and check points

We've already seen an outrageous and insulting proliferation of roadblocks and checkpoints throughout the U.S. Motorists are now being stopped to be checked for drunken driving, insurance, general criminal activity or outstanding warrants, and even seat belt use! Some east- and west-coast states now have, heaven forfend, pollution checkpoints; you can be stopped at random and your vehicle can be confiscated on the spot if it fails to meet the very high standards.

Courts have deemed nearly all of these outrages constitutional. (That sound you hear is the proverbial Founding Fathers — and a few Mothers, too — spinning in dirt.) The Supremes have done nothing more than quibble over details.

For instance, if cops were stopping only blacks or Hispanics while looking for drugs, that might be a no-no. But if they stop *every passing car* or cars selected at random, well, that doesn't violate the Fourth Amendment at all. (It even seems to be okay to single out blacks or Hispanics — as long as you have a "drug-dealer profile" that indicates they'll have loot you can confis... um... as long as you're Nobly Fighting the War Against Drugs or... well, I'm sorry, I just can't keep track of all the ins and outs of this thing. Darn, you know it was *so much easier* when we just had a Fourth Amendment.)

The short version of this long and depressing tale is that — at any of these checkpoints you'll have to fork over your driver's license. And you can bet your booties (and your brand new Toyota) that checkpoints expressly to verify driver's license possession are just around the corner. If you are caught in one,

you may, at the very least, lose your vehicle and all the cash you're carrying, if not also go to jail.

As of this writing, it *is* legal to avoid a checkpoint, if you do so in a safe manner. Speed while evading a checkpoint, however, and you are liable for a fine and five years in *federal* prison. That's according to the same Public Law 104-208 that gave us the national ID license. Ya just gotta love those Republicans!

Anyway, if you simply turn around, or park at the side of the road until the checkpoint folds up for the day, *theoretically* the cops have no bone to pick with you. In fact, of course, they'll come after you, intimidate you, attempt to pick a fight with you, and otherwise come up with something one of their black-robed accomplices will accept as "probable cause."

Not having a driver's license — or having a fake one — is a handy-dandy little probable cause. Theoretically, your lack of a license shouldn't enable them to search your car for drugs or guns. But hey, once you're being hauled off to jail, who's gonna stop the bastards?

Eventually, we just may have to shoot them. That's all there is to it. (Leave us alone, you little Stormtroopers, and we'll leave *you* alone!) But in the meantime:

- If you turn around or otherwise dodge to avoid a roadblock, do it as carefully, legally, and innocently as possible. If they come after you, claim you lost your dog a mile back or something and just had to turn around *now*. However, if you are an Undocumented Citizen, they'll already have asked for your ID — too late!

- Remember your rights. I carry a handy card in my glove compartment that has a number of Supreme Court cites on it, some from the days when they actually believed this country had a Bill of Rights. In some cases, you might actually benefit by letting the officer know you understand your rights. In others, it will only irritate him and he'll claim you assaulted him or resisted arrest or something, just so he can get back at you.

- Remember that police are trained to use a "command voice," so that when they say, "May we inspect your trunk?" they actually seem to be saying, "Open your trunk NOW, you muhfuh, or we'll spray your brains from here to Dallas and let our dog Cujo lick them off the pavement!" If you possibly can, take a deep breath, stay calm, and keep standing on your rights. Again, though, you now have this basic ID question that might get you busted before things ever reach that pass.

- If you are using a fake driver's license, don't expect it to get past the cops' computers. If you are using *alternative* (not fake) documentation, such as an International Motorist Qualification, which you can purchase by mail, you will benefit by researching *in advance* how police and courts in that particular jurisdiction handle your documentation of choice. Chances are, you may be arrested by an ignorant cop, then vindicated by a judge. Some organizations of freedom lovers issue their own driver's identification and vehicle plates; someday it may be a possibility for your Free Community as well. But so far, such alternatives tend to attract, rather than deflect, trouble.
- Keep detailed local maps, gazetteers, mapping software, or other such items in your vehicle and prepare to get out of there *before* you have to talk with the nice men in the ninja suits.

Which leads to the next aspect of travel:

Off-road

Those gazetteers and similar *accouterments* can lead you off-road where — unless someone is actually chasing you (or looking for illegals) — you aren't as likely to be found, stopped, questioned, hassled, arrested, and otherwise treated like a Jew in Nazi Germany.

Off-road travel can be handy for the import-export trade (a.k.a. smuggling), recreation, the underground railroad, jaunting off to hide goodies, and a variety of other activities.

It can also be dangerous and misleading, as anyone who's ever been stuck in a gully without four-wheel-drive can attest, and as anyone *with* four-wheel-drive can attest after being led in to very strange places by a half-informative U.S. Geological Survey map.

My S.O. and I recently had a laughable experience. We were setting off for a resort community about four hours from here and he, being a true computer geek, plotted a number of different courses on his computerized atlas software. One led interestingly across country. We hadn't even known there was a

road there, even though we'd been past the turnoff many times.

Well, what the heck, this being a long weekend, we had all the time in the world. So we turned off the main highway at the suggested spot... and ended up climbing a wheel-rut so steep even the mountain goats wanted nothing to do with it. There was no road at all, just a rubble-filled utility maintenance track heading up toward some power high-lines. And down below, a lake into which we, truck and all, could have slid and disappeared without a trace. But the atlas called it a 35-mph county road.

So, as they say, "Trust, but verify."

- If you travel often in a given area, know all the back roads — every one of them. Know how they are in spring flood and winter snow. Know what you'd do if you had to use them — or what you'd do if you *couldn't* use them.
- If you are going to be traveling through unfamiliar territory, but on a critical mission, learn the backroads there, too, as best you can.
- Consider getting a GPS (Global-Positioning System) unit. The prices on these are fantastic now — about $150 and up, last I looked. If you get lost in the middle of nowhere, they could save your life. Using satellites for navigation, they can tell you, within a few yards, exactly where you are on this planet. In conjunction with a USGS map or good gazetteer, they might be able to get you back to a road — or enable you to get *off* a road when need be. They're useful when walking, driving, boating, cross-country skiing, hunting, etc., and could save your life, even in our pre-totalitarian society. However...

A GPS unit could save your life if you're lost and far away from a main road. But like nearly all technologies, GPS has its dark side. And the dark side of GPS is as black as it gets.

Here's the charming news, as not-quite-stated by an article excerpt from the San Francisco *Examiner*, November 27, 1997. Comments in brackets are mine.

Global positioning technology can monitor criminals 24 hrs a day
by William Leinknecht,
Newhouse News Service

Corrections officials in four states are tapping into military satellites to track the movements of violent felons and sex offenders released into the community. [Ah, yes, the classic "violent felons and sex offenders" dodge to sell any potential misuse of law enforcement techniques.]

Through global-positioning technology, authorities can know instantly if a parolee leaves home or enters a restricted zone, such as a school area or the neighborhood of a former victim. [This would indeed be handy, if victim protection against violent felons were all it would be used for. Of course, one might ask why violent felons are roaming around on law-enforcement leashes, instead of making license plates in prison. And then again, how many crimes even *have* victims, these days?]

"You can literally track any place he goes 24 hours a day," said Keith Feilmeier, marketing manager of Advanced Business Sciences, a Nebraska company offering the technology. "We can pinpoint the location within 4 or 5 feet."

Satellite tracking of felons is only the latest example of military technology being adapted to the needs of law enforcement in the post-Cold War era. [An unholy marriage if ever there was one, putting everything from machine guns to spy tools to a really hostile attitude into the hands and heads of the folks who used to be our "neighborhood police."]

Better than anklets

ABS's system is being used to track juvenile parolees in nine Iowa counties and adult parolees in Dallas. Pro Tech's equipment is being tested by the Florida Department of Corrections in two Tampa-area counties. The technology is also planned for counties in Minnesota and Pennsylvania.

The companies say global positioning is a better way to monitor parolees than the use of electronic anklets, which tell the monitors only whether the subject has remained at home.

ABS's system, known as ComTrak, requires the person being monitored to wear a tamper-resistant wristband and be within a few feet of a four-pound tracking unit, which looks like a

laptop computer and can be slung over the shoulder or worn like a backpack or vest....

If the parolee tampers with the wristband or abandons the four-pound unit, the computer sounds an alarm and gives the subject's last coordinates.

Users of the system can check a subject's activities at any time, for example, at the end of a day or week. A complete record of the parolee's movements is archived at the ComTrak communications center....

William Lockwood, Pro Tech's vice president for sales and marketing, said global positioning could be used by law enforcement agencies to track the targets of investigations. He said a tracking unit could be *surreptitiously* positioned, for example, by attaching it to the bottom of a suspect's car or the side of a boat.

And there you have it, Mr. and Ms. Suspect America. Once again the media reports with total gee-whiz credulity a tool that law enforcement is bound to abuse against folks like you and me.

Right now, the four-pound unit (and no doubt its unspecified cost) does present a drawback to Big Brother's scheme of monitoring us all. But examine the pace of technology, the shrinking size of technological wonders, and the shrinking cost of technological wonders — and fear for your future.

In the meantime, check under your truck, thoroughly and often, okay?

On-and-off road: convoys

As an individual traveling in restrictive conditions, you face one set of problems. As a trader to or representative of a free community, you face even greater ones. That truckload of "hoarded" food or van full of Undocumented Citizens may attract unusual official attention.

A few things you might consider (in addition to the above) before setting out:

- If possible, travel in a convoy. The lead vehicle is your scout. The driver of that car or truck can travel a mile or two ahead and, if he spots a roadblock or other suspicious gestapo activity, can warn the following vehicles by coded CB or digital communications. If using CB or similar methods, make sure all vehicles stay in range! If using cellphones, make sure they'll be operable in every area you're going to be passing through.

- The lead driver should be "clean." If possible, this should be someone with a real state ID (or, at worst, a substitute known to be effective with police in the area). This person should have no police record, no known political affiliations, and, if possible, look like (and be!) a sweet little old lady. Since this is the member of the convoy most likely to get caught in any official web, she should be a person well equipped to escape suspicion.

- Ditto the lead vehicle. It ought to have "legal" state plates, current registration, insurance, fully functioning safety features, and the whole kazoo. Even if your Free Community objects to the state's quasi-ownership of such vehicles, you might keep one in that condition, just for convoy purposes. The title could be in the name of a trust or corporation to keep it from being identified with you.

- Remember that convoys can operate off-road, too, at least for modest distances. Across many rural parts of the country, you could convoy by horseback, snowmobile, or ATV, carrying goods in saddlebags or other portable containers. While this may sound quaint to a New York City-zen, trail riders still draw only minimal attention in such places as the mountains of Montana. And there aren't — yet — too many roadblocks set up across bridle trails or desert gullies.

Other things to consider: When transporting, it may be better (though tedious) to travel in a sport utility vehicle or pickup truck than in a semi or delivery van. You're less likely to be subjected to a cargo inspection. (Though this can vary! When crossing borders, even ordinary pickup trucks are sometimes just about taken apart by government agents.)

Don't equip your vehicles or yourself in any way that might draw attention. If you're crossing into Canada, for instance, having a sticker in your truck window that identifies you as a member of a gun-rights group is an invitation to agents to search you from top to bottom. Same with baseball hats with political or gun-oriented slogans. Same with anything that sets you apart in any way from Mr. or Ms. TV-Sucking Average American.

Before setting out on the road in dangerous times, think like an actor putting on a costume. Think of your vehicle as a prop for a play; make it just right for the scene.

Buses

City buses — except for those with surveillance cameras in them — are still anonymous forms of travel. Inflexible and often unpleasant, but at least they aren't prone to roadblocks and ID checks.

As of this moment, the good old Greyhound is also still E-Z travel. No IDs. No metal detectors. No baggage searches. No invasive questions about your habits or plans. No roving DEA agents or drug-sniffing dogs hanging around as a routine matter. No hassle at all.[1]

Except, of course, the hassle of riding the bus.

Ah, the joys of riding around the country with a collection of low-lifes and interminably talkative grandmothers! Stopping in such scenic wonderlands as south Cheyenne, Wyoming! Going where Greyhound goes, instead of where you really want to go! Breathing diesel fuel for days on end as you try to occupy your mind with something... anything... anything but the boring scenery and the even more boring company.

Okay, it's an ugly job. But it has its advantages.

You can buy a ticket right at the terminal, without even giving your name — and just go. It's cheap, too. Adult fare from Alachua, Florida, to Albuquerque, New Mexico, is just $145. Or you can get an Ameripass and go anywhere you want in the U.S. as long as the 7-, 15-, 30- or 60-day pass holds out. Anonymously. Or under an assumed identity that no one will bother to question.

It seems odd that the form of mass transportation most likely to be utilized by druggies and criminals is the one subjected to the least "security." That may be because nobody has (yet) hijacked a Greyhound or blown one up. But actually, I believe it's evidence that the Powers That Be really have little interest in

---

[1] Sigh — how things have changed since 9-11!

low-lifes.[2] It's the more solid citizens who need to be intimidated into silence or soothed into accepting airport Gestapos in the name of "safety."

Anyway, on the bus you are inherently anonymous. Unless the law has some reason to be looking for you, specifically, on that Greyhound (or that city bus or regional transportation system bus) you're in pretty good shape.

Even once the feddies institute driver's license checkpoints, they're *not* likely to check an entire bus full of sleeping grandmas and nodding ne'er-do-wells. (The one notable exception will be in border areas, where INS agents might think a bus full of Hispanic-looking people is an invitation to fulfill their whole month's quota of illegal aliens, or customs agents might see a veritable nest of drug smugglers.) As noted earlier, there's still no *legal* requirement that an innocent, nondriving citizen produce a state-issued ID. So even if a gang of Nazis did search the bus, you might get away with having no ID, except at a border crossing.

For the moment, and the foreseeable ID Society future, the admonition to "Go Greyhound" is still a good one, provided you don't develop a sudden need for evasive action. Then you might have to hijack that bus.

Gas scam?

There is, of course, a push to get us all on buses — a push that is particularly pushy in urban areas, or in states whose political power lies in their urban areas.

One strategy in accomplishing this goal — say, if an environmentalist like Al Gore were president — might be to manufacture another gas crisis, like that of the 1970s.

Or here's another possibility: As more people refuse to cooperate with national ID, both state and federal governments will crack down on them. Part of the crackdown might consist of laws requiring ID before buying gas. Or gas pumps might be altered "for convenience" to be activated only by a driver's license. (Some companies are already using trigger-

---

[2] I can just hear some devout bus rider getting steamed here. You're gonna tell me what salt-of-the-earth people they are on that bus. But dammit, they *are* low-lifes. You may like low-lifes. Some of them may have interesting life stories, which they will surely tell you *ad nauseum*. You might be able to learn some interesting low-living techniques from them, however, which might come in handy when dealing with cops or poverty.

ing devices on the dashboard of customers' cars to activate pumps.)

These scenarios might develop without warning. More likely, however, they'll be preceded by months of tongue-clucking about the "grave national problem" of fuel shortages or "anti-government extremist ID resisters."

If you can:

- Stockpile (and don't forget the fuel preservative, available at any hardware store)
- Get a gas-conserving motorbike or ORV
- Get a mountain bike
- Get a horse. Might not work too well if you're in Manhattan, but it works fine in some parts.

Trains

Good old Amtrak.

Much as I hate to say anything nice about government transportation, there's something refreshing about looking up safety guidelines for a train service.

Instead of things like:

- *Do not accept any mysteriously ticking packages from strange men in robes or buzz-cut guys wearing Thomas Jefferson quotes on their tee-shirts.*

Amtrak's safety rules say:

- *Use handrails when boarding.*
- *Walk, don't run.*
- And the ever-popular, ever-sensible:
- *Never exit a moving train.*

Damn! It makes one positively nostalgic for the days when travel didn't automatically make one a suspect in terrorism.

Amtrak, like Greyhound, still operates in an atmosphere of sanity and humanity. Even if it does also operate in an atmosphere of taxpayer-robbing. As a vehicle for Undocumented Citizens, it has many of the same attributes as the bus, with some notable exceptions:

- Fewer low-lifes
- Higher prices (much, for a person traveling alone)
- More comfort
- More places of privacy (therefore opportunity to hide objects or drop messages)

However, if you cross the U.S.-Canadian border on Amtrak, you'll be expected to go through an en route customs and immigration inspection, and to produce citizenship papers (passport, birth certificate, naturalization certificate, etc.).

And here's the really bad news....

Crossing the U.S.-Canadian border used to be a civil and casual affair. Here's an e-mail I got from a friend in January 1998:

> I talked to Sheldon this morning. He took the train up to Toronto for the big English professor conference (MLA) and said that returning through customs was a bitch. The train was stopped for an hour and a half and the custom cops were really bad. Basically they were grilling all the blacks, making their "suspects" go down to the dining car for even more grilling.
>
> A very bad scene, hearing it from Sheldon. I had no idea things had gotten that bad. He said it was like being in Eastern Europe — just like that, in fact. He sounded pretty weirded out about it....
>
> The MLA conference told U.S. participants to "bring your passports" ...and warned that Canadian customs had gotten rougher in response to what Amerikans were doing.
>
> Sheldon is white, 50, upper-middle class, and he used to be a liberal, but I think he's waking up.

Planes

I was tempted to dismiss this entire section in two words: "Forget it!"

I used to fly a lot. I no longer fly, except in direst emergencies. The Gestapo Gauntlet every airline passenger has to run is illegal, infuriating, and conditions the best of us to behave as unquestioning sheeple. Now that the Authorities have added their requirement for showing *government-issued photo ID*, it's become too ridiculous to bear. And, to the extent that requirement is enforced, it has become *impossible* for ID-resisters to bear.

My personal preference is not to fly at all or to fly on private planes from small airports, rather than commercial airlines. (Private charters, though expensive, might become a future alternative for the Numberless.)

However, there may be hope for asserting our rights against the cattle-herding process of commercial flight. And if so, it lies in the attitude of people like Jackie Juntti, the self-described "Old Polish Woman." Her story of how she beat the ID requirement is told below, in her own words. I still won't fly. And what she had to go through to board a plane was in some ways as bad as being forced to have ID. But I admire her guts and grit — and principles.

Before moving on to Jackie's story, I have just three other quick thoughts to add about flying. One came from my S.O., Charles, another from my correspondent Badsheep. One is my own. None may be practical for the in-a-hurry business flyer, but they're worth keeping in mind.

- If you must fly, try flying out of smaller airports, where security is more relaxed and you're likely to experience less hassle.
- Avoid flying out of the U.S. when going to another country. Drive to Canada or Mexico, or take a boat to another country, then fly from there. It's a small thing, but it cuts down on some of the "other people's business minding" by the fedgov.
- When recruiting members for your Free Community, try to find one or more good pilots — preferably people who own their own small planes. Settling near a small general aviation airport is helpful, if your community can't have a private airstrip of its own.

Speaking of which, I think we all know by now not to pay cash for airline tickets, since that's considered evidence of "drug dealing," particularly if you're black or Hispanic. (My god, the fedgov is appallingly racist!)

And beware of taking large amounts of cash out of the country through airports.

Now onward with Jackie's story. Remember: You fly, if you fly at all, at your own risk.

Flying on My Costco Card
by Jackie Juntti

Did you know you have to provide "GOVERN-MENT ISSUED IDENTIFICATION" to travel?

As many of you know I took one of my very infrequent trips on an airplane last week. I had been forewarned by one of my daughters that I would HAVE to produce a Driver's License in order to get past the baggage check-in desk. Well, this just happens to be an extremely sensitive issue with me and I said, "NO WAY"; I will get on that plane using my Costco Card as it has my photo on it.

I did call the airline and ask what the deal was on identification. I did this as the plane tickets were a gift from my brother and sister-in-law and I couldn't goof up their gift to me to prove a point. The person I spoke with on the phone was very polite in telling me that I would indeed need GOVERNMENT ISSUED ID to board the plane. I asked what is considered Govt. Issued ID? She explained that would be a state issued Driver's License, a state issued Identification Card, or a Passport.

I asked what a person can do who has none of those items. She replied, "Then you must get one of them."

I told her my flight was scheduled the next day, so there was no time to get any of those items and just whom would I talk with to discover what other options would be available? Her response was to tell me to go talk with the airport security at the airport.

I did not do that, choosing instead to take my chances of just going to the airport and seeing what would happen. I love real life adventures.

Upon arriving at Sea-Tac, I gave my daughter the usual hug and kiss and said, "Bye, see you in a week — or whatever." I grabbed my luggage and headed towards the baggage/ticket counter.

When my turn came I placed my suitcase on the proper spot and handed the clerk my tickets. She looked at them and asked for ID. I opened my purse and my wallet and pulled out my Costco Card and handed it to her. Believe me, this was a KODAK moment!!!

She recovered and then explained that I needed to produce GOVERNMENT ISSUED IDENTIFICA-TION. The ensuing discussion was long (took about 15 minutes to get past this point to the next step) and I will just summarize for this writing. Oh yes, there were many people standing around who heard all of this.

We went back and forth over GOVERNMENT ISSUED ID and my comments about why did I need a driver's license — that I wasn't driving the plane — that I thought I lived in America and we had freedom here and hadn't reached the point of having to PRODUCE OUR PAPERS.

Next we discussed how someone who flies only every few years is to know of these socialist rules. The requirement of needing GOVERNMENT IS-SUED IDENTIFICATION is not printed on the tickets or the envelopes that contain the tickets. AND, as I looked around where I stood (where they sell tickets) there was not any notice concerning that rule.

She explained that I would have been advised at the time I purchased the tickets of the ID requirement. I told her I didn't purchase the tickets, they were a gift and had been mailed to me.

"Well, it is FAA rules," she said.

I asked for a copy of those rules so that I could see for myself if that was indeed true. She didn't have a copy and told me to contact FAA for one. I explained that it was odd that IF that is the rule then it should be readily available for the public to see. The conversation then went to how safe she feels knowing that everyone on the plane has GOVERNMENT ISSUED IDENTIFICATION as it makes everyone SAFER and more SECURE.

I remarked that false identification is not that hard to get and I didn't understand how the possession of possibly false GOVERNMENT ISSUED IDENTI-FICATION could make anyone feel safer. I certainly didn't feel any safer or more secure knowing that all passengers carried GOVERNMENT ISSUED IDENTIFICATION. We agreed that we seemed to have different views on what constitutes SAFETY and SECURITY.

(I really wanted to explain how the FBI, BATF, CIA, had GOVERNMENT ISSUED IDENTIFICA-TION and I wondered how SAFE & SECURE the Randy Weaver family and the Branch Davidians felt knowing that those firing on them had GOVERN-MENT ISSUED IDENTIFICATION. I don't think she would have comprehended the relationship at all.)

I Am Not a Number!

brianleesblog.blogspot.com

I finally asked her point blank if the fact that I didn't produce any GOVERNMENT ISSUED IDENTIFICATION was going to create denial of my boarding the plane. She was very exasperated at this point as I am sure they have not been taught how to deal with nice little old ladies that aren't nasty or threatening but are just asking honest questions. She then reached down below her counter area and pulled out a very bright fluorescent orange strip of card stock, approximately 18 inches x 1.5 inches that she folded around my purse strap and stapled.

I was told NOT TO REMOVE it either. She then explained that I would HAVE to submit to a physical search of my purse upon passing through the metal detection area. AND, be sure they punch this strip after you have been searched or YOU WILL NOT GET ON THAT PLANE!!!!!!

I looked at her and asked if the searchers were aware that they had to punch that strip of bright orange paper after they searched my purse? "Yes, they know that," she replied. Well then, I guess it is their responsibility to punch it and not mine to be sure they do, right? She didn't really answer me but made it clear in motions that she was done with me and for me to proceed so she could help the next person.

I proceeded to the metal detection area where a long line was waiting to be "detected." I was not carrying anything other than my purse, which had this BRIGHT orange flagging on it so that everyone would know I was some sort of criminal and not a compliant little sheep following the dictates of the NWO. I enjoy watching people so this gave me a lot of entertainment as I stood in line.

When I reached the position of approximately 7th in line, the man that I presume is an observer was saying something. I didn't realize right away that he was talking to me. When it dawned on me that he was directing his comments to me I asked him to please repeat what he said as I had not heard him. He smiled broadly and pointed at the BRIGHT orange flagging and asked me WHAT I had done to deserve that, as they rarely ever see that on a passenger.

Keep in mind this area was crowded and the voice level had to be raised in order to be heard. I made sure my purse became very visible and smiling I told him (loudly) that I was guilty of NOT ACCEPTING GOVERNMENT ISSUED IDENTIFICATION as I thought I lived in AMERICA and didn't realize I was living in NAZI GERMANY!!!!

This definitely caught the attention of many, and the observer smiled and said ok, he understood. By this time I was at the metal detector and placed my purse on the conveyor belt and walked through to be "detected." A nice young woman took my purse and asked me to please step to the side with her as they needed to physically search my purse. I said fine and followed her to a window sill.

She explained she had to call for a supervisor; so that took a bit.

When the supervisor appeared, she began to remove the items from my purse. I love these exercises. I have a well-stocked purse, too. In fact, it was even more so than usual as I had my 8 oz. bottle of Colloidal Silver in my purse so that it wouldn't spill in my suitcase. I am an E'Ola Distributor and I take the C.S. daily as a preventative antibiotic (I am allergic to all but two prescription antibiotics) so I had to have it with me.

I had to explain what was in the bottle which I did. I told both of them they were lucky I had not brought my little C.S. Maker (for making the C.S. myself) as it has three batteries and wires and silver probes. That would have made them all nervous and probably landed me in a cell somewhere.

Both of them were very nice and polite through this process. After all items were removed and those that needed explanation were explained, the woman attempted to replace the items in my purse. After a while of watching the attempted repack I asked if there was any rule that prevented me from repacking it. She gratefully said no, so I did the chore.

As I was repacking my purse the supervisor (he was of Asian descent) asked me WHY I went through all of this. I explained to him that I was born in America almost 58 years ago and I still believed in ALL the freedoms that Americans are supposed to have. Also, that I would continue to exercise my rights as I understand them until the day I die in spite of the Socialist restraints being imposed upon the people of this Country.

This man looked me square in the eyes and told me thank you and to please continue doing it. He wished more people would stand against these things as I have chosen to do. I wish I would have had more time to find out where he came from and hear his story but flight time was fast arriving so off I went to the boarding area. I made mental notes of the expressions on the faces of those that would see my BRIGHT orange flagging (reminded me of the YELLOW STAR during WWII) and wished I had time to explain to them the reason why I had it. Perhaps a few understood.

I boarded the plane without further stops and arrived in Reno on time. An amazing event took place in spite of my not having produced GOVERNMENT ISSUED IDENTIFICATION but only using a Costco Card to get on board — all of the passengers on that flight arrived SAFELY, can you believe it?

As I was recounting this trip I felt I should add the experience of seeing the high-flying planes in the sky over the Reno area that trailed the white contrails in grid formation which in turn released a black shadow that floated to the earth. I wonder if those pilots had GOVERNMENT ISSUED IDENTIFICATION?

Getting out without a passport

U.S. passports will be denied to those who refuse to take the Slave Mark. This is going to require yet more coping on our part. But we're getting kind of used to that now, aren't we?

Until the turn of the twentieth century, passports were largely unknown. The first country in the world to institute them? That historic bastion of freedom: Russia. As in so many other matters governmental, the alleged free nations rushed to institute their own citizen controls once a tyrant had come up with the idea.

A passport is just another government travel permit, like a driver's license. And once again, we've gotten sucked into using it for reasons of convenience or security. Yes, if you're abroad and in trouble with the local law, it might be nice to wave your British or U.S. passport and claim protection of your citizenship. And passports, particularly well-used ones decorated with visa stamps, are a glamorous item.

All that would be well and good if you didn't have to take the Mark to get one. But since you do, here are some alternatives:

- You'll always be able to get into Canada and Mexico without a passport, no matter what the laws say — even if U.S. borders are eventually barricaded as firmly as those of old Berlin. You'll still be able to sneak across. Both borders are too long to be fully guarded, and there will never be a government security system that can't be gotten around by determination or money, or both.

- From Mexico or Canada, you might be able to fly, sail, or (from Mexico, at least) drive elsewhere "under the radar" of immigration authorities. Not every country is obsessed with the necessity for passports. Some small ones will welcome you and your American money, documents be damned. But find out about the habits of your destination country *before* you go.

- You might — I am definitely not recommending this — experiment with a passport from a fake or obsolete nation. While personnel at airports, ship ports, and border crossings no doubt have databases of valid and invalid "nations," you might also luck out. If an agent is busy, inattentive, or doesn't give a damn, you might get away with crossing a border on your passport from "Rhodesia" or "Dutch Guyana." (Who can keep track of all the nations that have gone under in the last few decades?) However, this is extremely high-risk behavior.

- Another experiment: A fake passport from a real nation. Expert forgers are already creating such things, and I'd expect the number of forgers to increase with market demand. CIA agents and similar belly-crawlers already get passports that way (when they don't get "real" passports in reciprocal agreements with governments of other countries). If you can plausibly pass as Irish, Canadian, or Zimbabwean, it's worth a try.

- Get a "real" passport from a real nation. As the situation begins to get desperate for people in the U.S., you can expect embassy and consulate staffers from other countries to be willing to sell "real" passports. They already keep such documents on hand to replace lost passports of their own citizens, so why not for you? This is a relatively safe option, but you must have good contacts to take advantage of it.

- And speaking of that… You could also "help" a genuine Zimbabwean or English person to "lose" a legitimate passport. It might take some luck to find a foreigner who looks like you (or whose documents could be altered to look like yours), but it can be done.

- Another possibility — though another one that's not for everybody — get a really real passport from another country. This means either 1) being entitled to a legitimate second citizenship through the circumstances of your birth or achievements, 2) giving up U.S. citizenship and going through the always-arduous process of becoming a citizen of another country, or 3) buying an official second passport. (If you recall Chapter Three, the prices start at around $35,000. If you have that kind of money to spend, enjoy.)

If you want to play games with second or suspect passports, you must, above all, be able to put on a plausible show of *being* of the nationality you claim to be. If you hand the agent a passport that says you're from Argentina, you'll have more chance of success if you look or sound plausibly Argentinean. If you show up speaking Texan or looking Scandinavian, you're going to create suspicion.

Oh, no doubt there are Texans and Scandinavians with genuine Argentine citizenship. But if you're not the genuine article, it's even more important that you look like you are in order to avoid arousing suspicion.

I'm thinking of a story I heard just this week that didn't involve passports, but did involve plausibility in crossing borders. A man was trying to get his golf clubs through customs, but in casual chatter (which was certainly not really casual), the customs agent began to suspect that the "golfer" didn't really know the game. When he asked the man to demonstrate his swing, the man did — backwards. He was arrested with a golf bag full of cocaine.

Whatever you do, always be plausible!

I make two illegal border crossings

I have two personal experiences going into and coming home from other countries without required documents. The first occurred in such an unusual circumstance it might not be helpful to anyone else, but I'll throw it out because you just never know…

I had gone to an American island resort in the entourage of a wealthy business owner. (Me, I was just a serf whose only purpose was to write about this rich dude's Glorious Self. Nevertheless, there I was at the edge of the inner circle.) On the spur of the moment, the Grand Dude decided to carry the entire gang of flunkies off to a decidedly non-American country.

When I explained that I had no passport, Mr. GD just gave me a sardonic look, as if passports applied only to far lesser beings than he — and loaded me on the airplane with all the executive vice presidents, harried secretaries, security thugs, and high-class hookers.

At Country X, no one even asked for documents, not from any of us. They were too busy throwing their bodies under the Grand Dude's shoes so they could revel in being trod upon by his Rich and Famous Feet.

Coming back into the U.S., our little party was personally shepherded past two full 747 loads of mere peons and personally presented to Customs by airline VIPs. The Customs agent fretted over my undocumented status for about thirty seconds before taking the attitude that, if I was with Mr. GD, I must be okay. They did no more than give a cursory glance to anyone's documentation, and checked no one's baggage.

I could have carried a suitcase full of white powder or a backpack nuke and they wouldn't have cared because I was third-flunky-once-removed to a hotshot.

My other experience without proof of citizenship came when I flew to Canada from the U.S. a few years ago. Previously, I'd driven across the border several times and not been asked to show ID at all. (DL was, at that time, sufficient, and even that was often not checked).

I was unaware that, when flying in, new arrivals were even then expected to show proof of citizenship — passport or birth certificate. I had nothing but a driver's license. They made some display of frowning over me — but after talking with me long enough to believe that yes, I really sounded like an American businesswoman, they let me go.

Now, in both these cases, I did have a driver's license. But I also believe that, in both cases, I could have gotten into (or out of) the country without even that. The first time I was protected by a circle of privilege. The second time I simply looked, dressed, and sounded like what I claimed to be, an innocent American who'd just screwed up, so they had no reason to suspect I was "up to" anything. I was plausible.

Always be plausible. It may not be good enough in the future. But it will help.

The underground railroad

In pre-Civil War America, slaves began escaping the U.S. by "following the drinking gourd" into Canada. Traveling at night, walking with their eyes toward the Big Dipper, they fled the slave states of both south and north[3] and made their way to freedom.

They were not alone in their escape efforts. But neither were they helped by the kind of government program or "corporate initiative" we now imagine are necessary to make anything happen.

Hardly! The U.S. government — demonstrating the power-grabbing nature of all governments everywhere — passed the Fugitive Slave law to repel and halt this freedom effort. The notorious Dred Scot decision put the stamp of highest officialdom on anti-freedom. And the Underground Railroad to Canada rolled along, in secret, as a private volunteer venture. A venture of sheer necessity for those who would be free at any risk and those who would help them do it.

---

[3] It's one of the myths of government education that slavery existed only in the south. Although most northern states had abolished that abomination by the time of the Civil War, some members of Lincoln's own Union were slave states. As Jeffrey Rogers Hummel details in his book, *Emancipating Slaves, Enslaving Free Men*, slavery wasn't even abolished in the Union's own capital, the District of Columbia, until April 1862. In early 1863, when Lincoln issued the famous Emancipation Proclamation, "It did not emancipate any of the slaves in the four [Union] border states. Nor did it emancipate any slaves in those sections of the Confederacy that Union armies had already reconquered, including all of Tennessee and large portions of Virginia and Louisiana. The only slaves covered were the ones beyond the reach of Union authority." In other words, the famous Proclamation we were taught to honor in school was a PR gesture so hypocritical and so dishonest as to be worthy of a Bill Clinton. Of course, it also was intended to provoke slave rebellions, and thus weaken the South. But the slaves Mr. Lincoln could have helped free, *he deliberately and specifically chose to keep in slavery*. So yes, those slaves were fleeing from the north, too, both before and no doubt during the Civil War.

The railroad was so well hidden that even now, nearly 150 years after it ceased operating, historians are still working to trace its routes and discover its stations.

Who was the Underground Railroad? Among others, it was Quakers and other conscience-following Christians. Free blacks. Magnificent, courageous women like Harriet Tubman. Abolitionists of all stripes. Perhaps even slaves sneaking out of their hovels to help other slaves at night. It was simply moral people, whether atheist or believer, who believed they had to do the right thing, even when it meant breaking the law. And of course, the escaping slaves themselves, dying to be free. People a lot like us.

We will need an underground railroad. Soon. In the near future. We will need to help Undocumented Citizens get out of the country, or to hide them from pursuit after they've broken one of the millions of meaningless laws or regulations. Frankly, we already need that *now*.

We may need, simply, to reach each other across hostile territory, where the most innocent of us could be in danger from the forces of tyranny (or, in the event of collapse, the almost-equally dangerous forces of freelance criminals).

At any time, and for any reason, that we need a network of safe houses on a road to freedom, we need an underground railroad.

Computers and the Internet already serve as a kind of intellectual underground railroad, enabling us to pass ideas and information through networks of freedom seekers, unobserved (if we are careful) by government enforcers. And the Internet may help us establish a physical underground railroad of the future. It has already performed a basic miracle of organization by putting far-flung freedom fighters in touch with each other.

How do we build an underground railroad?

I'm sure a lot of us would say we won't have to "build" anything when the time comes — that when there's a need for Jefferson Henry to escape the People's Republic of Colorado and run for the Mexican border, Henry's friend John Paine will get the word to Abigail Hancock, and she'll get the word to Betsy Madison, who will get the word to Otis Revere, and it will be accomplished.

There's some truth in that.

Informal underground railroads will exist (and certainly do exist) among small groups of people. And necessity will direct the creation of more as the government becomes more oppressive.

But that's true of many things. And, as with a lot of other possibilities we face, I believe it behooves us to be thinking about them in advance. Planning them, too. Quietly.

When I was thinking about examples of groups who are (or might) already be laying the groundwork for underground railroads, the first ones that came to my mind were the militias. Through loose networks around the country, militia groups are already in contact with each other and already thinking in terms of defense against tyranny.

In some ways they're a natural.

But militia groups also bring to mind the two biggest problems a future railroad is likely to have:

- Too much visibility
- Being compromised

These problems are related. Groups become visible for being "anti-government," and the next thing you know, there are more agents and informants in their ranks than there are real freedom lovers. And with all the laws nowadays, there are plenty of genuine freedom lovers (but without backbone) who can be co-opted; break a law, inform on your buddies or go to prison.

Militias have already responded to both these problems by going further underground. I hate to say militia-baiter/master fundraiser Morris Dees is right about anything, but he's right when he says the militia movement is now dominated by "leaderless cells" and even "cells of one."

The great advantages of the underground railroad of the nineteenth century were these:

- The need was urgent and obvious to moral people.
- The people who maintained the stations were truly principled.
- They worked, in large part, through churches and other small groups that had little relationship with the government, while most of our churches and alleged "service" organizations have sold out.

- And (alas!) the fedgov didn't, in those days, have the nation so caught in a net of laws and spies.

There's little we can do about the latter, except be watchful, route around known or suspected fink-agents, and lick our wounds when we have losses. Or inflict wounds upon those who sell their friends. It's already obvious from such tragedies as the death of Gordon Kahl and the targeting of the Weaver family that even the smallest and most intimate groups contain people who'd sell their grandmothers for a dollar.

Nevertheless, we will need to build our railroads, and we have some examples we can learn from — not only from 150 years ago, but from contemporary experience.

One modern variation on the underground railroad was the sanctuary movement of the 1980s, in which church groups brought undocumented refugees from Central American wars to the U.S. and gave them refuge, sometimes within the walls of churches. (Churches will still do the right thing when it's left wing.)

Another modern variation are the networks that help abused adults and children escape their tormentors — whether those tormentors be spouses, parents or the state. These networks may spirit mothers and children, occasionally fathers and children, away from abusers (or alleged abusers). Some of them will take in children who've run away from their families. They may also spirit children away from government institutions, where the poor kids are drugged, beaten, and intimidated into submission "for their own good."

In a December 1997 series, the Pittsburgh *Post-Gazette* identified at least four such independent networks operating within the U.S. If journalists were able to track down four, there are certainly many more than that. One, run by an Atlanta, Georgia woman, Faye Yager, operates in open defiance of the law, while the rest keep a low profile. Yager claims safe houses all over the U.S. and in several other countries.

The owner of a safe house that sheltered a 14-year-old runaway said:

> We know it's a risk. We could be sued, lose our home if it was ever discovered we had

helped her. But we knew the Lord would want us to help if it's a matter of a child in danger.

The Underground Railroad Quilt

It was just an ordinary quilt design. If you encounter it in a quilting book or on a bed today, you might think it was just one more antique American pattern. It is that, but not *just* that.

The ladies who were the mainstay of the underground railroad used a distinctive quilt pattern as one way to identify stations along the route to freedom.

An escaping slave might know, for instance, that there was a safe house at the edge of Liberty Gulch, Pennsylvania. Beyond that, she might not understand exactly which house to look for. But the pattern of the quilt, hanging in a window or from a porch rail, was as clear as a neon sign.

The underground railroad quilt helped guide the way from the South to Canada.

People who enter the program change their names, adopt disguises and often end up moving from place to place, without permanence or security. But for them, it's better than the alternative.

For us it might be, too.

The Appendix lists several books that might be useful sources for information on underground railroads, both historic and modern.

So what do you need for an underground railroad?

- A network of people — anywhere from two to who knows? The larger the network, the more versatile, the smaller the more secure.
- People with a variety of help to offer:
  - Transportation
  - Temporary housing
  - Long-term housing
  - Money
  - Contacts with border guards or other law-enforcement types
  - Protection services
  - Good communications channels
  - Forgery skills for false documentation
  - Acting skills
  - Disguise techniques (either for themselves, or to help hide the identity of the escaping person)

  - Medical services
  - Food
  - Survival and orienteering skills
  - Name a whole lot more
- "Stations" that are a useful distance apart. Depending on your needs, this might mean different things. It could mean four or five locations around a single city, where someone could be moved rapidly without ever leaving the area. On the other hand, it might mean homes and businesses located a hundred miles apart on a route from Iowa to Canada or Nevada to Mexico.
- A network of Free Communities makes a natural foundation for a series of stations on an underground railroad — though serious gulchers would have to balance their desire to do good deeds against their need to maintain invisibility.
- "Stations" might also be campgrounds or hidden camping places. So far, national ID hasn't stretched into most campgrounds. And even if it does, it's possible to cache minimal camping gear at different locations — or to prepare backpacks of gear for an Undocumented Citizen to use in an escape and still use camping as an alternative to indoor "stations."
- Means of getting from station to station — which could include anything from walking to private plane.
- A destination where escaping freedom lovers will be welcome. Or will at least have a chance to live and breathe.

Keep in mind that an underground railroad doesn't in any way need to be a formal, organized network. If an effort has enough popular support, you'll inevitably find "volunteers" springing up like weeds in a garden — thousands of whom you may never even know about. Parallel and overlapping networks will appear. Interestingly perpendicular networks, too.

For instance, a symbol — like the underground railroad quilt — could be adopted by people everywhere who stood ready to help Undocumented Citizens. Jackie Juntti, the Old Polish Woman, has come up with the orange ribbon campaign for ID opponents, based on her airport experience. Jackie's orange ribbon is like the lapel ribbons worn in support of AIDS victims, or the ribbons on web sites to show opposition to censorship.

Perhaps orange ribbons tied around potted plants — or curtains tied back with orange ribbons — could identify safe houses, as well.

Obviously, there's danger in such exposure. I can just see the feddies now, tying the orange ribbons on their porch rails, then rounding up the folks who showed up looking for shelter. But this danger can be circumvented — not infallibly, but in several ways.

For one thing, there isn't necessarily a need for the underground traveler to identify himself or "confess" his reason for needing shelter. He can simply be a modern-day hobo looking for shelter or a meal, an innocent person economically crippled at the hands of The System. To put it in terms the Clinton era can understand: "Don't Ask; Don't Tell."

In fact, people who want to participate in an underground railroad may find a variety of ways to communicate with each other — certainly including the Internet.

Don't forget, either, that a "sign" could be posted on a Web page or in a chat room. To those who didn't understand, it would mean nothing. To those who knew to look for it, it might be a signpost on the road to freedom.

As with so much else, we will need an underground railroad and we'll have to take some risks to get it. We'll have some losses. We'll learn some hard lessons before we can do better. But it's all preferable to staying put and dying of the pain (or the ennui) of being regulated and owned to death.

Update 2002
What's New
Since Chapter Six

Few things have changed more — and for the worse — than access to transportation. September 11 was the excuse for some of this, but the trend was going on long before (as the very fact of national ID being introduced via our drivers' licenses reveals). The Drug War has been a long-time excuse for transportation crackdowns of various sorts. Now — different villains, same "solutions." But it's all excuses.

The bottom line is that there are certain fundamental things police-statists *must* control, if they are to seize control at all. One is firearms. Another is data on the populace (like that that helped Hitler be so successful at disarming enemies, then rounding up and murdering Jews and other minority groups). Two others are communications and transportation. If you can monitor, then limit these, you've got a population whose ability to rebel against you or threaten you is largely choked off.

So what's happened in transportation? Far too much to cover. But again, I'll shoot for a sampling here.

Does anybody have a valid ID?

Here's one development to make an ID resister smile. It's just a hint so far, a glimpse of what might really be going on out there. But a liberty outlaw should enjoy it: A series of those checkpoints I predicted to catch "undocumented citizens" was set up in Dayton, Ohio, beginning shortly after *I Am Not a Number!* was published. (It was a "public safety" checkpoint, looking for unlicensed drivers. It was a money-raising checkpoint, issuing tickets. An ID checkpoint by any other name would smell just as bad.)

The checkpoints revealed, as Ohio state supreme court justice Paul E. Pfeifer wrote, that, "Of the two million or so drivers in Ohio, approximately 800,000 have their license under some sort of suspension, and an estimated 1 in 8 drivers in Dayton doesn't have a proper license."[4]

Now *that* is a phenomenal percentage of resisters and scofflaws! (It's also nearly impossible to believe that more than one-third of all Ohio drivers have their licenses under suspension. But that is what Hizzoner wrote.)

It's difficult to interpret what this really means. If the checkpoints were set up in poor, ignorant, or high-crime neighborhoods, for instance, the percentage of ID resisters might not reflect what's going on on an average American highway, but might only say that people with little money, education, or regard for

---

[4] "Justice Paul E. Pfeifer's Weekly Column: Checkpoint Charlie," May 16, 2001. Found at http://www.sconet.state.oh.us/Communications_office/Justice_Pfeifer/2001/jp051601.asp.

law are likely to ignore licensing requirements or to drive after revocations.

(Even that would be interesting in a way; it means many of those "ignorant" folks are smarter and a lot braver than all the Good Little Citizens obeying their way into a police state.)

But if there's a possibility that one in eight Americans is actually saying no to government ID — for whatever reason — then there's more hope than you might think for freedom. *Think about all those people the government will have that much harder time tracking and controlling!*

More checkpoints

In 2000, the U.S. Supreme Court, in *City of Indianapolis v Edmond* 531 US 32 (2000), outlawed checkpoints whose sole purpose is to snoop for drugs. But the Supremes have been unusually schizy on the constitutionality of checkpoints. (Apparently the eminent justices have never read the plain words of the Fourth Amendment.) They've allowed nearly every other form of random checkpoint, including stop-and-search for DUI, insurance, safety, seatbelts, "security," ad infinitum. (And the Ohio state Supreme Court found the above-mentioned ID checkpoints to be constitutional, as well.) So if the law enforcers really want to randomly check the population for drug possession? All they have to do is *say* the stop is to check for something else altogether.

An individual-rights organization, The National Motorists Association, is dedicated to helping us protect our rights in random checkpoints. While it can't tell us how to do away with the very notion of random checkpoints, which steal our rights by their very existence, it does offer helpful tips on how to protect yourself. See the Appendix for contact information.

GPS

In this chapter I wrote about the benefits and potential misuses of GPS technology. Since then, we've seen more of both. GPS units are now being installed by the manufacturer on many vehicles for helping drivers find their way around (not a bad use when you're lost in the middle of nowhere). But

courts have also ruled that police can attach a GPS tracking unit to your car or truck without a warrant. Their reasoning: Since all it does is give officers an alternative way to follow you, GPS tracking is no different than having a cop physically follow you in his squad car or unmarked vehicle.

Courts have seemed spectacularly oblivious to the fact that electronic devices *expand* the capabilities of the police. To say that attaching a tracking device to a vehicle is no different than physically following a vehicle is like saying a phone tap is no different than overhearing a spoken conversation. Most judges know nothing about technology and their willful ignorance and disregard of liberty is helping turn America into a surveillance state. But then, what do you expect? Judges are government employees, paid for by tax money, and they usually serve their masters. (As Gerry Spence said, they're the lions guarding the throne of power.)

In any case, bear in mind that GPS units attached by police can be used not only to follow you "in real-time," as the computer people say, but also to give Big Brother a record of your movements after the fact. This is no doubt a valuable tool for legitimate law enforcement (in one of the early police uses of a GPS unit attached to a vehicle, a murder suspect unknowingly led police to his victim's burial site). But used without a legally obtained warrant, it's yet another theft of your privacy and your self-ownership. And the really fearsome thing will come — probably in the not-too-distant future — when every passenger vehicle is equipped by law with some sort of GPS-based tracking device that will enable police to locate any car or truck anywhere in the world at will.

Again, such technology has potentially beneficial uses. (Say your car has gone into a wooded ravine and you're trapped inside, unable to reach your cellphone; your spouse calls the police when you don't return on time from that business trip, and zap, they're at your side with assistance.) But the presence of such devices should generally be voluntary and police should not be able to use their tracking capabilities without either a warrant or that kind of life-saving emergency need.

Combine this with technology that now exists to stop a vehicle at will and you have tools that will not only be abused by police but by freelance stalkers as well.

Auto-tracking

Some states have also begun tracking "traffic patterns" (they swear they're not tracking individual vehicles) using the radio-based sensors mounted on the windshields of cars and trucks that have "EZ-Pass" electronic toll-payment devices. There have also been serious proposals for states to use similar monitoring to tax vehicles according to how many miles you drive on certain highways. So far, public protest has kept this from happening. But you can see where the trend is heading. Familiar story, get you used to some "helpful" little use of monitoring ("traffic patterns"), then whomp you with individual vehicle tracking.

Public transport

Since *I Am Not a Number!* was originally published, ID-checking has been extended to other forms of transport like Amtrak and long-distance busses. So have random searches for weapons, drugs, and the like. What was sweetly true in 1999 about the friendliness of mass transit is now yet another sunny part of America's past. Read and weep.

Well, even then things behind the scenes probably weren't as cheery as I painted them. In fact, not long ago Amtrak was caught sharing a direct computer connection to the Drug Enforcement Administration, so that any time a passenger did something "suspicious," like pay cash for a ticket or buy a one-way ticket, DEA agents could rush right over and shake the hapless innocent down for any cash or expensive goods he might be carrying.

Public outcry forced Amtrak to say it was giving up the direct computer link. But the practice of informing on passengers continues, of course. Sharing in Drug War asset forfeiture shakedowns has become a profitable business for the otherwise unprofitable railroad, which can make far more on a single shakedown that it would ever make on some poor soul's one-way ticket to Albuquerque.

If you must use public transportation, do your best to learn what various government agencies consider "suspicious" travel patterns and avoid those behaviors. Some of them are fairly obvious, like the aforementioned purchase of one-way tickets or buying tickets with cash. But some "suspicious" travel activities are incomprehensible to any but the most governmentally paranoid (for instance, paying for a ticket with a credit card, but buying it at the last minute before you travel). And some "suspicious" behaviors are unavoidable. Notoriously, you can draw suspicion merely for being black or Hispanic, for carrying "too much" luggage or "not enough" luggage, for seeming "too tense" or "too relaxed," or for a whole host of other things you could never figure out in a million years.

Passenger Profiling

Speaking of passenger profiling, since 1998, all airline passengers have been screened using a system called CAPPS — Computer Assisted Passenger Pre-Screening. This system is designed to catch "suspicious" characters, including terrorists. According to the *Wall Street Journal*, CAPPS actually did spot two of the September 11 hijackers, but human error (in the form of those good old airport security screeners) intervened. Instead of searching the passengers, they searched only the luggage and missed those little box cutters.[5]

The version of CAPPS in use on September 11 was a politically correct one. Its passenger profiling carefully did *not* include race, religion, or national origin. All passenger profiling is loathsome. And racial profiling is a particularly obnoxious kind of profiling. However, if you're going to profile at all, the data are meaningless if you're not including enough data to come up with a real threat profile — like a bunch of Moslem young men from Saudi Arabia, all buying tickets together on the same credit card. Duh.

But don't worry. CAPPS is being "fixed" and the new system, CAPPS 2, will be online by the time you read this. Nobody, but nobody, is saying what CAPPS 2 searches for in your "passenger profile." But the word is it does very much what Larry Ellison

---

[5] The moral thing to have done would not have been to search anybody, but to let the passengers and crew defend themselves — and let potential hijackers know that they'd lose their lives *before* they ever got control of an aircraft. The vast majority of what's being done in the name of "airport security" is not only ineffective and in stark violation of the Bill of Rights. But it's only "necessary" because passengers have been reduced to the state of helpless victims.

wanted his national ID system to do. If the most authoritative reports are true, it not only will (or can) profile your ticket-buying method, travel history, race, national origin, and so on, but also your consumer credit history, medical records, educational records, and anything else it can scoop in about you as an individual. In other words, it's the Ellison plan, and you can view it as a pilot national ID database program being introduced via air travel and eventually to be extended to other areas of travel, then to work, shopping, and other activities.

We can hope that by the time this book is issued, more will be known about CAPPS 2. Then you can do everything possible to avoid being a Canadian woman who buys clothes from Land's End and knits for a hobby or an Armenian fruit merchant with a limp — or whatever else it is that the data doctors are going to consider "suspicious" next year.

CAPPS also illustrates another trend that's naturally arisen out of universal gathering and storing of data. You are simply no longer treated as an individual. Having so much data on so many people has enabled mathematicians to develop algorithms and researchers to produce "sophisticated" predictions of what people who fit certain profiles will do. Just as you are now being investigated for crimes you didn't commit, you're also suspected of crimes based on completely innocent patterns of behavior in your life. Your most truly harmless personal habits can potentially result in anything from being refused permission to board an airplane to being arrested — or as they now say (Soviet style), "detained" on suspicion of heaven knows what. (And I really do mean your most innocent habits — like the way you buy pizza, as we shall see after Chapter Seven.)

Once again, the best solution for true freedom lovers is simply to keep your purchasing habits, hobbies, financial records, and everything else about you out of databases. However, this too has its drawbacks. An absence of data may also be considered "suspicious." So those among us who desire to be "moles," living in society but not of it, may do best to ensure that a certain amount of totally innocuous data shows up, but not the whole picture. (In other words, buy your bird-watching supplies by credit card, but your political literature, firearms, and sex toys for cash — as long as you can.)

If you're interested in knowing more about fighting intrusive transportation ID requirements, profiling, and other government snoopery "within the system," you should follow the legal cases of John Gilmore, the powerful, and powerfully fierce, privacy activist. A URL for *Gilmore v. Ashcroft* is in the Appendix.

Airport screening

Airport screeners have gone from being minimum-wage, uneducated, untrained and largely inept airline employees to being better paid, uneducated, semi-trained and largely inept employees of the federal government's new Transportation Security Administration (TSA). According to the latest tests run with dummy weapons, screeners were still missing at least twenty-five percent — and at some airports much more — of all the weapons people attempt to carry on board aircraft. (This would be good if it meant they weren't conducting any illegal searches; but sadly it means they're conducting illegal searches but merely aren't competent thugs.)

Passports and SSNs

Passports are not yet being denied to all people without Beast Numbers. This is a mixed bag. I have two acquaintances without SSNs who got their passports in about ten days without anyone even batting an eyelash. Another SSN-resisting acquaintance, on the other hand, was told to fill out an absurdly snoopy form (asking things like who her grade-school teachers were) and was denied a passport when she refused. This person, however, lacked a government-issued driver's license, while the former two had valid state licenses issued before the SSN requirement took effect.

The really bad news is that passports are in the process of going digital (now) and biometric (in the near future). This was in the works even before the Bush administration's July 2002 announcement of its Homeland Security Policy. As mentioned earlier, the policy contains a provision to let no foreigner enter the U.S. without a biometric ID, and to work with unspecified international bodies to develop biometric standards for *all* government-issued travel documents. Don't rejoice if, ten years from now, the U.S. State Department removes the SSN fields from its passport applications. It will probably only mean that the old-fashioned SSN has been replaced with a different and even more dangerous form of Beast Number — the digitized (that is, numeric) representation of your fingerprint, DNA pattern, or eyeball.

An apology to Russia

I was wrong when I said Russia was the first country to institute passports, though Russia was an early adopter (and one of the first, in the early 19th century, to introduce an internal passport). Modern passports were actually the work of that other great bastion of justice, freedom, and human decency, the security state of post-Revolutionary France. See *The Invention of the Passport: Surveillance, Citizenship and the State* by John Torpey (Cambridge University Press, 2000) for more detailed historical information on how governments have used passports to control their citizens. The book is deadly dull, but its information is historically valuable.

Underground railroad

Here's a book that should be helpful to anyone interested in running or participating in an underground railroad. *Underground Railroad: Practical Advice for Finding Passengers, Getting Them to Safety, and Staying One Step Ahead of the Tyrants,* by Jefferson Mack (Paladin Press, 2000). Mack is also the author of *The Safe House: Setting Up and Running Your Own Sanctuary* and *Invisible Resistance to Tyranny: How to Lead a Secret Life of Insurgency in an Increasingly Unfree World.* Both of these are also from the great folks at Paladin Press. I don't know who Jefferson Mack really is, and I gather that few people do, but he writes good stuff on covert freedom operations.

Break out

Today, the only way to avoid violations of your rights in travel is ...sigh ...not to travel. Short of that level of frozen paranoia, the best bet is to use your own vehicle, travel only domestically (unless you're escaping from America), and make sure that both the vehicle and your behavior in it are innocuous and nondescript in the extreme. Don't have expired plates or burnt-out taillights. Don't paste on controversial bumper stickers. Don't look any different from a typical local. Don't push any yellow lights or go too fast over any speed bumps. Don't travel in areas of known red-light cameras or checkpoints.

Don't, don't, don't, don't, don't. Until you're ready to rebel and strike back.

Ultimately, if mass resistance — *adamant, unyielding resistance* — doesn't develop and take hold — and there's not much sign that it's going to — the government and its partner corporations are simply going to get away with everything you're reading about. You can read all the privacy-protection books in the world. You can use all the EZ Tips for privacy protection you wish or for getting around the system — and good for you. By all means, look out for your own backside; it's the only one you've got. You can lobby all you want, join all the civil liberties groups you can afford. Great, good, all of it. But until enough people simply break out of the system ...the system will continue to break America.

Get mad. But don't get even. Get smart.

Chapter Seven
Finance and Trade
in the Free Community

"In the 1200s, the bankers of Florence adopted Arabic numerals without hesitation — and the city council outlawed the new system. Of course, this was futile. In our age, the invention of public key cryptosystems is also well-received and also subject to government controls. Such controls cannot last."
— Michael E. Marotta, *"Money in the 21ˢᵗ Century"*

With a lot of the usual avenues of finance and trade cut off by our lack of government ID, we have some improvising to do.

Well, good.

The "usual" banking and finance systems in America have become *way* too elitist and governmentalized, anyway. Even without problems of ID and Year 2000, it's time to get away from them.

Your banker has long since become a federal snitch. And if you're a basically poor person or a working class type, that friendly teller is just the falsely smiling face of an institution that actually looks down its patrician and patronizing nose at you.

Have you ever witnessed someone trying to make a large cash withdrawal from their very own account? Have you watched the teller call over the manager, who browbeats the mere account holder, humiliating them with a "You *really* don't want to do that" lecture?

I saw it happen a couple of months ago with a Southeast Asian gentleman who'd gotten an insurance settlement. He simply didn't see why he had no "right" to pay cash for his new car. He didn't understand the bankers' dire warnings about how they'd be "...*forced* to report the transaction, which could set

off investigations." He understood the English. Perfectly. He just didn't understand the reasoning behind such silliness. He stood there, small and confused, while the teller and manager loudly lectured him for the benefit of everyone else in the bank. Finally, still confused, and now utterly humiliated, he gave in to their (and the federal government's will) and took his cashier's check.

I opened a checking account with $1,000 a few years ago. It was a non-interest-bearing account, but they still demanded my Social Security number "...just long enough to run a check on you." Uh, s'cuse me? I'm giving *you* $1,000 of my hard-earned money and *you* want to run a check on *me*? Hey, what's *your* Social Security number and home address, babe? And how about your boss'? And how about the numbers and home addresses of the board of directors, while we're at it?

And let's not even talk about what it's like to apply for a mortgage (especially if you're self employed)!

Well, screw 'em all, for a thousand good reasons. We'll create our own systems of banking, and even of money. We have the opportunity to make them more private and more humane than the corrupt institutions we're bailing out of.

And to do that, we can hark back to some ancient models, look forward to some digitized miracles, and look offshore for our salvation. Necessity might just be the most nurturing mother we ever had.

Alternative forms of money

Checks and credit cards on U.S. banks will largely be denied us. (Or we'll deny them.) We won't want to use, even if we can get, ATM cards or smart cards issued by banks or government agencies. Let's look at some alternatives.

Cash

Cash is fine — to a point. But it has been and is being made more dangerous. First, we have to cope with assumptions from *Les Jacquebootes*. The most notable of these is, "Any amount of cash over $300 is evidence of drug dealing." Good grief! A month's grocery money, evidence of drug dealing? Whatever will they think of next? If you're ever caught with more than pocket change, you can count on it being stolen by police. Not only that, but they may use your possession of cash as an excuse to turn your house, your car, or your luggage inside out, looking for even more "contraband."

You say searching you on such flimsy grounds is against the law? Yeah. Tell it to the judge…

Cash is also becoming detectable. As the *Pittsburgh Press*[1] revealed several years ago in its groundbreaking expose of civil forfeiture, as much as ninety-six percent of U.S. currency in major cities was then tainted with traces of cocaine. That police dog at the airport or the roadblock is going to sniff out your cash, and if you protest when the agents pocket your cash, you might be arrested for drug dealing.

And what about the rumor — I stress, rumor — that the tiny fiber strips now placed in U.S. money can, in large quantities, set off metal detectors? I haven't seen any verification of this, and have in fact read some credible debunking. The persistent stories, circulated on the Internet, that "a friend of my cousin's went through an airport metal detector with cash in his wallet and…" have all turned out to be elusive when investigated.

However, the fibers in U.S. money *can* be detected by specially designed scanning equipment (used in some stores and requiring close contact with individual bills), and you will, occasionally, if you use an older bill without the fiber strip, be questioned as if you were a counterfeiter. The fibers in the new $50 and $100 "funny-money" bills fluoresce — yellow for the $50, red for the $100.

So the fibers are detectable, under certain conditions, with current technologies. Whether or not they set off metal detectors becomes moot, if the airport and courthouse Gestapos install other equipment that *can* detect your money. If the technology to do this isn't available, it's on the horizon. Is government motivated to track the amount of money you carry on your person? Especially the amount of money you carry through airports and at border crossings? Of course. Will it do so, given the slightest opportunity? Of course.

Therefore, whatever the current status of cash-detection equipment, your future ability to carry cash undetected probably will be compromised.

Even without increasing detectability, cash isn't quite the totally private, totally anonymous medium we like to think it is. Unless you send it by mail (not very smart) you still have to hand it across a counter or a desk, observed by the person on the other side and possibly by others.

At present this is no big deal. Unless you're wearing a parrot on your shoulder, have a Heidelberg dueling scar, are wearing Don't Tread on Me tattoos, or reach over and smack the clerk upside the head, who's going to remember you an hour later? But as we roll toward the cashless society, cash transactions will stand out more and more. They might eventually become illegal.

Of course, cash is also vulnerable to theft. And the present, debased U.S. currency and coin is vulnerable to losing its value overnight or being called in and replaced by scrip.

So cash is okay for now for small transactions and for transactions among trusted fellow freedom lovers. But it has a lot of drawbacks and may not have an infinite life span.

Money orders

Money orders have been good — particularly the anonymous ones peddled by the Post Office. Hand over the cash and get the money order. You don't even have to sign your name.

---

[1] In their six-part series, "Presumed Guilty," 1991, The Pittsburgh Press Co. by Andrew Schneider and Mary Pat Flaherty.

It's not always that simple, however. Here's what the U.S. Postal Service's web site has to say about the matter:

> You can buy domestic and international money orders at all post offices in amounts up to $700. You can purchase multiple money orders at one time in the same or different amounts. There is a $10,000 daily purchase limit, and customers who purchase more than $3,000 in Money Orders in a single day are required by federal law to complete Form 8105, *Money Order Transaction Report*.

When you fill out Form 8105, you must provide your Social Security number and show your ID card. Under the terms of PL 104-208, that means your state-issued, federally designed ID card, based (of course) on your SS number.

At present, you can avoid the ID requirements by purchasing multiple MOs in lower amounts, in different places, and over a period of time. But then you're committing that creative new crime of "structuring." "Structuring" is the dastardly deed of conducting financial transactions in small, perfectly legal steps, in order to avoid transacting them in one, large, illegal step. So of course, Congress made it illegal.

As columnist Vin Suprynowicz points out, this is rather like being arrested for going 43 mph in a 45 mph zone. But what can I say? That's our good ole U.S. government and there ain't nothin' we can do about it for the moment.

Money orders are still safer than cash for mailing. If lost or misused, they can be traced. (Assuming you're in a position to ask for a trace without revealing your own violation of yet another stupid law.)

So they're not hopeless. But I can't imagine the present, no-ID requirement for small purchases can long survive the ID State. And most *bank* money orders, as opposed to postal money orders, already carry a paper trail that makes them undesireable.

Gold and silver

These are, of course, America's traditional, real, valid form of money. They will *always* play a role in freedom lovers' lives. That role is well known enough that there's little need to discuss it here. Just a couple of points, then: Metal detectors and government policies make silver and gold exceptionally vulnerable as a widespread spending medium; however, your Free Community might want — or need — to adopt them as a local medium of choice. In times of hardship, small-denomination U.S. silver coins may be the most versatile, recognizable currency available to you and your fellows.

Smart cards

For all our disparagement of smart cards and the cashless society, this particular cash alternative really has some potential advantages.

The smart card issued to you by a government agency or bank is a trap. Stay out of it! But when the day comes (soon) that you can purchase a smart card in the way you now purchase phone cards, it'll be a hopeful day for freedom.

The smart card, as we've seen, uses a datachip to store information. That same chip can store the electronic information that is, increasingly, used for money in this society.

Here's how the smart card can help guard your financial privacy.

Let's say you go down to your local Target store and pay $260 cash for a smart card that's pre-charged with $250. (The extra $10 is the cost of the service.) You don't give your name, Social Security number or anything else, other than cash, to the store clerk.

You may or may not have to call an 800 number to be assigned a PIN. (Make the call from a phone booth.)

Now you have $250 to spend, wherever smart cards are accepted.

Currently, this doesn't include many places. But that's changing rapidly. Within a few years, every business that now "swipes" your credit or debit card through its scanner will be able to do the same with your smart card. Then you tap your PIN number into a keyboard, demonstrating that you're the owner of the card. (Hope it never comes down to a fingerprint, rather than PIN.)

The system automatically subtracts the amount of your purchase from the card. If you buy an $18.95 box of .44 magnum cartridges, for instance, your card now contains $231.05 in value.

You may also be able to use your smart card, just as you now do your credit card, over the Internet or phone. But unless the transaction is accompanied by strong encryption you run the same risk you do with credit cards; someone can snatch the data out of cyberspace and use it to run out the value of your card.

If you're the merchant, you are protected by systems that instantly verify the purchasing balance left on the card. Although it would be relatively easy for someone with technological skills to program fake information into the card itself (say, to tell the chip that it has a $250 balance left, when in fact there's only $13.98 of purchasing power remaining), the database to which your scanner or other electronic verification system is linked contains the accurate amount for that card. Unless the two match, the system will hiccup and reject the purchase.

Everyone is safe. But no one's privacy is violated because the data is linked to the card, not the user. And the card is a temporary instrument that can be thrown away or destroyed at will.

Bank-issued smart cards will almost certainly be rechargeable; go to an ATM and use money in a checking or savings account to refill their money supply. The card you purchase anonymously may be disposable, instead. Even if it is rechargeable, you'll need to be sure that the recharging method is as anonymous as the method of purchase.

Caution

Just as phone cards are anonymous *only as long as no one can link a particular card to you*, a smart card can be anonymous only as long as enforcers and other snoops can't identify it as yours. If you get "caught" for violating some law and you have a used smart card in your pocket, purse, or desk drawer, the transactions on it can and will be traced.

With some caveats, anonymously issued smart cards should be a very useful medium of exchange until the day the government or card vendors begin requiring fingerprints or some such thing, rather than a PIN number, to activate them.

And of course, the government *will* do all it can to close this avenue of financial privacy. Count on it.

Another caution about smart cards

We should have lots of cautions about smart cards. But here's one in particular. The current leader in smart card technology is a company called Mondex.

From a report circulating on the Internet:

It is apparent [that] TNO (The Netherlands Organization for Applied Scientific Research)

broke Mondex. At Eurocrypt this year, TNO's Ernst Bovenlander gave some details of these attacks (though he didn't mention Mondex as the target). He showed an electron micrograph of a fuzed link in a smartcard; while intact, this link activated a test mode in which the card contents were simply dumped to the serial port. The TNO attack was to bridge the link with two microprobes. At the last RSA conference, Tom Rowley of National Semiconductor reported a similar attack on an unnamed chip using an ion beam to rewrite the link....

Bovenlander also told the Eurocrypt audience that microprobing attacks get harder when the feature size drops below one micron. However, there is a simple fix — to use a focused ion beam to plate a nice large contact for the microprobe on each bus line. He showed a micrograph of a 0.8 micron chip treated in this way. He also related that undergraduates at Delft University routinely break smart card chips using microprobe workstations, and as part of their assessed course work rather than as personal hacking. So it looks like the current version of Mondex (3101) can be broken by undergraduates.

In other words, the contents of a smart card — including all data on your life (if you are foolish enough to allow any there) and all the "electronic money" carried by the card — can be stolen by hackers, from college students, to freelance thieves, to government thieves.

Barter and other informal "finance"

Barter, of course, is as old as history. I'll swap you this basket of Ugh-root for that haunch of Grmp-meat. You inscribe this papyrus for me, I'll brew you a vat of beer.

It's useful to us now and could become more useful in our free communities.

The classic problem of barter, as everyone knows, is that the thing I want might not match the object you have, or the service offered by Person X might not mesh with the service Person Y has to swap.

So X and Y have to find Person W and maybe Person Z before they can come up with enough different objects and services to fill everyone's needs.

And then there's the question of how to swap items or services of different value...

Which is where barter clubs enter the picture. Barter clubs, which (in their modern incarnation) have been active since the early 1970s, exist to arrange swaps among a large network of members. Some operate internationally. Some specialize in business equipment and services. There are a variety of clubs to meet a variety of needs.

Most barter clubs don't simply match Person A with Business R, Service G with Product T. They use a system of credits: Person A has given twenty hours of consulting services to other members of the club, while Business R has supplied 100 gross of Acme Widgets. Person A has thus earned X-number of credits which can be "spent" on the services and products of other members, and Business R has also earned X-number of spendable credits.

You can easily see how this could develop into a monetary system... which is exactly what happened with the barter systems of thousands of years ago, and how barter systems became one of several avenues through which modern money evolved.

The "credits" become not just a unit of exchange, but a commodity that can, itself, be traded to others. They can be printed on paper, plastic, or some other medium. They can be tracked and transmitted via computer. They could even be transferred back and forth on smart cards.

Alas, drat, and no big surprise, the IRS also regards barter (in some cases) as income. It's silly when you're simply swapping equal value for equal value. But then, that's all you're doing when you're earning a wage or billing for X-hours of services, too. And that never stopped the IRS from claiming its unfair share.

So...one more gummint intrusion you've got to plan around. What else is new?

Also, all barter clubs charge some sort of membership and/or transaction fee, so you have to work with that as well, and determine for yourself whether the fees are excessive. A URL pointing to various barter clubs and other information about barter is listed in the Appendix.

Community money

If barter clubs can evolve into money systems, then communities can also take the direct route and de-

velop their own money systems. This is something many free communities are likely to do, either from necessity or desire.

Perhaps the best-known community money system operating today is "Ithaca Hours." In Ithaca, New York, Hours (in the forms of paper certificates) are accepted for rent, groceries, massage therapy, roofing, baked goods, dog grooming and a host of other products and services. The promoters of Hours also sell starter kits for other community money systems, and have exported their system to cities and towns around the world.

Since a well written account of Ithaca Hours is already available, I'll forego my own blather and give you words straight off the Ithaca Hours web site:

Ithaca HOUR Factsheet

Since 1991, we've issued over $62,000 of Ithaca HOURS (6,200 HOURS at $10.00 per HOUR). Five denominations: 2 HRS, 1 HR, 1/2 HR, 1/4 HR, 1/8 HR. Includes a commemorative HOUR, the first paper money in the U.S. to honor an African-American.

Over 2,000 people, including 360 businesses, have earned and spent HOURS.

They have made an estimated $2,000,000+ value of trades with HOURS, representing 100 job-equivalents at $20,000 each.

HOURS are thus real money — local tender rather than legal tender, backed by real people, real labor, skills, and tools.

Most HOURS have been issued as payments to those who agree to be published backers of HOURS, listed in our bimonthly directory HOUR Town. Every eight months they may send the coupon again to receive a bonus payment — which gradually and carefully increases HOUR supply.

10% of HOURS are issued as grants to community organizations. 35 nonprofits have received grants totaling 600 HOURS ($6,000) since we began.

5% of HOURS may be issued to the system itself, primarily for paying for printing HOURS.

Loans of HOURS are made with NO IN-TEREST CHARGED. These range from $50-$1,000 value.

HOURS are legal. Professor Lewis Solomon of George Washington University has written a book titled *Rethinking Our Centralized Monetary System: the Case for Local Currency* (Praeger, 1996) which is an extensive case law study of the legality of local currency. His number is (202) 994-6753. IRS and FED officials have been contacted by media, and repeatedly have said there is no prohibition of local currency, as long as it does not look like dollars, as long as denominations are at least $1.00 value, and if it is regarded as taxable income.

HOURS are protected against counterfeit. They are multicolored, with serial numbers. The 1995 Quarter HOUR and 1997 Eighth HOUR use thermal ink, invented in Ithaca, which disappears briefly when touched or photocopied. The 1993 Two HOUR note is printed on locally-made watermarked 100% cattail paper, with matching serial numbers front and back. The 1996 Half HOUR is 100% handmade hemp paper. Our District Attorney has declared HOURS a financial instrument, protected by law from counterfeit.

BENEFITS:

- HOURS expand the local money supply

- HOURS promote and expand local shopping, with an endless multiplier

- HOURS double the local minimum wage to $10.00, benefiting not only workers, but businesses as well, who find new and loyal customers.

- HOURS enable shoppers to afford premium prices for locally-crafted goods and for locally-grown organic food

- HOURS help start new businesses and jobs

- HOURS reduce dependence on imports and transport fuels

- HOURS make grants to nonprofit community organizations

- HOURS make zero-interest loans
- HOURS stimulate community pride

The Ithaca Hours promoters have also started a local Hours-based health fund and plan to use Hours to finance projects such as weatherization of homes.

Even if you don't endorse all the implied political goals of Ithaca Hours, these folks have a great idea that could be adapted to meet a lot of needs.

Electronic cash

We who prefer money we can clutch in our hands find the concept of electronic cash baffling. Electronic cash is nothing but strings of digits moving back and forth between computers. But if that sounds strange, it's really nothing more than an individualized version of the way banks move money around the globe every day. You don't think the Federal Reserve or the Bundesbank move FRNs and Euros in trucks, do you?

When this book was first written, the electronic cash system that was getting the most press was e-cash by DigiCash. The company has since gone broke. And, as marketed, its technology was far from perfect for seekers of true anonymity. However, the basic method is worth looking at.

E-cash works by storing "coins" (long strings of digits) on your computer. Then, when you purchase something over the Internet, it sends strings, equal to the amount of purchase, to the computer of the e-cash account holder from whom you're buying a product. The software on your machine debits your account. The software on the vendor's computer credits the vendor's account.

For mainstreamers, you can see the first problem of this system is getting enough buyers and sellers to make it all worthwhile. If you're a merchant, there's no point setting up an e-cash system unless the buyers are out there. If you're a buyer, there's no point setting up an e-cash account unless you can find something you can buy with it. A certain critical mass has to be reached before it's all worthwhile. Reportedly, DigiCash's eccentric founder turned down several huge deals with Visa, Microsoft, and others — and that critical mass never developed.

For us nonmainstreamers, there's a more fundamental problem. And that is that the use of e-cash begins with an account at a bank. Ten or fifteen banks around the world offered e-cash accounts; some certainly offered a degree of privacy. But for our purposes, an electronic cash system would be better if it didn't use the conventional banking system at all. (More about that later in this chapter.)

E-cash used cryptography techniques developed by Dr. David Chaum. Chaum's original vision was to give anonymity on both sides of the transaction. DigiCash does give the payer the choice of anonymity — at least in any specific transaction. But there's no anonymity for the entity receiving the money (the payee). And the payer still has that bank account to worry about. Banking privacy is another question. And in America, banking privacy is an oxymoron.

Still, e-cash had three important advantages over credit cards for electronic transactions: 1) Encryption ensured that only the authorized payer could make the transaction (nobody could "steal" access to your e-cash), 2) There's nothing like a credit card number, which can be snatched out of cyberspace and reused, and 3) Transactions were cheaper than those using credit cards.

The cyber-community of Laissez Faire City (see Appendix) is also developing its own electronic cash system; early word is that it will be more secure and more private than current systems.

Electronic cash is interesting. But some other folks have declared they've come up with something better. They call it e-gold.

E-gold

E-gold is a new exchange system that also operates on the Internet.

It's a modern take on one of our old, legitimate systems of money, the warehouse receipt or metal certificate. In other words, it's like the old silver and gold certificates, back in the days when the U.S. had real money. The papers you held in your hand then were actually receipts for gold and silver, and you could trade the slips of paper in for the metals. In this case, the digits you hold in your computer represent quantities of metal.

With e-gold you purchase a store of gold, silver, platinum, or palladium. This is held for you in a warehouse (or, for safety, several warehouses). You can then use this store of value to make purchases or do other types of exchanges with e-gold account holders.

One nice thing about e-gold: the transactions can be of any size. If you want to buy a $6.00 paperback book on your e-gold account, you can. If you want to buy a car, and another e-gold participant has one to sell, you can.

Six percent is the maximum cost for a complete transaction (currency to e-gold and back to currency).

E-gold's proponents claim to have made electronic cash obsolete. Among other things, they point out that their system allows rapid conversion from one form of money to another, which e-cash does not. Your gold store can be used to make payments in silver or in dollars, for example; present electronic cash systems don't offer that flexibility. Also, the need for establishing a separate account with a bank — an institution which must, by law, consider privacy seeking customers to be criminals — is a huge flaw in e-cash. E-gold overcomes this, but adds the risk of trusting your precious metals to a third party.

And e-gold still is not a truly private medium of exchange. The Gold & Silver Reserve, which came up with e-gold, is adamant that it should not and cannot be used to hide from the swarms of financial laws descending upon us. And this isn't just a pro forma, CYA declaration. Although the transactions themselves are conducted in privacy, G&SR maintains records of your account. I can't speak for G&SR, but all too many institutions, like banks and phone companies, have handed over customers' private records to any ole government agency that asked, often not even requesting a subpoena, let alone a warrant.

Another disadvantage is that, as with electronic cash, the people on both sides of the transaction must be subscribers to the system. You can't spend e-gold at your local Wal-Mart. You can't even spend it at your "local" Internet bookstore — yet. You can spend it only with businesses or individuals that also hold e-gold accounts.

So it's caught in the same Catch-22 as e-cash.

E-gold, however, solves one of the chronic dilemmas of those who like precious metals. While metals have been a historically good medium for storing value, they haven't always been the greatest method of exchange; gold is great for stockpiling, but try buying a hamburger with a one-ounce Maple Leaf.

The big advantage of a system like e-gold (provided the proprietors are honest and reliable) is that it gives you a relatively stable store of value while you retain the ability to spend in small increments.

This still isn't the perfect system, though. We need total anonymity from the beginning to the end of the process. Soon, perhaps.

Alternative banking systems

Federalized banks suck. But we still need banks for commerce and as a secure place to store value. So what do we do? Here are a few ideas:

Offshore banking

Offshore banking is becoming an increasingly popular alternative. Once it was available only to the rich. Even now it's difficult for a person of moderate means to find a secure offshore banking haven, as many countries want $25,000 or more before they'll deal with you, and some want more than that.

(If you're a U.S. citizen, it's also illegal to have more than $10,000 in foreign banks without reporting it to the fedgov. Just in case you still care about such things.)

Still, there are an increasing number of countries getting into the offshore banking business. Would you believe *Latvia* as a bank haven?

There are a number of possible havens and their contact information listed in the Appendix. A few of these will accept deposits of $500 or less. Again and always, investigate carefully before handing over your hard-earned money.

Here are a few things you should look for in an offshore banking system:

- Reliability of the bank and/or the broker setting up the account. Always. How long have they been in business? How's their credit rating? Are there any legal actions pending against them? Are they making promises that sound too good to be true? Is their snail address a real location or just a mail drop?
- The country's history as a bank haven. This isn't everything, because the value of havens change. Switzerland, long *the* banking haven, has recently caved in to a lot of pressures from other governments and opened some once-secret records. In fact, once a haven gets a reputation for excellence, that's when it's most likely to come under political pressure from the U.S. and might be pressured into changing (or compromising) its laws. So the next island in the chain, or the country just across the border becomes the next bank haven. Still, before investing with any new-comer to the haven business, find out what their virtues are.
- The country's virtues as a tax haven. Look for a country that, among other things, has few taxes and low taxes of its own, particularly one that has no income tax or capital gains tax. Try to find one that has no tax treaties with the U.S. or other countries. Such a country would probably still help the U.S. in a criminal investigation (prepare to be accused of drug smuggling if you keep large amounts of money offshore), but would just shake its head if asked to help the U.S. investigate a tax matter.
- Costs of setting up the account. It's common for offshore banks or investment brokers to charge between $750 and $1,500 (sometimes more) to establish your account. There may be excellent reasons for these charges (see below). But be aware of these, and any hidden charges as well.
- Denomination of the account. Some banks establish all accounts only in the local currency. Others offer a variety: accounts in dollars, gold, pounds, sterling, the local currency, other commodities. The less money you have to invest, the fewer choices you're likely be offered. The choice you make might depend on a lot of things: whether you need quick, spendable access to the money here in the U.S.; the stability of currency A vs. currency B; the security of gold, etc.
- Ease of access to your money. How quickly can you get your hands on it when you need it?

One common way of setting up an offshore account is to create a corporation in the haven country. This 1) keeps the money out of your name and 2) avoids some of the problems of being a foreign account holder. I can't address the advantages or disadvantages of that for your circumstances, but many brokers are simply doing it automatically, and that's a common reason for the relatively high fees to open some offshore accounts.

Many banks that are courting offshore investors make a point of having either a branch or an agent in the U.S. A friend with several offshore accounts warns against using these offices, however, since it creates a paper trail *conveniently available to U.S. snoops and enforcers.*

Besides, with the Internet, it's often just as easy to use an agent in the haven country.

A lot of people speculate that offshore bank havens will eventually become a thing of the past, as a bullying U.S. government scares small countries into compliance with its dictates, or as the UN eventually forces the standardization of all banking laws. I used to envision this myself. And certainly *specific* bank havens have been pressured and forced to compromise in the name of the War Against (Some) Drugs, the war against money laundering, or the war against anybody who might be hiding loot from World War II.

But then Charles Curley, who wrote the first mass-market paperback on legalized gold investing back in the 1970s, pointed out something I hadn't thought of. As soon as he spoke it was as if one of those cartoon lights went on over my head. He said, "Government officials and their wealthy friends will *always* need places to hide their own stolen money. So they'll never close down the banking havens — because they need them more than we do."

Oh, of course…!

And of course, as governments become more corrupt, they'll need money havens more than ever. Which might mean opportunities for us as well.

Underground banking systems

Some island or some newly entrepreneurial nation of the former Eastern Bloc might be a great place to *stash* money, but for most of us it probably won't be a convenient place to keep money we want to use — until truly private, easy international electronic transactions make the location of our bank almost irrelevant.

Under mattresses and in hidey-holes is also a fine place for money sometimes. And it may have to do us for a while. But commerce functions most smoothly with banking.

The electronic money systems mentioned above, or their descendants and cousins, have strong potential for becoming the banking systems of the future.

But some of us are going to prefer to stay low tech. Or are going to *need* to stay low tech because of our particular life choices.

In that case, we could benefit by having community banks of our own. Or, more accurately, something like savings and loans used to be before feds and high-flyers got hold of them. In other words, not institutions designed for high international finance, but cooperative, local ventures established to help people build houses and small businesses — institutions in which we invest our money so that our friends and neighbors can use it to benefit themselves and the community.

The Sovereign Society

Whether you wish to remain in the U.S. or find your future elsewhere, there's an interesting organization that might help.

The Sovereign Society is the creation of Bob Kephart and Bill Bonner (owners of Scope International) and is supported by such figures as Lord William Rees-Mogg, Douglas Casey, and Vince Miller (International Society for Individual Liberty). It offers members a variety of benefits, including:

- A bank account with Robeco Bank, Switzerland (minimum opening deposit: $5,000; the account remains "dry" but available until you activate it with your first deposit).
- The book *The Whole World Catalog* (offshore products and services). Several freedom-oriented newsletters and reports.
- The services of JML Swiss Investment Counseling.
- Mail and fax forwarding services from Ireland.

While naturally geared to the affluent, the Sovereign Society hopes to keep its membership fees within range of the middle class (between $195 and $295 per year). You'll find contact information in the Appendix.

Our first unofficial "banking" systems in our underground Free Communities might be as simple as this:

Ten people want to build homes. Each has $10,000. The ten pool their money and one member of the pool is chosen (perhaps by lot) to be given the $90,000 contributed by the other members.

That person builds a house, then begins paying back the money. At a certain point (perhaps when the entire $90,000 has been paid back in, plus the homebuilder's $10,000, or at some earlier, agreed-upon point) the next person begins using the funds that have been returned to the pool.

Of course, you can see flaws in this right away.

This puts the last few people in the pool at quite a disadvantage. They not only have to wait ages to have a house, but they stand the risk that, somewhere along the line someone might not pay back the money. (Well, that's what knee-capping is for. A fine deterrent. Naw, just kidding, just kidding…)

Who'd want to be tenth… or ninth… or even fifth, in a scheme like this?

Okay, then let's introduce interest payments into the mix, so the last people in line stand to gain more, financially, than the first. Each time their $10,000 recycles into another house, it gains another round of interest.

Interest is paid to the individuals in the case I just described. However, there could also be arrangements by which all interest went into the pool, or by which it was divided between the pool and the contributor as it came in.

Suddenly the pool looks interesting to people who have $10,000 to invest but already own a house, or don't want to. And *voilà!* you've got your own little S&L or "building society." Your organization can then grow and start taking deposits of varying amounts, instead of the fixed $10,000 investments. The more who participate, the more flexibility you have in the operation.

What I've just described is based on history. It's probably very much the way some financial institutions actually got their start, and the way some of ours may get started in the future.

The history of banking and money-lending offers lessons to anyone setting up systems of finance in a free community. Take a look at how pawnbrokers, goldsmiths, and other commodity dealers evolved into bankers and see if any of those evolutionary adaptations have a place in your little society.

Microbanking

Another easy-to-develop system is microbanking. Microbanking has gotten much favorable press over the last decade, and for good reason. It has helped ordinary, even desperately poor, people in third world countries buy the small amounts of equipment needed to establish businesses and hire others.

Microbanking is, in its simplest form, the lending of small amounts of money, at interest, to new, independent businesses. People receiving microbank loans may also be required to attend business seminars or meet other requirements (such as teaching business techniques to others, once they themselves have become successful).

Since this requires little in the way of resources, it's perfect for small community and individual development, and involves minimal risk on the part of the lender, it could be perfect for our free communities as well. A single individual with a few thousand dollars to spare could make a substantial difference in a community.

Done carelessly, microbanking is risky. Most small businesses fail. But the risk in any one loan is small, and the lender — and former recipients of loans — are often in a position to watch newcomers and help them along.

Fei-ch'ien: flying money

Here's an underground banking system ethnic Chinese have been using since the Colonial days (if not before). Because it relies heavily on family connections and the kind of trust most of us aren't prepared to give or accept, it might not work for us. But it's an ingenious way to move money and goods around without moving very much at all.

It gives international law enforcers hissy fits because a large part of the Asian drug trade is conducted and financed through fei-ch'ien. And as far as I'm concerned, anything that's nonviolent, nonfraudulent, and gives law enforcers fits has serious potential for freedom lovers.

Here is how fei-ch'ien was described by William L. Cassidy of W.L.R. Cassidy & Associates in a speech before the International Asian Organized Crime Conference in June of 1996:

Suppose that I wish to purchase 500 kilos of opium from you. You live in Burma, I live in China. I do not want to transport 50,000 taels of silver [assuming one kilo per 100 taels of silver as the going rate of exchange], so I tell my cousin in Burma to pay you and I promise to settle with him later. You deliver 250 kilos but you receive 50,000 taels of silver. I now have a 50,000 tael liability on my cousin's books, a

25,000 tael asset on your books and a commodity worth 25,000 taels on my books.

I sell my opium for double its unit cost and have 50,000 taels of silver in my possession. My cousin tells me to pay a 50,000 tael debt he owes in China and thus settle my debt with him in Burma. I have caused the transportation of 250 kilos of opium from Burma to China without moving my silver and have 25,000 taels in Burma which the Chinese authorities will never see.

…And you're still owed 250 kilos of opium, though Cassidy doesn't specify that. So the beat goes on. See the Appendix for the URL where you can find the complete speech.

Personally, I find this a bit dizzying, but this is basically how certain entire banking systems work in the east. Many of the Asian businessmen bribing Bill Clinton and the DNC are known for operating this way, so presumably Bubba Bill can understand it. And anything Bubba Bill can understand, we can understand.

Can this be applied in America — that is, anywhere outside of clannish groups like the Mafia, the DNC, or the Fortune 500? I don't know. But if this whole notion of freedom communities works out, we may find ourselves developing relationships of greater trust (and, alas, the enforcement systems needed to deal with those who breach the trust).

Truly private electronic banking

One thing a free future society needs is totally anonymous electronic banking — a system we can enter anonymously and use in complete privacy. No snoops allowed. No compromise unless the user "blows his own cover" or the user's own private records are discovered by snoops or "authorities."

That is, in a truly private banking system, there would be no cheap-and-easy subpoenaing of third-party records, no routine reporting of transactions by the bankers. The "banker" wouldn't even know who you are or where you lived. She would have nothing but your electronic ID.

Such a system is already technologically feasible (with some bugs still to be worked out). However, it's too much of a political hot potato. Anyone operating an anonymous banking system could be held liable if criminals used it, say, to collect a ransom for a kidnapping, or if free-marketers used it for "money laundering" or "hiding drug profits."

But eventually, someone will have to develop a private banking system and put it into use in some cyberlocation outside the easy reach of law enforcement. Criminals, including government officials, might use it for their own benefit. But so what? Criminals and government officials always use everything for their own benefit. Aren't you tired of having *your* privacy and *your* rights stripped away from you on the excuse that the protections that benefit you might also benefit some crook?

Let's put a stop to that nonsensical excuse-making for tyranny and get on with regaining our freedom from the snoops!

Such a system might use your PGP key as your "unique identifier" — without requiring you to identify yourself in any other manner. (If you are a computer user and you aren't familiar with PGP, Pretty Good Privacy, you owe it to yourself to learn to use the software. One of the most powerful encryption programs in the world is at your fingertips. Some versions of it are even free. The federal government is having a fit because We The People have such a potent privacy tool. And that, right there, is reason enough for all computer-literate people to be using it.)

All transactions in this perfect, anonymous system would be made electronically.

Using your key, you would make your first deposit into the system anonymously. The PGP key, and perhaps a code word or phrase generated by the banking system, would be your only identifier. It would be used to prove you are the person who owns the account — without anyone having to know your name, age, location, financial status, Slave Number or anything else about you.

This is rather like a numbered Swiss bank account, or one of the anonymous bearer accounts available to Austrian citizens.

Though your key is as unique as an SS number, it is private because it is generated by you and can be changed by you at will. You can also withdraw a key if you suspect it has been compromised in any way.

Every transaction is encrypted. You use the banker's public PGP key to encrypt outgoing transactions. The banker uses your key to encrypt transactions going to you. You both use each others' keys for *all* communications.

To decrypt transactions, you use your secret key and secret pass phrase, which the banker does not have and does not know. (In fact, no one but you should have a copy of your secret key; and no one but you should ever have your pass phrase.) The banker likewise uses a secret key and secret pass phrase to unscramble your transactions.

Even if someone else, for some reason, opened an account using your public PGP key, he couldn't take any money out because he doesn't have your accompanying secret key and secret pass phrase.

This is a very rough description of such a system. Questions abound.

Where is the money stored? What form does it take? What's the best, most undetectable way of putting money into the system? How can you be sure the banker is honest? What's the best way to avoid liability?

These and others are questions that will have to be answered by developers of any anonymous banking system. But these questions *are* being answered by the cypherpunks of the world, who are developing such systems right now. When the *political* problems of a totally private banking system can be solved (or ignored with outlaw jauntiness), the technological problems will present a relatively small hurdle to leap.

The same techniques used to give us totally anonymous electronic banking can also give us *almost* totally private electronic commerce. In fact, the transactions, as we buy and sell goods over the net, can be anonymous. It's in delivering the product that anonymity is most likely to be compromised.

Nevertheless, once we have totally anonymous banking, we are very near anonymous purchasing and selling, as well.

And if you still like the government's little partners and want a "regular" bank account...

Here's a story from the web site of the National Organization for Non-Enumeration (NONE):

> On April 24, David... and two companions serving as witnesses appeared at the bank at lunch hour to open an interest-bearing checking account.

They spoke to Barbara, a customer service representative. He stated he wanted to open a personal account. But first, David went out of his way to praise the bank and its reputation.

Now, to business.

David asked if the bank had any policies on discrimination: "Does the bank discriminate on the basis of gender?" On race, sexual orientation, birthplace or origin, religion?

"No, it doesn't," came the reply. David handed her a copy of a letter. In it the bank's compliance officer had assured him that the bank did not discriminate on any basis.

As Barbara looked at the letter, David thanked her that the bank was eager to treat all people alike.

He handed her the bank's regular application form. She looked it over carefully. "She said he had to have a Social Security number to verify past checking and past savings history," recounts eyewitness Farrell Carney, a homeschool dad and home-based entrepreneur.

"He offered her a sample of his current checks. She then asked if there was a reason for not giving a Social Security number, and at that point [David] stated for religious convictions."

After a phone call or two, Barbara insisted she had to have the number — again, to verify "past checking history." David held his ground. He had no criminal record, a stable job at the newspaper for 10 years, had banked 10 years at a local credit union.

Here now he presented the NONE document "Notice of Limitation on Social Security Number Use and Demand for Compliance with the Laws Relating to Requirements Governing Requests for Disclosure of Such Number." Each witness had signed it.

No less troubling for administration was the application form, which David had completed prior to coming. With his edits, David asserted other legal arguments not directly related to his refusal to provide an SSN.

Looking perplexed, Barbara got on the phone. Would David mind chatting with Pat, the compliance officer downtown?

Pat asked David to undo editing on the bank's application form. David held firm, saying he had no federal identifier on the basis of religious convictions. David and the compliance officer agreed David would add the following to the form: "Because of my private religious beliefs, I refuse to use a Social Security number. David X."

The added language simply repeated the NONE form. David's other edits stood as well. Now it was time for the applicants to withdraw — temporarily — from the scene, as NONE's R. Kenneth Potter had suggested in two phone consults.

"I realize my requirements may be a bit unusual," David said, "so why don't we leave and come back in an hour to open up the account, since probably you need to consult with the legal department?"

He then asked, "Should I write my check to open the account now, or when we come back?"

"When you return," Barbara said.

The men returned an hour later. A clerk who had helped Barbara in the first visit had taken over, and invited the men to her desk next to the wall. Becky, a customer service officer, spoke pleasantly to David and asked him what kind of account he wanted. He chose an interest-bearing account, wrote a $1,500 check to open the account, waited for her to verify the check, received documents relating to the new account, and heard about the bank's many services. In all, the follow up meeting lasted 40 minutes.

"I was surprised at actually how easy it was to achieve," said Farrell the witness. "I was expecting a lot more of a fight from the bank. It was amazing to me the way people in general are buffaloed into thinking they have to have a number.

"I think you run into obstacles and you have to fight little short battles every time, because everybody's bought into it. But it's really not that hard to get by if you basically follow the rules and you point out to the people that you don't have to have a number."

Once the no-SSN issue was settled, a separate dispute arose over David's refusal to fill out an IRS W-9 form and give a taxpayer identification number (TIN). David defused the bank's threat to shut the account by citing the Code of Federal Regulations provision that requires banks to keep a special list of all people who don't have TIN's whom the bank has made a reasonable effort to obtain TIN's from.

The "Notice of Limitation" form mentioned in the text is available from NONE, which is listed in the Appendix. While I can't personally testify to its legal force, I carry a similar form myself. Merely waving it under the noses of clerks and bureaucrats often produces a desired result. Remember, these folks often don't *think*; they merely obey anyone who sounds authoritative and knowledgeable. So this is a method worth looking into.

ID in our free society

For many of the transactions described above, we'll still need ID. We won't have government ID — and good riddance to it — but we'll still need some ways of demonstrating who we are and finding out who the other guy is.

Some forms of electronic transaction already have ID built into them. PGP offers about as good a form of ID as possible, with both anonymity and verifiability. For other transactions, we may still need some documentation.

There is no such thing as a perfect ID system. There never will be, not even on the day that our "number" is a digitized reading of our fingerprints, retinal scans, voice prints, heartbeat and brain activity patterns, not even when our ID is implanted under our skin.

No human-designed system is ever going to be completely without errors. And no ID system of any sort will ever (as the government so eagerly claims) prevent crime. No government-implemented ID system will even *discourage* crime. More draconian systems will simply create new crimes, and even entirely new *forms* of crime, as people seek ways to subvert and resist the tightening ID net.

People will hack the databases, sabotage the scanning equipment and — being always more clever and more highly motivated than those attempting control — will invent technologies to jam, fool or mimic the control technology.

Yet, despite all this, some form of identification has a role in a free society. It's something we are going to have to deal with if we are going to do non-cash financial transactions, for instance. How?

Two major functions of ID

There are a lot of purposes for ID documents or procedures. But most of those functions fall into two categories. The first is:

Is this person who he says he is?

The second is:

Will this person do what she agrees to do?

The first is fairly straightforward (although the question of Who We Really Are can sometimes get as complicated as, "What is the Meaning of Life?").

The second has more ramifications and variations, such as "Is this person gonna pay me?" or, "Is this person gonna deliver the goods?" and, "If she doesn't, how do I find her and wring the money out of her?"

Before the government usurped the ID business, ID was private and could easily be again.

For example: A bank (the regular kind, not the anonymous wonder described above) might issue a customer ID, complete with photo. An insurance company could issue a certification of your driving ability, which could also be used as ID in situations involving your use or misuse of an automobile. Your employer or anyone else you dealt with regularly could (and may already) issue an ID card.

The problem lies not in ID cards, but in centrally issued ID linked to central databases.

But wouldn't a world in which dozens or hundreds of agencies issued ID cards lead to chaos? Wouldn't criminals take advantage by creating fake ID — say, a manufactured card from a bogus bank in a distant state — and using it to cash bad checks?

Certainly. And businesses would have a right to retaliate by requiring certain standards for the IDs it would accept. Or by maintaining databases of "legitimate" ID issuers.

Yes, a business might even get into requiring fingerprints and digitized photos and the other things we're trying to get away from.

Who is Patrick Henry?

I have a friend named Patrick Henry. I'm almost certain that's not his real name, but it was the name he was using when I encountered him on the Internet, it's the name we shook hands over when we met in person, and the name he wore when he came to dinner at my house and met my friends.

"Patrick Henry" has owed me money, and promptly paid it. I have borrowed books from him and promptly returned them. We have exchanged token gifts and many confidences. We have sat in the sunshine and discussed many personal aspects of our plans to survive and prevail. We have discussed our philosophies of nonviolence and our fears that violence will descend upon us.

So do I know "Patrick Henry" or not?

Of course I do. I know him at least as well as I know my next door neighbor.

But, you might object, this guy could be wanted in sixteen states under some other name!

Well sure. So could my next door neighbor. So could you. So could I. (In fact, the way laws are proliferating, we probably *will* be, before long.)

I have two points here. One is that people can use fake "ID" for many reasons, the vast majority of them totally innocent. I happen to know that Patrick is a fierce guardian of his own privacy, and I respect that. I, myself have written under three or four different names, as writers often do. Someone else might use a fake name or fake ID because he's hiding from the law — but it might be a really bad law, and he might be doing a really good thing in hiding from it.

My other point is that ID — genuine, real, meaningful ID — has absolutely nothing to do with "real" names, drivers' licenses, Social Security numbers or entries in databases. You *are* what you do, what you think, what you believe. Somebody could give you his real citizen ID documents, and still be the skunk of the universe.

The whole question of ID really comes down to this: If you're the purchaser or recipient of a service, you want the greatest anonymity possible. If you're the deliverer of a product or service, you want to make sure it's going to the right person, and that you will get paid for providing it.

I Am Not a Number!

Except in the electronic realm, where total anonymity is possible, we will *always* have to balance our privacy against someone else's need to know. The important thing is that we *do* maintain a balance. And that we, as individuals, have some control over the balance point.

As it stands, the entire ID question has been thrown out of balance by government and the institutions engaged in perverted congress with government. We have lost our say, our flexibility, our ability to protect our own identity. Government has taken our identity away from us — or rather, has declared our ID to be *its* property, merely to be used, with permission, by us.

And though we may always have to struggle to protect our privacy against businesses and officials, we need to shift the ability to do so back into our own hands — to level the playing field, to use a cliché — to remind ourselves and the people we deal with that we control our own destiny.

Update 2002
What's New
Since Chapter Seven

A couple of the earlier chapters now feel ...well, ahead of their time to me. They were written from an overly optimistic view of what freedom lovers might do when faced with Slave ID and an overly pessimistic view of how fast that state might move.

But in this chapter, it's all true and all laid out. I'll add a couple of cautions about our ever-tightening financial controls. But the basic situation and the basic solutions are as the chapter says. Anybody who's still dealing with SSN-based accounts in U.S. banks is leaving him- or herself wide open to being tracked, controlled, bought and sold. Alternatives exist, though the government does its best to limit them. Some of the best alternatives, like the obvious one of dealing in cash and money orders, have been slowly squeezed over the years and may soon be squeezed just about to the shut-down point. But as long as they exist, we should be using them. When those are closed down, we should invent better ones.

So what's new?

Know your customer

In the last few years, the obnoxious program with the pleasant name — Know Your Customer — appeared as a measure in the War on Drugs, seemed to disappear under howling public protest, then re-appeared attached to the War on Terrorism — bigger, nastier, and more far-reaching than ever.

KYC, as you may know, is a customer-tracking and profiling operation. It means no bank, stock brokerage, or other financial service business will open an account without investigating your "real" identity and verifying the source of any funds you ever deposit. Thereafter, any activity in your account that can be classified as "unusual" is also analyzed by those infamous algorithms and reported as suspicious. (If you receive an inheritance, sell a house, or win a contest — all these larger-than-usual deposits become causes to suspect you of drug dealing, money laundering, and now, of being an international terrorist.)

But it gets worse.

If you loved KYC when it was just for banks, you're really going to love it now that it also applies to insurance, credit cards, art galleries, coin dealers, and dealers in automobiles, airplanes, boats, and real estate — just about every type of business with which you might ever spend any serious money. That's thanks to the infamous USA-Patriot Act, signed into law in October 2001. The new requirements took effect in October 2002.

Previously, financial service businesses, from banks to Western Union offices, had various cash-transaction reporting requirements ($5,000 for banks, $750 for international money-wiring, $3,000 at the post office, $10,000 for stockbrokers and other non-bank financial service businesses). Now those requirements are still in place, but virtually *every* U.S. business you spend major money with is required to report any customer who spends $10,000 or more in their establishments.

As has become typical, this outrageous requirement isn't clear cut. It comes with all sorts of vague provisions that no one can really interpret or understand. For instance, if you make three purchases of $3,333.34, that counts as $10,000 and must be reported. (But make them over what period of time?

Who really knows?) If you make a single purchase of $9,998, or maybe even of $8,673, or maybe even two purchases, one of $4,500 and one of $4,600, those purchases, too, must be reported as "suspicious." Why? Clearly, they're all under the $10,000 reporting threshold. Because any purchase is suspicious if any government agent or store clerk might *think you're trying to beat the $10,000 limit by deliberately spending less than $10,000.*

You figure it out. I can't. But that's the way things are done these days.

Two other things about KYC we all need to know. First, is that this program, as with so many other financial programs, is global. The U.S. government has been the driving force behind it, but some variation on it is being put into practice all over the world — including most offshore banks. The offshore institutions may still not ask for your Slave Number, but they will want government ID, a home address (P.O. box won't do, and neither will a maildrop unless you're very clever about using an unknown drop, not the local Mailboxes Etc.), and other data handy to anyone investigating you.

Also, the genesis of KYC is another example of how dedicated, but naïve, political activists may think they've achieved something when they haven't. The FDIC first put forth the regulation in conjunction with the Board of Governors of the Federal Reserve System, the Office of the Comptroller of the Currency, and the Office of Thrift Supervision. Led by the U.S. Libertarian Party, Americans bombarded the FDIC with so many e-mail protests that the agency appeared to back down. Then of course a couple of years later, with Americans understandably outraged over terrorism but not asking enough questions about the real nature of some of the government programs labeled "anti-terrorist," KYC was back in the USA-Patriot Act. And as you see, during the lull during which we thought we'd beaten it, it was simply being prepared to expand.

How many times does this sort of thing have to happen before some freedom activists realize that while you can always get *more* government through activism, you can *never* get less government that way?

Opt-out

One more quick reminder on domestic bank privacy. In the late 1990s, several banks were caught selling customers' account information, including Social Security numbers, balances, and records of account activity. This was ever-so-slightly illegal! But barely had the prosecutions and lawsuits begun to crank up when the fedgov — in its eternal wisdom and boundless desire to protect the rights of us little people — passed new "privacy regulations" custom-tailored to the banking industry. These regulations made it 100 percent legal for banks to sell you, body and soul (well, sell any information about you) — unless you "opt out."

It also made it legal for the banks to send you "opt-out" notices that looked just like junk mail so you'd ignore them. When only about five percent of customers said, "Don't you dare sell me out that way," bankers and Congressthings took it as a sign that Americans weren't really concerned about privacy. Ugh.

Foreign bank accounts

The U.S. government has also continued its long-time crackdown on offshore banking and financial dealings. This, too, was done originally in the name of the Drug War and money laundering, and is now done in the alleged cause of anti-terrorism. (Isn't it funny how all the proposed "solutions" to two such diverse problems are always *exactly* the same and always involve investigating you and me?)

In addition to not opening a foreign bank account through a U.S.-based agent, you should look for a country that doesn't have a treaty with the U.S. under which it agrees to help the feds bust tax avoiders. You definitely need a country that will cooperate with the fedgov only in legitimate investigations of the most serious violent criminals.

To keep up with which countries are standing firm against U.S. bullying and which are being newly targeted and pressured by the feds I recommend once again that you subscribe to the best of the financial privacy newsletters and/or join The Sovereign Society (listed in the Appendix). These frequently updated news sources can best help you distinguish a haven from a soon-to-be hell.

Offshore credit cards

Many financial privacy seekers were shocked when the IRS demanded and got the offshore credit card records of somewhere between one and two million Americans. MasterCard and American Express both turned them over without a flicker of regard for their customers' privacy.[2] Once again, you were put under investigation without the slightest probable cause to indicate that you were guilty of anything.

This also ties in with Know Your Customer. The IRS's agreement with American Express specifically allowed the agency to get your passport number, driver's license number, and other personal data, including your credit-card transactions from those allegedly offshore banks. They were looking specifically for purchases of $2,500 or more on hotels, boats, cars, and other items and activities the government crowd considers (is this getting familiar, or what?) "suspicious."

Before this happened, in the spring of 2002, most privacy seekers probably thought that if your Visa card was issued by a bank in the Barbados or your MasterCard came from Monte Carlo, it would be difficult for the feds to snoop into your activities without a very serious investigation and strong suspicion of wrongdoing. We (and I plead guilty to this) forgot that the Visa, MasterCard, American Express and other credit card companies themselves are vulnerable to all kinds of governmental pressures — *and that because they process their transactions in the U.S., the feds have a grip on their cojones.*

And please don't give me that old, "If you're innocent, you don't have anything to fear" fallacy. You have *many* things to fear from a paranoid government with too many agents and too many agencies looking for trouble. The worst thing you have to fear is the loss of liberty.

For anyone who hasn't read the Bill of Rights or the most recent newspaper, here's a lesson in 21st-

Century Civics: The constitutional method of conducting a search of someone's private data is this: You suspect an individual of a crime for some specific reason like finding a dead body or an empty bank vault, you take those reasons to a judge, and only if the judge agrees do you get a legitimate court order to seek more information. The new and outrageous method is: You investigate anybody, you get any information you want either through sheer brute force or political pressure, then you use mathematical algorithms, your bad mood, and your politics to select which poor saps look guilty today. And you prosecute them under vague statutes (racketeering, tax evasion, conspiracy, terroristic activity), lock them up for decades, or at least make their lives miserable for a while, ruining their reputations and possibly bankrupting them along the way. Then you go on to the next victim.

Loyalty cards

The next item just goes to show you that you can't predict the risks you actually face when you let your financial transactions be trackable. The *Village Voice* reports that just after September 11, a major grocery-store chain turned over its entire database of "preferred customer" transactions to federal anti-terrorism investigators.

And they not only did it without anyone presenting a warrant or a subpoena. They did it *without the feds even asking them to.* Some marketing geek just thought it would be a patriotic thing to do, to let the fedgov search for "terrorists" among its customers by examining years of data on their potato-chip buying habits.[3]

Now, of course anyone who makes purchases using one of those grocery-store "loyalty cards" is a damn fool, anyway. Unless she lies like a rug about every bit of information on the card application, therefore turning herself into a fictional person (a lovely way to screw up the datamasters). But how

---

[2] As of this writing, the U.S. Justice Department was trying to force Visa to turn over its records, as well.

[3] This is not a joke. Apparently, in their zeal to profile "terrorists," investigators have decided, among other things, that people who order pizzas and pay by credit card are more likely to be terrorists than those who don't. You'd better hope your college-aged son isn't also named Mahmoud. If so, his dining habits could get him into deep trouble.

many of those innocent fools ever thought that their foolishness would turn them not only into marketing targets, but into subjects of federal investigation?

By the way, there's a vibrant and wonderful anti-loyalty-card organization called CASPIAN (Consumers Against Supermarket Privacy Invasion and Numbering). By focusing doggedly on this one issue, it's doing great things. Check it out in the Appendix.

Anonymous debit cards

Here's one relatively new way of avoiding betrayals by companies who no longer think you are the customer, but who serve the government instead. You can get anonymous offshore debit cards, identified only by number. You send a deposit to the issuer and this becomes the fund from which the card draws.

These cards have a number of drawbacks. Some of them are useable only at ATMs, not for making point-of-sale purchases. And they can be extremely expensive to purchase (some are several hundred dollars — aside from the deposit that covers your withdrawals). So for most people, they're not all that great an option.

Search the Internet under the term "anonymous offshore debit card" and *caveat emptor*. Or for more authoritative information, consult those good financial newsletters, the ones who have the resources actually to send people overseas to investigate which privacy-protection deals are legitimate, or who have the legal savvy to scope that out at a distance.

Trackable Euro dollars

Something else to be aware of for the future: As of 2005, all Euro paper notes are to become trackable. That is, they'll have a tiny, tiny transmitter — made up of a computer chip and a bit of copper antenna — woven into their paper. This radio-frequency ID (RFID) tag can be read by a scanner from a distance of several yards. And the chip also records each place a Euro note is spent. According to Paul Saffo, director of the Institute for the Future in Menlo Park, Cali-

fornia, "The RFID allows money to carry its own history."[4]

The RFID will help confiscators more easily identify people who are carrying large amounts of cash, will enable them to find out from whom you got your cash, and will help the algorithm boys and girls identify more "suspicious" spending patterns to include in future laws and regulations.

I know of no plan (yet) to do this with U.S. currency, but I'd be astonished if U.S. Treasury, Justice, Homeland Security, and even the Bureau of Statistics officials didn't find this an irresistible idea.

"Suspicious" money orders

The U.S. Postal Service is currently in the process of destroying most money-order privacy, as well. Postal employees are already taught (through one of the most creepy police-state videos you'd ever want to see) how to detect "suspicious" customers and report "suspicious" purchases of money orders. (You can, for instance, be reported not only for buying "too many" money orders, but for deciding *not* to buy them after being informed of the paperwork requirements. And the clerks are encouraged to smile to your face and tell you everything is just fine, but if in doubt about *any* activity, to report you as soon as your back is turned.)

But worse, the U.S.P.S. is setting up a "real-time" tracking system for money orders. The moment any M.O. is sold, or the moment one is cashed, the transaction is reported to a central database. Once again, those mathematical algorithms analyze any transaction that might be "suspicious" and send an alarm to enforcers. This system isn't online as I write this. And perhaps we'll luck out and the Post Office's computers will be as screwed up as those of the IRS. Or very likely the system will be so overloaded with data and alarms that human investigators will never be able to follow up on all your "suspicious" activities. But beware. Watch out for this.

Even with this system, you should still be able to receive M.O.s in small denominations from your customers or employers — without the TO field

---

4 Yoshida, Junko. "Euro bank notes to embed RFID chips by 2005." *EE Times*, December 19, 2001.
http://www.eetimes.com/story/OEG20011219S0016

filled in — and pass them along to your creditors to pay bills. That is, this time-honored financial privacy-protection system should still work unless you or the person paying you is under serious investigation, in which case personal investigation will uncover even this.

And do remember, always, that a blank money order is a bearer instrument. Misplace it or lose it in the mail and anyone can fill in the TO line and cash it.

Anonymous smart cards

In this chapter I speculated upon the future of anonymous smart cards — like phone cards you can purchase at Wal-Mart or a truck stop, but charged with cash, not phone time. This exact thing hasn't emerged yet, to my knowledge. But a very similar tool is making an appearance for those who are now called "the unbanked." (You see, there are enough resisters that they've even got a name now.)

These are precharged debit cards, which could be either smart cards or the more old-fashioned kind of mag-stripe cards. Some you can buy yourself (for fees way less than their offshore cousin cards) and some are issued to you by employers or contractors as an alternative to a traditional paycheck. (They issue the card once, then charge it up when pay is due.)

Now, there are a lot of varieties of these things. Some are useful to privacy and some are very much the opposite; they're part of the Evil Plot (I'm only half joking) to get the "unbanked" into the system where, instead of trading their paycheck for cash at a storefront business and spending the cash untraceably, they'll be forced to make trackable purchases and withdrawals.

Look for cards that don't require you to give an SSN or a lot of other personal information about yourself. And don't use them to make purchases, but only to get modest amounts of cash from ATMs which you can (until the advent of the RFID tag) spend privately.

For more on these cards see the resources listed in the Appendix, including my *Backwoods Home* magazine article, "Bye Bye Banking."

A new label

The "unbanked." Now, there's an interesting phenomenon. In the last few years, the Federal Reserve has become very upset that a certain percentage of Americans — 13 percent, nearly one in seven families — happens not to use banks, particularly not those nice checking accounts, so useful to the government when it comes time to track our spending habits.

The Federal Reserve has done several studies on this. They find various reasons that people don't use banks, but a large percentage of those reasons amount to either "I don't like banks" or "banks are irrelevant to my life."

This particular spate of federal fretting over untrackable financial dealings was spurred on by the Debt Collection Improvement Act of 1996, the law that pushed people to receive their government payments electronically. The Federal Reserve further makes the pious case that people who go bankless cut themselves off from many benefits of prosperity. And there's some truth in that. But frankly, if they'd quit turning bankers into Junior G-men reporting us to the feds, or worse, Junior CIA agents spying on us as if we were all international terrorists, maybe more of us would be willing to trust and do business.

The URL of the latest Federal Reserve study on the "unbanked" is in the Appendix, along with the URL of my article, "Bye Bye Banking." Hm... wonder how many of these bankless folks are also among the one in eight who (if data from the Dayton, Ohio, ID checkpoints is valid) may be resisting all possession of drivers' licenses? Interesting how similar the figures are.

NONE

The National Organization for Non-Enumeration, mentioned in this chapter, appears to have gone defunct. Although you can no longer get its forms, information on how to get a bank account without a Social Security number is still available. Some sources are listed in the Appendix.

A little good news

Let's have some good news, shall we? Two items:

First, the 1998 Taxpayers Bill of Rights, passed by Congress and signed into law by Bill Clinton, actually accomplished something good. To the surprise of cynics, the legal requirement that the IRS prove the guilt of taxpayers, rather than demanding that taxpayers (impossibly) prove their innocence in disputes over taxes, actually stopped the IRS in its tracks.

This burden-of-proof requirement applies only to good citizens who file their taxes, not to outright resisters (although, when the IRS brings criminal cases, the burden of proof is back on the IRS). And it's too good a thing for innocent citizens. So I don't expect it to last. But for a while, it's nice to know that one of the two most brutal and unjust police-state agencies in the U.S. has had its jackboots replaced by fuzzy bunny slippers.

Also, in 2000, Congress passed some very mild reforms to federal asset forfeiture (The Civil Asset Forfeiture Reform Act, aka CAFRA). These are not enough to prevent, let alone undo, the great injustice that legalized theft-by-government has caused. But at least the legislation was a step in the right direction. One of the most sanity-making of its provisions was the addition of an "innocent owner defense." Prior to CAFRA, the Supreme Court, in the *Bennis* decision had upheld the completely idiotic idea that an innocent person could and should have her property seized by government (without any compensation) if a guilty person used it to commit a crime.

Chapter Eight
Medical Care in the Free Community

Experience should teach us to be most on our guard to protect liberty when the government's purposes are beneficent. Men born to freedom are naturally alert to repel invasion of their liberty by evil-minded rulers. The greatest dangers to liberty lurk in insidious encroachment by men of zeal, well meaning but without understanding. — Justice Louis Brandeis, *Olmstead v. United States*, 277 US 438, (1928)

Next to travel, one of the earliest things to be restricted from Undocumented Citizens is medical care. This is thanks to the "beneficent" zealotry of a federal government that increasingly believes we must be taken care of "for our own good," from womb to tomb. As a natural consequence, we must submit to our caretaker's numbering and tracking system.

Well, bull-oney!

Not that long ago, health care was strictly between us and our doctors. Then it was between us, our doctors, and our insurers (or our insurers and our employers). That seemed to be a boon. But this has led, sadly, to health care being between *our insurers and the government*. Increasingly, it is leading to the government *being* our insurer, or being in such a cozy little snuggle with our insurers that it's hard to tell where business ends and government begins.

Oh, yes, the state and doctors will still take care of us in the ID Society. Even if we don't have money. But not if we don't have our Number, boys and girls. In California, a physician told me, county hospitals are already, under law, denying medical care to people who can't prove citizenship. And remember that the Health Care Portability and Accountability Act of 1996 (PL 104-191) set up those federal "standards" for the transmission of your medical data. Have no number? Eventually — if not in the near future — you'll get no medicine beyond the basics you can pay cash for.

For the moment, perhaps you can lie about your number. However, as federal funding and federal rule-making increasingly dominate the medical profession... and as scannable SS cards or other scannable ID become required for each medical transaction, don't count on care if you won't submit to Cattle ID.

We might also lose a great deal of medical access in an economic collapse. Older readers could be caught in a crash of the unstable Medicare program.

So what can we do about it?

A lot. And I believe our hopes lie in two areas:

- The increasing number of medical people who are becoming disenchanted with their highly controlled profession.
- A selective turning-away from some of the more dubious benefits of modern medicine, coupled with better self-care.

A lot of doctors, nurses, and therapists are just plain fed up. While the neurosurgeons, cardiologists, and other high-status specialists will no doubt go on enjoying the conventions and satisfactions of their institutions, we are already seeing an enormous rebellion among:

- Chiropractors
- Osteopaths
- Midwives
- Nurse practitioners
- Nutritionists
- Naturopaths
- Pharmacists
- Veterinarians
- And many others on the less gloried ends of medicine.

Some of these specialists were never really *in* the mainstream of medicine. Midwives have only recently and grudgingly been admitted to "respectability" by their OB-Gyn "superiors." Theirs is often an uneasy relationship, even though both specialists have valid roles to play. Chiropractors have always been outsiders, fighting the scorn and legislation of the medical profession. The nurse practitioner often does the work of a doctor with nowhere near the pay and respect. Pharmacists are often frustrated at the restrictions placed on them and the drugs they sell (or the helpful drugs they are forbidden to sell).

So a lot of these people are going to be willing — even happy — to work for cash or barter in a society that seeks their services, respects them for their skills — and doesn't demand that they spend their lives filling out *&@)!$$! paperwork or living in terror of breaking regulations.

What we do when we need a more recondite specialist is a question that has no satisfactory answer. I can only touch on the question. Perhaps some knowing reader of this book will come up with the answer. Perhaps some cardiologist or neurosurgeon is sitting out there right now, getting fed up with tyranny. Perhaps some skilled professional like that is about to have her door kicked down by fedcops from the FDA or DEA or some other alphabet soup agency that covets her nice home or valuable office. Maybe that oncologist or neurologist has never before given a thought to our cries for liberty… but she will.

Our other hope, self-care and a rethinking of what medicine means to us, has many aspects to explore. So once again, this chapter will be a beginning, a tossing out of ideas for consideration. The world you create is largely up to you and will depend on many factors. I can do no more than mention a few considerations.

First things first: decisions

If you accept the premise that medical care — and a lot of other things — will be difficult for Undocumented Citizens, then there are a lot of basics to take care of *before* that day comes.

First of all, if you have a medical condition that requires constant and sophisticated care, you should certainly consider *staying within the system*. I don't envy you. For some Christians, particularly, this could mean a conflict between your health and your soul — remain within the system to stay well, while risking your soul to the Beast's number and databases.

Even for non-Christian people it's a toughy. I can sit here glowing with health, and say, "I'd rather *die* than live in the Slave System." But I know darned well it would be another matter if I were in pain.

We healthy people can be very arrogant toward the less healthy — and very short-sighted about our own potential vulnerability.

Nobody like me can make decisions for you. I have true freedom-loving friends who have *grand mal* epilepsy, diabetes, or potentially fatal lung conditions. I wouldn't blame them one bit if they accepted the ID system and went along for the sake of their health. In fact, I'd be grateful, because I know those folks would use their position within the system to become moles. And I know they'd use their rage at being tied to a Slave System in order to fight even harder for freedom.

First things first: actions

If you do decide you're going to defy the numbering system and all that goes with it, and if you do believe this could cost you access to much medical care, the first thing to do is to take care of necessities *now*.

Medical necessities aren't cheap. So most of us won't be able to do everything on this list. (Fortunately, most of us don't need to do all of them, anyhow.) But here are some things to think of taking care of now, while you still have some freedoms:

- First, adopt the healthiest lifestyle you can. If you drink or smoke to excess, or live on jelly donuts, consider cutting back. If lifting a Bud Lite is the heaviest work you ever do, start moving around

— whether in exercise or physical work. We all get tired of the health fascists yammering at us and changing their recommendations every other week, so don't listen to those folks. Listen to your own body. If the food you're eating makes you sluggish, bloated, and cramped, switch. If cigarettes make you cough or reduce your endurance, stop. But if you're fine as is, fine. It's your body.

- Ditto with your weight. If you're comfortable and energetic at your present poundage, terrific. But if you need either to bulk up or to lose fat, do it now. Gradually and carefully, I hope. But determinedly.

- Have your eyes checked and, if you need glasses or contacts, buy extra pairs. I know one man who even had radial keratotomy to correct his nearsightedness, precisely because he didn't want to have to fret about equipment in a future of turmoil.

- Have those teeth checked. And if it looks as if you might soon need a crown or a bridge, try to get it done. (This is *very* expensive and most of us still don't have dental insurance, but do what you can.) Of course, get those cavities filled, too.

- If you believe in 'em, get your shots. And your childrens' shots. I'm coming, increasingly, to share suspicions about vaccines that I would have considered crazy a few years ago. Vaccines certainly can *cause* disease, as well as prevent it. And the next time the fedgov, or the UN, announces some universal vaccination program, I'm going to ask, "What the hell are those bloody control-freaks actually putting into people's bodies?" Still, at this point, I'd rather update my tetanus shot than to risk tetanus.

- Buy a good water purification system — perhaps two, if you can afford them, one for your kitchen tap and one you can use if you need to drink stream or lake water.

- Lay in supplies you know you need. This might include medicine or medical appliances. It's difficult to stockpile medicine, since it loses its potency after a while. But a year's supply is possible, and can be rotated and replenished. This includes both prescription drugs and over-the-counter — as well as other supplies, from bandages to syringes.

- Don't forget birth control!

- Keep a first-aid kit on hand. Boy Scout manuals and Red Cross pamphlets list ingredients, and emergency survival stores sell ready-made kits. Stock up on self-care books.

- If you aren't already "into" herbs, food supplements, and "natural" disease cures, consider taking a look. Frankly, I'm very, very skeptical about most claims for this stuff. And being disgustingly healthy, I've never had motivation to investigate. But plenty of my friends swear by everything from colloidal silver to shark cartilage. Even I have a health-store herb or two I wouldn't do without. The simple fact is that many of the claims made for "modern" medicine are bogus, too, or the powers of the therapies are real, but so are the drastic side-effects. We need alternatives.

- Buff up on your own skills in first-aid or disease treatment. If my notion of Free Communities pans out, you may never need them. But if you find yourself on your own... that's a different matter. And certain skills, like CPR, just make good sense in any case.

What about the things we can't do for ourselves?

We must probably face the fact that, as Undocumented Citizens, we'll have no access to MRI or CT scans, kidney dialysis or heart transplants.

If you suspect you have a brain tumor or a degenerative heart disease, the lack of these sophisticated tools and procedures looms frighteningly.

I hope someone monkeywrenches the medical system to the point where we Undocumented Ones could still avail ourselves of high-tech, expensive care, if we want and need it.

But we should also do some rethinking about the value of these tools and procedures.

We aren't — and we're not going to be in the near future — immortal. The fact is that (if the government's reports are to be believed) over half the money spent on health care in America is spent on people who are in the last year of their life.

Insurance companies and the government are spending half their medical budgets on people who are *already dying*.

I'm not against care for the dying. Humane care, yes. That we need. I'm not even against heroic, desperate attempts to reverse the course of fate. If you can afford it and you want to cling to life at any cost, go for it. If you have private insurance, you're entitled to get your money's worth and to wring every last drop of value out of your life.

Personally, however, I believe I'd simply reach a point where I'd want to say, "Stop, dammit! Let me go and go in peace."

I don't know because I ain't been there yet. But I do know that doctors have made a cult out of preserving the last scraps of life, and that billions of dollars in tax-looted money have encouraged them to do so. They have taken people who could have died at the end of their "natural days" and twisted one or two more years of life out of them. Often life without value. Life with nothing but pain. Immobility. Vegetation. Nothing but breathing and horror. All at enormous emotional and financial expense.

And to benefit whom?

Please understand, I don't advocate state-euthanasia. Nor do I advocate the state setting "quotas" on who gets medical care. Either is barbaric. The government simply has no business — zero — none — in determining who lives and dies, who gets medical care and who doesn't.

No state euthanasia. No state quotas on care. State preservation of a death-in-life condition, however, is as barbaric as state decisions to kill. Many years ago, I watched cancer doctors torture a beloved relative. They knew she was dying. But because Medicare funds were available, they pumped her full of puking-retching chemotherapy drugs to the point where there was nothing left of her but a brown, dried, depleted shell, nothing left to stick their accursed needles into. They didn't do it for her sake. She suffered endlessly. They did it for their own sakes.

Too much of modern medicine is done in exactly that spirit. If it isn't done for the sake of sucking up taxpayer dollars, it's done for the golly-gee-whiz sake of, "Well, we have this technology, we might as well use it." (And out of fear that patients will sue if the doctors *don't* use every possible means of diagnosis and treatment.) Or for the sake of doctor's egos. Or the sake of defying death. Playing god.

I want my 30-year-old friend who was healthy one day and had ruined kidneys the next to have access to dialysis and a transplant. I want my old grandma or a young AIDS sufferer to have morphine to ease the pain of dying. If I get headaches that drive me mad, I want a brain-scan to see if I have a tumor. When my best friend's child gets hit with appendicitis, its wonderful there are surgeons to prevent the boy from dying in the agony of peritonitis. And for crying out loud, let's have anesthetics and antiseptics, please. I'm grateful to the doctors who ease pain and cure disease, and to the nurses who administer medicine and comfort. But don't just prolong death!

I don't mean to take any of this lightly. But a great deal of modern medicine is… well, modern medicine. Humanity survived, and even thrived, without MRI scans and chemotherapy. Antibiotics didn't begin performing their miracles until my grandmother was a grown woman. (And we're now beginning to see that those miracles may have merely set the stage for more dangerous epidemics, as harsher, drug-resistant "bugs" sweep the world.) Most of the increase in longevity in the last 150 years has been due to sanitation and decreasing childhood mortality, not to treatments at the end of life.

Surgeons and machines perform miracles on individuals — and bless them! But for most of us, the greatest miracles lie in some simple treatments, a clean environment, good sanitation, and a healthy life.

Yes, there will be hardships if we must give up any of "modern medicine." For some of us, terrible hardships. But we, as a free people, will survive. And we, as a free people, may win back some of those technologies by our principled perseverance. Even more… If freedom prevails over control and stagnation, our hidden societies will give birth to a future explosion of human inventiveness that will make MRI machines look as primitive as leeches to a future historian.

But let's not be too flipping self-sacrificing!

I still want all the medical care my body needs. I presume you do, too. So how do we go about setting up the systems for *getting it*, in these burgeoning little communities of ours?

It's going to work differently in every circumstance. But in every case a medical system is going to need at least:

- One skilled health care professional; preferably a variety of them

I Am Not a Number!

- A building or buildings in which to function — and with sanitary conditions, please
- Tools, at least basic ones
- Curative medicines
- Painkillers and anesthetics; antiseptics and sanitizing instruments, too
- Security against raids by the Slave System's health police
- Labs in which to run tests
- (Maybe) labs in which to produce medicines
- Transport systems to bring in medicines and supplies
- Communications — between providers and patients, and between providers who may be able to assist each other
- Reference books
- Financing or cash to set up the operation
- Means for patients to pay for medical care when insurance isn't available
- Ambulance, EMT, and paramedic services
- (Ultimately) education to produce more health care professionals

In the tidiest scenario, most of us won't have to worry about any of this. Some small-town doctor is simply going to begin treating Undocumented Citizens as a matter of course. Well, she does so already, in these pre-totalitarian days. She doesn't ask her patients for their ID or Slave Number. Or if she asks for the SSN and they refuse, she shrugs and proceeds.

When the rules close down, ultimately requiring everyone to give a Slave Number for anything beyond a routine office visit (and even for that, in many cases), this human and humane doctor is just going to go on treating her patients as individuals, rather than as numbers.

When patients need a few thousand dollars in treatment and have no access to the insurance systems, she'll carry them or let them work it off.

It won't just be small-town doctors, already accustomed to viewing their patients as people. It might be fed-up residents from huge, impersonal hospitals as well, or nurses willing to do a little unauthorized medicine on the side.

Ah, yes! Ordinary, freelance criminals, just like us!

The quality of this sort of freelance medicine will vary (as quality varies now — though the licensing agencies and medical associations don't want to admit it).

I can envision free-market surgeries being performed after hours in existing clinics and small hospitals, with sterile conditions and proper assistance.

I can also see veterinarian's offices becoming unofficial clinics — an idea that bothers me very little, but might freak out those with less trust in their vets. Possibly, a freelance doctor could share a vet clinic's facilities unofficially.

Envisioning the worst of the worst of these freelance scenarios, I can picture (though God forbid!) kitchen-table surgeries with alcohol as an anesthetic — nightmare echoes of the Old West. The doctor goes home with a couple of chickens in trade and the patient might even survive.

But in each of these cases, the doctors, nurses, or other practitioners responding to market need and their own disgust with the system, take the steps to provide the service and arrange the facilities. All you, as a prospective customer, need to do is find a service you can afford and trust.

Paying for it

We should remember that insurance, government, and corporate medicine, whatever else they've done, have been the main factors driving up the cost of medicine. Although the aging of America does play a role, much of the current "crisis" in health care costs is manufactured.

I can go to my veterinarian and, if he's as willing as I to scoff at the law, I can get sheep medicine for $5 that would cost $100 if it was prescribed by a people doctor. Same exact substance. But different profit structure, different name, different government testing requirement.

For other drugs, you can go across the Mexican border and buy them at a much-reduced cost.

I'm not advocating doing this. Some vet medicines will hurt you. Some over-the-border medicines may be of dubious value or purity. I'm just making the point that paying for our own medical care may not turn out to be as terrible as it looks from here.

The outrageous costs we associate with health care haven't been with us very long and don't need to be with us at all, in most cases.

To give one simple example — a doctor who has dropped out and isn't giving half his income to his masters at the IRS can charge half as much for services.

There's little reason, aside from corporate bloatedness and government regulation, for hospital rooms to cost $2,000 per day or tissues beside your hospital bed to cost $20 per box.

If a vet can spay a dog for 100 bucks, why should it cost $10,000 to perform the same operation on a woman? (Even adjusting for factors like age and disease, that difference is a little crazy. And if it came right down to it, I'd trust any of my last three vets to perform a hysterectomy on me. In a heartbeat.)

When we are paying for it ourselves, negotiating with free-market providers, using simpler facilities, we can expect much of medicine to cost less.

Some things may cost more. Black market medicines may bear the price of the risks taken to import them and deliver them to you. But even there, we may get some pleasant surprises. "Store-bought" medicines are in some cases so drastically overpriced that the same drugs — bought covertly from an employee of the manufacturer, or made "generically," transported and sold on the black market — are actually *cheaper* than the same products peddled through the bloated and regulated medical system.

Setting up a practice from scratch

What if you're establishing an independent, self-contained community?

Or what if there are no health care professionals in your area willing to form underground practices, or willing to extend their existing practices to underground care?

In that case, you'll need to find, or become, a medical entrepreneur.

I've never done that. I've never known anyone who's done that in the kind of circumstances we're facing. So excuse me while I talk off the top of my head, and call this the beginning of a brainstorming session. (Your turn next.)

Is it legal?

That's the first thing. Is your free-enterprise, non-regulated, non-medicare-medicaid-food-stamp-wel-fare pay-as-you-go medical practice legal but unorthodox? Or is it illegal?

At the moment, it would be perfectly legal, assuming your providers were licensed and met all the usual requirements. But its unorthodox nature would probably make it a target for investigations by a variety of agencies.

In the future, medical care with no government ties might be banned or effectively regulated out of existence. Or you might be dealing with competent, professional, but determinedly unlicensed medical professionals — people who want no more to do with the government than you do.

Then your practice would be illegal and vulnerable — but no more vulnerable than so many other of the businesses we'll be engaging in.

Is there any possibility of patients using insurance at such a practice?

Insurance companies already like to use Social Security numbers, and once the federal standards are in effect, they'll be required to. It's possible (though no one can say, yet) that exemptions to the feds' "unique identifier" requirement will be given. Perhaps a set of null SS-type numbers will be set aside as identifiers for those with religious objections to using the SS; these could be assigned by the insurance company to a customer. Thus the insurance bureaucrats are happy, you get a number you don't have to label yourself with forever, and the federal system has its "unique identifier" for you.

Of course, this will drive the federal control freaks wild. And since the different number effectively divorces your medical records from all other records on you, it just isn't likely such an exemption will ever be given. Or, if given, that it will be maintained. They're *going* to number you and make you number yourself, if you try to stay within the corporate-government system. And they want it *universal*.

So the only type of insurance an underground practice could possibly accept, once the ID State has come to full fruition, is something different than what we have now. Among possibilities:

- A practice could eventually offer its own insurance. (But this takes big bucks, and also leaves customers unprotected when traveling. So it's an option for later, when underground clinics are well established and when they might be networking and making formal agreements with each other.)

- An underground insurance company could also offer policies. (Hey, you gamblers out there; want to go into a more respectable version of your trade?)
- A practice could sell memberships. Those customers who are well, subsidize those who are sick. (Again, though, this limits customers to business at the one clinic.)
- Customers could take out loans from the local underground bank when medical needs were high.
- Customers could rely on medical savings accounts.
- There may be other cooperative or business arrangements yet unthought of. What about local employers and their employees pooling resources to support a local clinic? What about your Free Community pooling funds to do so?

The market will provide. It may take some time before it does, and until it does, the risks may be unacceptable for both patients and doctors. But if enough of us free ourselves, the market will provide.

How can you attract doctors into a pay-as-you-go underground practice?

This could be difficult. If you're actually trying to put together a group of specialists tailored to the needs of your community, and they can't take advantage of all the varieties of funding that now pay their bills, you're going to run into resistance. "You want me to do *what*? Go into a practice exclusively dedicated to *uninsured criminals*?"

So your most fertile field for recruitment is probably those doctors and other professionals who are themselves fed up and just looking for an opportunity to drop out.

Chances are very, very good that these people already exist within your circle. Aside from computer professionals, writers, and other "rational hermit" types, I simply know of no other trade with more angry rebels than medicine.

If you have even one in your militia group or your supper club or your prayer circle, it might be enough to begin a small practice. And that person could spread the word to someone in her reading group or

his gun club and their networking might be all you need.

If you must recruit, various publications come to mind. (And I'm sure you could think of a dozen more.)

- *Backwoods Home* magazine
- *Prevention*
- *Liberty*
- *The New American*
- Local and regional alternative 'zines
- *The Washington Times*
- *Media Bypass*

Assuming, of course, that any of these are still alive in the world we're envisioning. I presume they, or their cousins, will be. I don't expect things to get so bad that the print media ceases functioning for long.

Although I can easily imagine the most "alternative" of the alternative media being prosecuted, legislated against, even shut down by FEMA in a manufactured "crisis," I expect the fedgov always to pay lip service to the notion of the free press. When all else is crushed under the boot heel of tyranny, our rulers and their minions can always point to a noisy media and say, "See what a free country we are?"

If those publications or their equivalents aren't around, then things will probably have gotten so bad that you'll have doctors roaming the roads, looking for safety. And safety — relative safety — is something you might be uniquely prepared to offer them.

Where to put a clinic

- An office building
- A storefront
- A converted house
- A house with a converted garage

…Hey, all this is sounding just like the kind of places where a lot of private practices are located *now*.

I think, in our high-tech and highly specialized world we sometimes forget that medicine wasn't always a profession apart, that it didn't always operate in an atmosphere of chrome and chilly tables.

And while we can all be grateful for *clean* chrome and *sterile* tables, we might also benefit by having medical professionals work with us (and not just *on* us), in surroundings that are more comfortable and more casual than we've been used to. Like the charming birthing rooms that have, for routine births, replaced glaring and terrifying operating theaters.

What do you offer the doctor?

Everything is negotiable.

Whether you provide the facilities and tools, or whether the doctor does. Whether the doctor sets his own rates or you set them jointly. Whether the doctor pays you rent for your facility or agrees to a percentage of profits. Whether the doctor is an employee or an independent contractor. What type of security you can, or need to, provide. All negotiable.

Should the diagnostic lab be part of the medical clinic? A separate business? An existing "legitimate" lab whose services can be purchased under the table? Negotiable. Flexible, depending on circumstances.

Can some drugs be manufactured locally? Must all be imported (smuggled)? Is there a local pharmacist who can provide them legally or quasi-legally? (Depending on a doctor's license status, the future of regulation, and the state of the economy, you may have no problem getting prescription drugs.) Negotiable and flexible.

If the world has really gone to hell and the medical schools are no longer producing professionals you can (or want to) hire, would your doctor, chiropractor, or nurse-practitioner be willing or able to take on an apprentice? Would your customers be willing to deal with this sort of home-trained healthcare worker? Negotiable.

But it strikes me that there are many things an underground clinic has to offer a medical practitioner, — things that would appeal to any professional looking for room to breathe free:

- Freedom from paperwork
- Freedom from control by government agencies
- Freedom from licenses
- (Maybe) freedom from the crushing premiums of malpractice insurance. (This is a problem that needs to be worked out. The need for malpractice insurance is real, but the premiums, in this lawyer-ridden, government-ridden world, have become insane.)
- Freedom from taxes
- Freedom to prescribe drugs other than those approved by fed-o-crats

- Freedom to use other unapproved treatments, with the informed consent of customers

If I could stand the sight of blood, I'd sign on myself.

Freelance ambulance services

If you remain within a "found" community, chances are good that its emergency medical services, including ambulance and EMT care, will remain available to you.

When you're bleeding all over the roadway or turning blue, nobody asks for your SS number or the name of your insurer. So emergency transportation and care on the way to a hospital probably won't be denied you. Even on the day when the paramedics routinely scan your skin to read your identity off a chip, they probably still won't deny you transport and life-sustaining care if they can't find what they're looking for.

But if you're operating your own independent community — or if things have really gotten bad enough that the local ambulance can't or won't come for you, you'll need an alternate.

Again, we need to remember that "modern" ambulance service is *modern ambulance service*. Until the Vietnam War, ambulances were specially modified Cadillacs or vans that came, picked you up, and hauled you away. The folks who drove the ambulances were simply attendants. While they certainly had first-aid skills, they were by no means the awesome EMTs and paramedics we have today.

In other words, just thirty years ago, if you were hurting, you wouldn't have gotten defibrillation or chemical stabilization until a doctor delivered it to you at the hospital. The techniques so important to us now were developed as military field techniques in war and brought to us in that war's aftermath.

Even if worst came to worst, we'd be very unlikely to have to return to that old, primitive level of aid. EMT and paramedic training is readily available, and even the tiniest volunteer fire departments usually have such skilled and helpful people in their ranks. There should always be someone with emergency medical training in your community. And even if the transportation available is nothing but a jerry-rigged van or sport utility vehicle with a medical kit in it, you will be better off than your father was when he had to be rushed to a hospital in 1965.

Still a daunting task

I'm probably being more glib than I should be in this chapter. I know medical care is literally a life-or-death business. I know there are many possibilities for abuses in *any* medical system, and that an underground system — regulated mainly by the goodwill and trust of its participants — can have special dangers.

There is the danger, already discussed, of simply not having the tools, facilities, and skills you really need. And of not having enough money to set up a system or pay for its services.

There's a danger that some of the providers who drop out and join alternative systems will be charlatans, defrocked incompetents, pill pushers addicted to their own drugs, perpetual malcontents, psychiatrists with more emotional problems than their patients — Lord knows. You might end up with a monster who performs medical experiments upon patients without their consent or knowledge.

Of course, that last paragraph of abuses exists within the regulated medical system as well. Licensing boards and medical associations are notorious for hiding abuses from patients, for protecting doctors from valid accusations of wrongdoing, and for delivering wrist-slaps in lieu of sincere penalties. And when it comes to medical experiments on an unknowing population, the federal government has been doing it for decades (from the Tuskeegee syphilis experiments to the bio-agents released over San Francisco in the fifties, to the various nuclear tests performed over the people of Utah, to the whole train of abuses still in the stage of rumor and question).

You may get one monster who does demonic harm. But you will be escaping a system that does monstrous harm as *a matter of policy*.

While an underground system may receive more than its share of suspect characters, chances are great that it will also receive more than its share of the most talented, principled, and dedicated people. After all, these are the ones who most hate to be put into narrow boxes of rules. These are the ones most likely to value their passion for their work over their pas-

sion for money. These are the ones most likely to give a good and true damn about the purposes of their life and yours.

There are huge challenges to setting up any business, and I can think of few more challenging than a medical business. Even if we remove a lot of the regulatory barriers, the task is still enormous. I admit again that I have only the sketchiest idea how to go about it, and would never want to be responsible for establishing a clinic or any medical system from scratch.

Entrepreneurs, this is a great opportunity.

But my fondest hope lies in the medical people already practicing, who will break the future laws and return to free trade, beginning within their own practices.

Medicine is an area of both greatest risk and greatest hope for us. A lot of us will lose our health and our lives by alienating ourselves from the "safe" system of the present. But to the extent that we prevail, we may both bring medicine back to affordable, human proportions *and* help it escape its bonds and leap into a future of technological progress.

And if today's "safe" system collapses — as it could for a variety of reasons — our rickety underground construction may actually put us ahead of our more cautious contemporaries who believed in the lying promises of the federalized, corporatized medical system.

Medicine on the move

I see these semis going up and down the highways hauling (so the side of the trailer says) MRI scanners. Once every couple of weeks I see one of these trailers parked beside my local hospital for a day or so, probably busy scanning away.

It's medicine on the move for small-town America. I wonder how much other medical equipment moves that way?

Trucks can be hijacked. Drivers of trucks can also be bribed into pretending their cargos were hijacked.

It's a very messy business, of course. Dangerous. And not nice. On the other hand, if the equipment belongs to the government — or to companies that live hand-in-pocket with government — who cares about "nice?" They sure ain't "nice" to us.

Update 2002
What's New
Since Chapter Eight

Once again, this is a chapter where nothing has changed and everything has.

In most cases, access to medical care is very much what it was four years ago — except for higher prices and ever-more services falling under the bureaucratic scope of "managed care" and federal law. Both these changes, however minor and incremental they may seem to someone protected by a good insurance policy or HMO membership, are the result of the creeping control government is exercising over the entire health-care industry.

Although some doctors and dentists do refuse to treat patients who won't give their Slave Numbers (even when those patients pay in cash), this is so far largely a private decision and not the result of government policy. However, some medical providers are getting downright creepy about it, too. One of my friends who refused, on principle, to give her SSN, and who explained her objections to the office staff, went back for her next treatment and discovered that they had obtained her number (from what source she doesn't know, as she wasn't using insurance; probably from a data warehouse or credit bureau) and added it to her files.

This is important because, remember, the systems are being set up — now, as you read this — to make your medical records sharable to bureaucrats, law enforcers, researchers, marketers, and anyone else with access to the database systems under the notorious HIPAA (Health Insurance Portability and Accountability Act of 1996). And either your SSN or some custom-created "unique health-care identifier" will be the open sesame for the most personal information about you. Your records are already broadly sharable, anyway, through the vast network of insurance-company and bureaucratic information swapping and product marketing.

Although you should never lie to your doctor about the realities of your symptoms or the things that might have brought them on, lying about your birthdate, the spelling of your name, your home address, and other nonessentials becomes a more and more important factor in protecting your privacy. This is still easy for cash-paying customers to do; far more difficult for those relying on third-party payers, whether private or government. But no matter what your circumstances, you can *always* write an "E" instead of "F" for your middle initial, and put down that you live on Smith Street instead of Smythe Street, or "accidentally" record your birthdate as June 4, 1973 instead of June 3, 1974. (People do make innocent mistakes, you know.) That is, you can do it until all health-care records are under The Number, at which point it doesn't much matter what you put down on a form at the doctor's office, because nothing will matter except what the digital database says is so.

I wouldn't tell you to lie under any circumstances where it might be illegal. (Heavens, not *moi!*) But any little thing that can help confuse the data-gatherers helps the cause of privacy and freedom.

You can also get your doctor to sign a form saying that she won't ever share your records with anyone without your written consent. However, once HIPAA takes full effect, medical people will simply be forbidden to keep such promises. Even now, what with the wholesale peddling of data, few doctors would be willing to sign or honor such a document. (If you're interested, you'll find some wording for such an agreement in one of my other books, *Don't Shoot the Bastards (Yet)*, also published by Loompanics.)

Many of the solutions in this chapter still seem far removed from average lives. They are, for the most part, for freedom lovers engaged in setting up self-sustaining communities. And yet, while the average individual may not be ready for the medical black-market, the federal government's control of the health-care system (and its ultimate control of *you* at your most vulnerable moments) is crawling along with the subtlety and kindness of a tank.

Here are just a few of the developments of the last few years:

- A pilot program was adopted in Wyoming, North Dakota, and Nevada to require some recipients of government health and welfare services to use a "Health Passport" smart card. This card was advertised as giving more "convenient" access to medical and other services. Not mentioned were two other facts: every use of the card makes the user's activities traceable, and the card can be used to limit or deny services as well as grant them. Another interesting datum: This card, being introduced in these three heartland locations, is a project of the G-7 organization of nations. Its formal title is the "Official G-7 Global Health-Care Data Card" — which ought to tell you that the purpose is neither benevolent nor in line with traditional American freedoms.

- Every person in the U.S. now receiving home health-care services — *every person*, including those who privately pay their bills, is required to fill out the twenty-six page OASIS B-1 form, which provides bureaucrats and researchers with information on people's bowel habits, mental state, and ability to walk or dress themselves, as well as other medical data. Although only a few questions are marked as mandatory (and why should *any* be mandatory, if you haven't subjected yourself to government control?), if the patient refuses to, or can't, give the information for herself, the caregiver will go ahead and fill in any information she sees fit. This is all reported to the government. It's simply a vast research project in which the most helpless patients are forced to participate. And the information, of course, goes into a giant national database.

- Hospitals have become such enthusiastic participants in the Social Security Administration's "Enumeration at Birth" program that they have forced Slave Numbers upon newborns even over the objections of parents, and have in some cases threatened to have children taken away from their mothers and fathers, simply because the parents refuse to consent to numbering.

Raids

Raids upon alternative-care providers, which were already ongoing before *I Am Not a Number!* was written, are still with us. In February 1999, Dr. Frank Fisher and two pharmacists were violently raided, dragged to jail, and charged with multiple counts of murder. They hadn't killed anybody. But what they had done was become vocal advocates of more humane use of opiates for the terminally ill or chronically pain-ridden. (One by one, the murder charges collapsed and the three medical people walked free; but the message had been delivered — the same message the federal government continues to deliver to

anyone who advocates, grows, or uses medical marijuana. And this despite voters' repeated endorsements of the helpful herb.)

Internet pharmacies

Here's one helpful development, though, and one of the rare places in which the Internet really has lived up to its promises. You can obtain many prescription drugs without prescription by buying from pharmacies overseas. Of course, it's *caveat emptor* (and when, in reality, is it otherwise?) But in my experience and the experiences of my acquaintances, the prices are reasonable, the operations are often so professional you'd never realize they were "illegal," the products are the same ones you'd get at the corner drug store (although the labels may be in Spanish or French), and the mailings are discreet enough that they rarely arouse the suspicions of the U.S. Customs Service even in these post-9-11 days. (The best of these offshore pharmacies will warn you that confiscation of your delivery is possible, but in reality it rarely happens.)

While many of these services specialize in Viagra, hair restorers, and other such vanity and pleasure products, a few are true, full-service pharmacies. Their offerings include birth-control pills, anti-depressants, arthritis drugs, hormone-replacement therapies, allergy treatments, muscle relaxants, pain medications, and more. Names and contact information are listed in the Appendix.

Cash for treatment

I still like the idea of a pay-as-you-go medical practice. And so, apparently, do a few doctors. Over the last half dozen years, some small medical practices around the country have offered as much as a whopping fifty percent discount to patients who pay cash. (Yes, fifty percent is how much of the cost of medical care is sometimes due to paperwork and related regulation!) But this is difficult with costs of anything but the most basic treatments being so high and most patients being absolutely dependent on either insurance or government handouts. And in various ways that are beyond the scope of this book, the government has also been trying to put the squeeze on doctors who try to return to this sort of customer-first orientation.

Still, if you are without insurance because you are among the Numberless, talk with your doctor, nurse practitioner, or whomever you go to for basic medical care. You may be able to negotiate a substantial discount for cash.

I Am Not a Number!

Chapter Nine
Work in the Free Community

"Laws are like spiders webs which, if anything small falls into them they ensnare it, but large things break through and escape." — Solon

Work is a big topic that merits only a small chapter. While there's a lot to do to provide good work opportunities in Free America, the groundwork has already been laid.

- For one thing, we've already got a thriving underground economy. The largest task is to expand it, improve it, and dodge new controls on it.
- For two, if I'm right about the things I've said earlier in this book, it will be obvious where some new opportunities lie.
- For three, a lot of work opportunities will spring from the sheer need for economic survival. No one will need to "establish work systems" as if they were running some central-government project. New work opportunities will happen.

Ours will be a free-market economy in the purest sense of the word — albeit one that exists within the box of expanding state socialism.

What is the Free Economy?

Every person reading this book has probably participated some way in the underground economy, which I'm considering a precursor to the Free Economy that is yet to be fully developed.

Some portions of the underground economy are so well known and visible they can hardly be called "underground" any more.

We probably all have friends who earn their entire living as unreported and untaxed carpenters, musicians, software engineers, gamblers, delivery drivers, flea-market vendors, crafters, artists, investigators, or product dealers of various sorts. If we're smart and fortunate, we *are* such people.

Hire an independent electrician, plumber, cabinet maker, cement contractor, floor refinisher or handyman and you'll usually find they'll give you a ten to twenty-five percent (sometimes larger) discount for payment in cash. At the very least they'll "knock off the sales tax." The underground economy at work.

In fact, it's harder to find a contractor who *won't* negotiate such deals than it is to find one who *will*. That part of the underground economy is so visible it's almost silly to call it "underground."

Most of us have also been part of the underground economy, in some way, even when we've considered ourselves good, upstanding, tax-paying citizens.

If you've ever sold an old rifle and not reported the profit, peddled your baked goods to the neighbors, swapped your lawyering services for someone else's gardening skills, or shoveled snow for unreported bucks — and if you've earned enough doing that and other things, but didn't bother to tell the government — then you, too, my friend, are already a criminal "tax cheater" and a member in good standing of the underground economy.

If you've babysat the neighbors kids all year or sold friends a few bags of hemp... If you've groomed dogs for cash or not reported income from guests at your bed & breakfast... If you're a veterinarian who cares for goats in exchange for unreported jars of homemade pickles… If you're a college student who's earned $1,000 cash over the course of a summer helping people move furniture… or a restaurant owner who doesn't report every, single cash dime that drops into the till… Why, you hardened criminal, you.

I hope you're proud of yourself.

The underground economy morphs into the Free Economy

I'm assuming that most of us UnNumbered also prefer to be untaxed. This may not be true in every case. If you really like paying taxes, feel obligated to do so, or are simply quaking in your boots at the thought of what your Benevolent Leaders might do to you if you fail to placate them — you'll have to figure out how to do that without having a Beast Number. Or you'll have to use your Beast Number selectively, and good luck to you in spending your whole life tippy-toeing on a moral tightrope over a pit of alligators.

The fedgov, in making it hard to earn a living, or even live, without its Number, has also made it hard to pay its taxes without its Number. So being an untaxed worker is a very natural expression of being an Undocumented citizen.

In some cases, if you manage to work within the aboveground system while still remaining Undocumented, you may find that a lot of money is taken out of your paycheck. Being Numberless, you'll have a heck of a hard time getting any of your pay back. It's a kind of penalty for remaining within the system.

Although we each need to make our own decisions on this and determine how much energy we want to put into fighting which battles, I believe our best course is to stay out of government-run or government-approved systems as much as possible.

That emphatically includes conventional work situations — which provide the financing for the very system that wishes to make slaves of us. By creating entire alternative systems, we also build the network into which new escapees from Big Brother can slip when their time comes. Thus, we do a favor not only to ourselves, but to others who would be free.

The underground economy, in its broadest definition, is simply the sum total of all transactions the taxers think they're entitled to get their hands on — but can't.

Hey, Taxers: Pffffft!

The Free Economy is the underground economy, as run and enjoyed by those who are free in other ways. Those who are UnNumbered.

The vast majority of unreported "income" results from good old honest work — the kind that used to be encouraged rather than penalized. If what I'm envisioning is true, there will be more opportunities than ever for underground work. This will fall into two broad, overlapping categories:

- New cash, barter, or untraceable income opportunities in *existing* businesses
- New occupations and/or businesses set up expressly to meet the needs of Undocumented (and other dropout) Citizens

And, as is true today, workers themselves will fall into two broad categories, those employed by companies and the self-employed.

The nature of "employment" will change, however. And opportunities for independent contracting will not just grow, but explode.

Independent contractors in the Free Economy

It's always been easy for those who contract individual-to-individual to participate in the underground economy. That's true whether you're talking about a WASPy lawyer and doctor doing an unreported swap of services, an old Mexican lady negotiating at a flea-market table for a set of used curtains, or a black teenager going door-to-door offering to mow lawns for cash.

It's usually also fairly easy when the deal is between small businesses. The guy who owns the little print shop benefits directly when the cleaning service offers twenty-five percent off on the price of laundering ink-stained rags. The cleaning service owner benefits directly when the printer offers twenty-five percent off the cost of business cards and brochures.

Tunneling along underground

From a February 1995 article in *American Demographics* ("Digging into the Underground Economy" by Tibbett L. Speer)…

Each year, as much as $1 trillion of income goes unreported to the Internal Revenue Service (IRS). The amount appears to be growing, thanks to a rapid increase in small service companies and a large influx of illegal immigrants. The IRS estimates that this "underground economy," along with improperly claimed deductions and exemptions, results in an annual tax shortfall as high as $170 billion. The IRS is not the only government agency that misses out on vital income information. "Any notion that people would not report something to the IRS but would report it to the Census Bureau is nuts," says M. Leanne Lachman, managing director of Schroder Real Estate Associates in New York City. Lachman, whose company manages shopping centers and other properties valued at $1 billion, says that national retailers usually avoid rural and urban communities that look poor. The reality, she says, is that many downscale communities are packed with farmers, babysitters, handymen, and others who shop at major chain stores and have lots of money to do it.

Lachman and a colleague, Deborah Brett, discovered that the 1990 census reports a 1989 per-capita income of $12,200 in the Bakersfield, California, metropolitan area. But the Bureau of Economic Analysis reports that Bakersfield residents' average personal income that year was 21 percent higher ($14,800). Such differences show up across the nation, with BEA figures ranging from 10 to 25 percent higher than census data. BEA reports are based on administrative records combined with a macroeconomic model. They include transfer payments, in-kind contributions, and noncash income.

(The notion of handymen and babysitters in downscale communities having "lots" of money is a bit grotesque. *You folks in Manhattan paying any attention to how the rest of us are living, hm?* And the article's shocked discovery that "drug dealers and hit men" aren't the only people being paid in unreported cash is funny. But the fundamental point is obvious, even if both the statistics and the author's tone are dubious; we're hiding in plain sight and they don't see us.)

Where it's a lot harder is where employees are involved. It's hard if you're an independent contractor trying to negotiate a deal with an employee. It's hard if you're an employee who'd really rather be making unreported income.

Free Economy arrangements are especially difficult with big corporations. I spent much of my career as a contractor to Fortune 500 companies. As a freelance writer, I had a lot of benefits of being self-employed. But the Mega-Galactic Supercalifragilistic Corporations I wrote for had less than no interest in making deals for cash discounts.

I'm sure some of those companies were making sneaky deals of all kinds, way up on the mega-floor, but that's a different matter. That's not the Free Economy; that's the very kind of slimy benefit-trading governments love and encourage. Much of the benefit of those slithery executive deals goes to them. ("'Contribute' ten million dollars and we won't close your plant down — this year.")

A little guy who just wants to keep what he's earned is usually out of luck when employed by or contracting to a big company.

But us Numberless dropouts have the opportunity — and the necessity — to get ourselves mostly *out* of Mega-Universal Conglomerate Unlimited and into a place that might be less lucrative but more sane and personal. Hooray!

Or we may have the opportunity to maintain a relationship with Super-Mega-Colossal, Inc., if we prefer, but in a different role.

Conventional employers aren't generally motivated to try all-contractor shops because of IRS persecution. But those forced into outlawry probably prefer to work only with contractors. (In fact, it will be difficult for them even to *have* employees in the conventional sense.)

Besides that, new forms of business are developing in which nobody works at a central location. These, too, will surely expand in the Free Economy.

Pretty cool opportunity: offshore contracting

As every software engineer or freelance writer knows, plenty of the Mega-Colossals do use contractors. In some cases, they've gotten around the IRS by having those contractors be employees — not of Mega Corporation, but of employment agencies that specialize in supplying skilled "temporary" workers. Some of these "temporary" relationships go on for years.

Here's a scenario we're going to be seeing more of. It's another case in which technology will enable ordinary people and small businesses to take advantage of techniques once available only to the rich.

The scenario begins very much like any other contracting opportunity:

- Company A-for-America, located in Scotts Valley, California, is looking for contract software engineers. It routinely uses staffing services — companies that find independent workers and negotiate short-term contracts.

- The workers are technically "employed" by the staffing service (not by Company A) and receive their salary and benefits from it. Company A, in turn, pays the staffing service as a contractor.

- The "employees" are actually independents who may work out of their own homes and telecommute, or who may work temporarily on site. All the "required" income taxes, SS funds, Medicare extortion, and so on are deducted by the staffing service and sent to the IRS and state slavemasters.

- Up to this point, this is all standard stuff, as thousands of software engineers, technical writers and other contract employees know.

- But what if Company A-for-America, there in Scotts Valley, contracts with Staffing Service B-for-Bahamas? Or N-for-Niue? Or C-for-Caymans? The staffing service is incorporated on an island somewhere. It does its banking on an island somewhere. Where it's actually located may be another matter…

- And what if Staffing Service B-for-British Virgin Islands in turn locates and hires workers who live…well, anywhere? In Buenos Aires, Argentina. In Boulder, Colorado. Or in Scotts Valley, California, just down the street from Company A?

- And what if Staffing Service B or C or N deposits the workers' paychecks directly into offshore banks?

- The workers then use debit cards, issued by their offshore banks, to get cash, make payments, and buy goods. The records of the transactions are kept safely out of the hands of America's snoop establishment, in countries that have no banking or tax treaties with the U.S. The contractors never receive a dime in the U.S. from either Company A or Staffing Service J-for-Jersey.

The IRS and contractors

Hiring independent contractors instead of employees is a really good thing for a lot of businesses, and for freedom-seekers, too. That's why the IRS has been cracking down on it for the last thirty years.

In the early 70s, many small businesses, to avoid tax hassles, converted to all-contractor, rather than all-employee, operations. The IRS decided that, no, regardless of what companies and workers decided between themselves, it and it alone would determine who's an employee and who's an independent.

Do you work on site? Use the company's tools? Work under supervision? Work steadily for one firm for X-months? Over the years, the IRS has dinked with the definition, refined it, obfuscated it, ruled upon it — and not slowed the racing underground economy by one millisecond.

If you care about the IRS' position of the moment, you can look it up in their code or call their taxpayers' hotline. (Given the well-known accuracy of their hotline staffers, when you ask what distinguishes a contractor from an employee, they'll probably answer, "Maybe," or "42." Or refer you to a section of the tax code that covers special tax breaks for emu breeders in central Arkansas. But what the heck, you'll have made them feel appreciated by asking.)

Why anyone should care what their silly little code says, I'm not sure. But *they* seem to think it's important.

Depending on the laws of the countries where the staffing services are located, and the citizenship and residency of the employees, this payment might be legally tax free, and these employees might not have to have Beast Numbers or their local equivalent, either for employment or for banking.

The U.S., being one of the few "civilized" countries in the world to tax its citizens' earnings, even when the citizens and the earnings are both half-way around the world, won't like this at all.

But it's going to take a heck of a lot of doing to trace the arrangement.

With the Internet, the entire scenario — Numberless, taxless and all — is well within the realm of possibility for Americans of even ordinary means. Especially those who work with computers.

Potential contract workers might also want to cut out the middle person by incorporating their own small business offshore and having paychecks deposited directly to that corporation's offshore bank account.

As we saw elsewhere, offshore corporations, complete with addresses, local agents, and bank accounts, can be gotten by ordinary people for as little as $750-$1,500.

Will the U.S. government legislate against all this? Of course! It's doing so already. It cannot *stand* to see people evading its mania for control. It *hates* to see anyone freely investing their money in productive endeavors, rather than pouring fifty percent of it down government rat holes. It *detests* having individuals evade its numbering schemes. But remember, the corrupt and political rich need havens, too. Your congresscritter doesn't dare cut off all your hopes because doing so might also damage him and his buddies. Poor dears might have a harder time hiding their looted millions!

Anyway, laws are made to be broken, by those with the panache to break them — and when an operation exists in cyberspace across international borders, laws aren't made to be enforced very well.

Employment vs. self-employment

Self-employment is rapidly increasing in the U.S. and has been for more than a decade. Mothers have started home-based businesses for the lifestyle. Laid-off middle managers have started them out of necessity. People who hate taxes have started them to make nonpayment (or minimal payment) easier. Computer geeks have started them... well, because they can, and because they'd rather relate to their monitors than to coworkers. (Not an insult. As a hermit writer, I like my computer monitor better than I like some people, too.)

There is going to be more and more self-employment, of necessity, among The Undocumented. When Madame Manager holds out her hand for our scannable card and we don't have one to offer, it's going to make independence look very appealing to a lot of us.

Unfortunately, some people are absolutely terrified at the prospect of self-employment. In my experience, they give the same reason, over and over again.

"How do you stand the insecurity?" ask corporate drones, from their gray cubicles.

"It's less insecure than you think," answer the self-employed. "You could be laid off from your one-and-only employer *at any time*. It would take a major catastrophe to separate me from everyone who regularly uses my services."

"But you have to buy your own health insurance. And you don't get vacation pay. Or sick leave."

"Yes, but my hourly rate is double or triple yours. With that, I can more than buy all the things you think are provided to you for 'free' and still have more per hour than you do."

"I'd never have the discipline," they added when they run out of insecurity arguments.

"But the need to survive is an excellent motivator." And on and on.

For some, the benefits of employment are more than mere "silver chains." One friend of mine has such severe health problems that, without her husband's company-supplied insurance, they'd never be able to buy the coverage she needs to survive. An acquaintance is in the same position because of a severely disabled child.

If you are in a similar position, you should certainly consider not dropping out of the system. But if you're merely daunted by the prospect of independence, you'd better take a deep breath. Because a new independence is on its way.

But might there still be something like conventional employment, just without the government involvement? Sure. I'd expect independents to dominate in the early years of our Free America, as new "systems" come together in an ad hoc manner. But the same needs that spawned a system of employment are still operating, to one degree or another. There will still be offices and bosses and employees who receive traditional benefits. It's just that even those things might take an altered form.

The new office (and who'll be working in it)

Let's take one of our Free Economy doctors as an example. If she's doing well and seeing a lot of patients, she's going to need the same sort of support she needs today — receptionist, at least one nurse or assistant, someone to keep her accounts and do her billing, a lab to process test results, and specialists to whom she can refer patients with problems beyond her expertise. All pretty standard stuff, just as in the unfree economy.

The accountant, lab, and specialists could all be outside contractors. But the receptionist and nurse would traditionally be employees.

Now, this is a Free Economy doctor, and her nurse and receptionist are Undocumented Citizens. So, being unencumbered by the *federales'* endless rules, there are a variety of ways they could structure their relationship with each other.

With the whole operation skimming under the surface of the unfree economy, the three members of this team could simply agree that the doctor would pay the nurse and receptionist for their independent services — no benefits, no deductions. The contract would specify that everyone was to take care of her own retirement plan, insurance, sick days, and vacations.

But the nurse and receptionist are used to benefits. And the doctor, for her part, would like to encourage their long-term loyalty. The traditional way to do that is to offer more than straight money. So she agrees to give them paid days off and to help them fund an off-shore savings/retirement/medical care fund. Being a physician, she probably also offers them and their families free primary care while they remain in her service. This might be done via formal contract, mutually negotiated by the parties. It could be done in the form of a specific take-it-or-leave-it offer presented by one of the parties. Or it could be done strictly informally.

But, say, it's done. So now are the nurse and receptionist employees?

The IRS would say so. But the IRS, the SSA, and the rest of the alphabet-soup-puke agencies aren't involved in this relationship (unless they learn about it through informants and come busting through the door, which is, of course, always a possibility). The people involved can *call* themselves whatever they wish. They have the "security" of employees, cou-

pled with the freedom of contractors — and nobody takes an unauthorized, unearned dime out of anyone's pocket.

We can expect to see much more of this sort of relationship as we leave the control of the state and form Free Communities.

I don't intend to minimize the dangers of government agencies involving themselves, by force, in these private work relationships. Whether it be the IRS, OSHA, or the omnipresent EPA, government agencies have made it their mission to insert themselves into every action of every business they can reach.

Clearly, it's going to be hard for some companies *ever* to evade that scrutiny.

However, with the increasing ability to encrypt and/or move transactions offshore, it becomes that much harder for business relationships to be traced. If employers and employees adopt barter, cash, local money, and/or encrypted electronic forms of pay, the government must work harder to find out that one of its millions of pages of regulations is being broken.

We won't all be able to stay out of trouble with the government. But the more people who enter the Free Economy — and the better they are able to use technology to maintain privacy — the harder government will have to work. And bureaucrats and enforcers don't really like to work hard.

They will catch the foolish. They'll catch those who fall victim to informants. And they'll catch some people they're really motivated to target. But the typical small business in which all parties benefit by the Free Economy is probably going to be "safer" than the typical small business that now allows itself to be invaded by a steady stream of alphabet soup agencies today.

Growing occupations

What specific occupations might increase in demand as the Free Economy grows? And what entirely new occupations might spring up to serve the Free Community?

With fifteen minutes, with nothing but a brain in low gear and the aid of a small town's Yellow Pages, I came up with the following. A bigger phone book, a few additional minds, and some more time would —

no doubt about it — produce a more comprehensive list.

- Pawnbroker
- Private pilot
- Solar energy (or other alternative energy) manufacturer or distributor
- Radio equipment distributor
- Phone card/other phone service seller
- Auto mechanic
- Nurse practitioner
- Medical technician
- Physician's assistant
- Virtually any other "para-medical" specialty
- Hydroponic gardener
- Acupuncturist, massage therapist, or any other alternative health care provider
- Dispute arbitrator
- Cleaning service operator
- Flight instructor
- Gun dealer (unlicensed)
- Investment counselor specializing in offshore investment
- Business consultant specializing in offshore incorporation and operation
- Web masters
- Antisurveillance specialist
- Furniture restorer
- All-terrain vehicle dealer
- Survival goods dealer
- Beekeeper
- Brewer or dealer in brewing supplies
- Hardware dealer
- Handyman
- Computer repair technician
- Any type of construction tradesperson (for building of Gulches or repairing of old properties for people who want to hunker down where they are or can't easily trade real estate because of lack of SS numbers)
- Small-scale farmer
- Cellular phone dealer
- Equipment rental dealer
- Chemist
- Software engineer
- Computer system designer/retailer
- Precious metals dealer
- Grocery wholesaler (smuggler)
- Fitness consultant

- Home care nurse or assistant
- Mail drop operator
- Midwife
- Notary public
- Paging service operator; pager dealer
- Satellite equipment dealer
- Telecommunications service provider
- Internet correspondence school operator or teacher
- Vending machine route operator
- Health food dealer
- Unlicensed ambulance operator/EMT/paramedic
- Security guard for convoys
- Community protection contractor
- Intercommunity liaison
- Private insurer
- Small-scale banker
- Business consultant specializing in underground business needs
- Import/export specialist (smuggler)
- Coordinator of community money system
- Operator of private fire department
- Operator of private water or utility service
- Unlicensed radio station operator
- Pirate phone service provider
- Manufacturer and seller of fake IDs
- Courier
- Wilderness guide
- Pirate gas station operator
- Free-enterprise doctor
- Contract staff member in clinic or underground hospital
- Drug manufacturer
- Hunter for hire (poacher)
- Independent insurance adjusters
- Hit person (just a thought.)
- Guard dog breeder/trainer
- Independent teachers; operators of independent schools

Occupations in which you *miiiight* not want to start a career

You might want to reconsider before starting a brand-new career in these occupations:

- Tax accountant
- Attorney
- Lobbyist
- Grant writer
- ATF agent

I Am Not a Number!

Working across two systems

Some forms of employment in the Free Community will cross between the aboveground and underground systems.

They do already, of course. When American Pollution Spewer, Inc. hires Ms. Cleanit to buff up its corporate offices at night, it doesn't know whether Ms. Cleanit pays her taxes or not. APS, Inc. covers its backside by keeping Ms. Cleanit's "taxpayer ID number" on file and by reporting every dime it pays her to the IRS via 1099 form.

But if Ms. C has successfully faked her information, APS, Inc. might never find out. If she doesn't pay taxes and gets caught many years later, APS can wave its own paperwork under the IRS' nose to prove it was an obedient and careful little corporate citizen.

The corporation doesn't really know, or care, whether she's a pirate operator or not. So the underground and aboveground business economies operate side-by-side, and even one-within-the-other. Oh-so-correct corporation APS is actually financing the underground.

In the future, we can expect the IRS and the Document Police to crack down even harder on contractors selling their services to corporations. We can expect to see laws requiring contractors to present scannable Social Security cards, scannable drivers' licenses, or other documents verifying their "right to contract" before being allowed to work.

But this will no more halt contracting by Undocumented Citizens, or halt tax-code scofflaws, than any other attempt by the control freaks.

This will simply drive more and more contracting underground, as more people get fed up with over-regulation. And while the Mega Corporations may go along with the feds out of blockheaded conventionality and fear of losing their state-granted privileges, plenty of smaller firms and individuals will be motivated to hire even more independents under the table.

Really? I asked myself after I wrote that sentence. *What the heck would motivate a "within-the-system" business to hire UnNumbered independents?* The business operators would be risking their butts — and for what?

What might motivate them? Any number of things. Perhaps they might be able to get cheaper goods from untaxed Free Economy vendors. As with some underground economists of today, The UnNumbered might be willing to work for less than their competition; there's no telling what some business might risk for the sake of an excellent deal. In some cases, the "within-the-system" business people might just detest the government and enjoy doing whatever they can to thwart the growth of ruling power. In other cases, a system business person might be a sympathizer to freedom's cause. Maybe there's some reason that person can't, or fears to, drop out; but he's willing to do what he can for those bolder than he.

For all these reasons, and many more, I predict we'll see more and more opportunities for The Undocumented to sell their products and services to businesses operating ostensibly "within the system."

Honor among outlaws

So far, underground employment has been an amazingly civil field, showing a most shining aspect of the market in action. When two people meet and voluntarily exchange services or products, each benefits. And they usually benefit more by not having some third party standing there with its hand out.

Except for the occasional horror story, the non-drug portion of the underground economy has been overwhelmingly peaceful, fair, and mutually satisfactory. Or, if the parties end up unsatisfied, it's no different than what they might experience in an aboveground encounter — poor workmanship, lack of follow-through, etc.

True, you might not be able to go to small claims court if someone stiffs you in an underground deal. But you may be able to go to a private arbitration service in your Free Community. (And, in fact, you may be able to go to small claims court, if there's nothing in your case that reveals the underground nature of the deal.)

You probably can't complain to the Better Business Bureau or file a complaint with your state attorney general when an underground transaction goes sour. But good grief! Have you ever done either of those things and gotten any results from it, anyway?

Even the occasional horror stories about underground employment don't usually involve underground employment so much as a combination of immigration with *promises* of employment — Mexicans suffocating in a locked trailer after paying their life savings to be smuggled into the U.S. for a promise of work — Chinese being promised opportunity, only to find nothing but deportation. It's pretty darned hard to exploit a skilled worker or one who knows both his business and his rights. It's impossible to exploit one who can walk away and easily get work elsewhere.

For a while, as we establish our new nation, we'll have to depend on the same kind of honor among outlaws that has governed the underground economy for years.

Eventually, as arbitration systems grow and as Free Communities develop their own equivalents of unions, collection agencies, and employment contracts, we'll develop more safeguards and securities for both workers and employers. (And, I hate to say, we'll gradually come to look like what we walked away from. But that's another story.)

Generally, I think we're better off with the honor of outlaws.

Pure satisfaction

I woke up this morning, remembered it was Monday, and reflected on how little that matters to me anymore.

I often forget that other people have "job-jobs" — the kind of arrangements where they have to put on nylons or ties and go off to some dreary gray place. Or where they have to put on steel-toed boots and work for nasty people they'd like to give a steel-toed kick in the butt.

I have a job — a task, a mission, a purpose, a passion, a means of earning a little bit of a living. But I haven't had a job-job in years. As a writer I'm fortunate. I can crawl out of bed in the middle of the night when the world is mysterious and peaceful, roam to the other side of the house, cup of tea in hand, and do work I love.

When the gods of creativity are with me, I may tap away at this machine for twelve hours, forgetting that time clocks, schedules, staff meetings, or such other abominations ever existed. When the gods are off carousing and quaffing nectar and I just don't have it, I can walk away. I can do something else for a while. Bake a batch of cookies. Walk the dog. Conduct the

revolution. Whatever. And not have any supervisor ask me why I'm not at my work station. ("That was a fifteen-minute break you took, Ms. Wolfe. According to the manual, breaks are ten. That's t-e-n.")

But the only reason I can live like this is *because I long ago refused to settle for anything else.*

I have no great education, no special talent, and certainly no privileged background that enables me to live like this. I am an uneducated working-class kid who simply refused to fit into the uneducated, working-class box.

Writing ability has only a tiny bit to do with the way I live. I simply hate structured work *that much* that I'd do anything else. I'd dig ditches rather than go back to work in an office. I'd slop hogs before I'd work in a factory for dictatorial bosses, as my father did for his entire adult life. I will do *anything* (any honest thing) rather than put up with arbitrary rules and artificial conditions. If I didn't have this one, single, useful skill, I'd pluck chickens for a living — *anything* but put up with crap from corporations or government!

So I'm always puzzled by people who say they want to work in better conditions — but who *don't do it.* I'm amazed at people who, year after year, stick in some job they loathe (whether it be slinging burgers or slinging corporate baloney from a 12th-floor office). Why don't they fix their busted lives?

This ID-resistance business might be a golden opportunity for some of those people. (And, what do you want to bet, a lot of them won't take it.) It might be a golden opportunity for *anybody* who's tired of following orders or submitting to the tyranny of schedules. Or for anybody who wants a change of whatever sort.

If you're a nurse and you love nursing but hate being employed by Merciless Hospital, here's a chance to sell your independent services. If you work midnight shifts at a postal distribution center, here's your opportunity to get on the road as a courier between free communities. If you're a vice-president in charge of environmental affairs for Pan-Galactic Incompetent International, here's your chance to quit and become a dealer of environmentally friendly solar-power products for the new John Galt market.

Whether you want to stay in your own field or switch, whether you want to become wealthy or stay poor-but-happy, there could be great opportunities for you in the New America.

Sell fake ID. Be an inventor. Take care of old people. Grow veggies and harvest honey. Sneak tax fugitives across the border. Form a free-market insurance agency. Operate a pirate taxi. Salvage trash. Perform surgery (if you know what you're doing, please). Do physical therapy. Market herbs. Start a savings and loan circle.

I know it isn't as easy as saying, "Just do it." But neither was coming to America when our ancestors did it. Neither is building any business. Neither is being free. It can be a pain in the rear, especially when guys with black uniforms and face masks keep trying to barbecue you for it. It's damn hard!

I just personally think it's all worth the effort. Besides, if we don't die trying (and even if we do), we're going to have a hell of a lot of mischievous fun.

Update 2002
What's New
Since Chapter Nine

This chapter is still substantially fresh and applicable to individuals as well as communities. I could comment on a few small things (survival-goods dealer doesn't look like such a hot occupation in these years after the Y2K bomb — a trend that can suddenly change at any time), but the one basic truth remains: To stay free, earn your money where the government can't easily seize it. And when the government "zigs" to try to locate sources of cash income, "zag" to develop new ones. Slapping your Slave Number onto your sources of income ... well, it's where this whole Numbering mess started, and it's as powerful a place as any for us to take charge and end the mess — and the control over our lives.

Most of the important developments affecting free-market workers have actually been covered in the finance and banking chapter, since the central issue is getting cash payments (or, in the future, anonymous smart-card payments or anonymous electronic payments or old-fashioned in-kind payments) and keeping them undetected.

A fact about SSNs

Just remember that there is no law requiring you to have an SSN (although there are many laws and customs that make life difficult if you don't). An employer, client, or the IRS may tell you that they're required to seize thirty percent (formerly 31; changed as of 2002) of your income ("backup withholding") if you refuse to give a number. They may very well seize it; I'm not saying they won't. But this whole "requirement" is largely a cruel bluff. They'll take the money, but probably won't credit it to your mythical IRS account. Since the IRS keeps tax records only under your Slave Number, if you don't have a number, any money that is taken is often simply stolen. Either your employer keeps it or the IRS gets it but never credits it against taxes you supposedly "owe." So this isn't "backup withholding" at all, but merely a threat to hurt you if you don't cooperate.

Some employers or clients — a precious few — will hire or contract with you even if you have no SSN. The really good (and very rare) ones will also work with you when (and IF) the IRS ever makes the demand for backup withholding. They won't immediately cave and withhold the thirty percent, but will give you the opportunity to make your case with the IRS about why "backup withholding" doesn't apply to you. Some of the resources listed in the Appendix section on Chapter Three may help, but this is a difficult area in which there are no guarantees.

Although there are ways like this to finagle the system and many of us have to use them to survive, I still believe that being conventionally employed (and therefore in the Deadbeat Dad's Database and generally "within the system") isn't the way for truly free people to go for a variety of reasons, both political and personal.

Please remember that anyone who promises to give you an "EZ" no-risk way out of paying taxes or out of using a Slave Number is likely to be either a charlatan looking for suckers, an IRS mole looking for suckers, or a zealot who really believes in what he's doing but who therefore disregards any risks and realities that don't fit into his pretty picture. Everything we need to do to save our future and our children's future entails risk — some big risks, some minor risks, but always risks. Keep your eye on the prize —

freedom. And then take those risks you intelligently calculate to be worth taking in that cause.

I Am Not a Number!

Chapter Ten
And a Free World of Other Things

"We can't be so fixated on our desire to preserve the rights of ordinary Americans..." — Bill Clinton, *USA Today*, March 11, 1993, page 2A

At this point, Loompanics gently reminded me that entire forests would have to die for me to cover every aspect of life in the Free Community.

There is an endless amount to cover. My heart, head, and keyboarding fingers ache to cover it. But in fact, I couldn't "cover it" if I wrote another million words. Each community and each individual within a community is going to have different needs. Only a writer with more *hubris* than I possess would attempt to define every need or outline solutions to every potential problem.

Some tasks — such as building appropriate forms of housing — are so fundamental and so well covered elsewhere that there's no need to detail them here. (Although the question of buying or selling a house without an SS number is a dicey one, for which you may need to use some of the techniques and institutions in Chapter Seven.)

Other situations may be impossible to anticipate. Yet others may be so specific to one type of community that only the organizers of that community should really undertake to define and address those needs.

A few other needs cry for at least a mention. So before moving on to Part III and the final chapter, I'd like to touch briefly on a few additional topics involving daily life in the Free Community.

- Protection
- Utilities and local services
- Children and education

Protection in the Free Community

If you establish an independent community, you may need to provide all your own protective services. If you live within a found community, you may have full civic services available to you — or some — or none.

In the worst case, the alleged "protective" services may make you their target. As Mayor Richard Daley of Chicago said so famously at the 1968 Democratic Party convention, "The police are not here to create disorder; they're here to preserve disorder." And the increasingly militarized police of ID State America are becoming highly adept at that. The final chapter will touch on the times when you may need to protect yourself against *them*.

In the meantime, you should be thinking in terms of your own protection and security against freelance criminals and other human or nonhuman agents of harm.

In the broadest sense, protective services means far more than police. They might include:

- Police
- Firefighting
- Self-defense
- Neighborhood and community defense
- Ambulance and paramedic services
- Home or commercial security systems and services

I Am Not a Number!

- Privacy protection
- Insurance
- Dispute resolution

While it's unlikely that police or fire services will be denied to The UnNumbered, it's certain that many forms of insurance will be. Even where civic services are available, they may be of dubious value. How good are the police in your town? How fair and just are the courts?

You will, as always, need to determine your own requirements for all forms of protection.

So just a quick couple of notes on protection:

- If you haven't already done so, take a good course in defensive use of firearms. Skill at target shooting or hunting is great, but learning to blast an intruder while rolling on your back with blood spattered in your eyes is a different matter. There are several nationally known schools that teach defensive shooting skills, but local courses and traveling instructors are also available. See the Appendix for a few sources.
- Private dispute resolution is already becoming a popular alternative to the proverbial "going to court." Even in very small towns you may find private dispute mediators. Check "Arbitration and Mediation Services" in the Yellow Pages. In an underground economy, you may need to think about arbitration *before* problems develop. In his 1979 science fiction novel, *Alongside Night*, J. Neil Schulman draws a portrait of an underground, free-market economy which is interesting for a variety of reasons. Notably, Schulman proposes a "binding submission to arbitration" — a contract by which parties agree to private arbitration when entering into business arrangements with each other. In a situation where you can't subpoena a debtor or contractor who failed to complete a project, such a document could be very useful.

Utilities and local services

If you are establishing an independent Gulch, you may have to provide your own utility services. One of the unknowns for people within found communities or others who choose to utilize existing civic services, is the degree to which utilities might be available.

If you already have a home in a suitable location, fully equipped with water, electric, gas, sewer, cable TV, and trash hauling services, you're sitting pretty — until a government passes a retroactive requirement that *all* utility customers submit SS numbers. Or unless political chaos, weather hazards, or other problems deprive you of those services.

Those of you starting communities of your own would do well to be as self-sufficient as possible, even if city, county, or private (regulated) services are available. Remember that, even at present, SS reporting requirements extend to private utility companies.

They don't, however, apply to vendors of solar panels or wind generators, and they don't apply to any passive or active energy source you can devise for yourself. They also don't apply if your Gulch is one big trust or corporation, with residents not being customers, but grantors or shareholders.

In addition to utilities, local services might include such things as:

- Snow plowing
- Road grading
- Other road maintenance
- Maintenance of water and sewer systems
- Maintenance of power "infrastructure"
- Storm cleanup
- Flood control
- Transport and burial for the dead

While there are no SS requirements standing between you and the "right" to such services so far, in the worst case you may need to provide them all for yourself or do without.

There are a lot of options, and there's a lot of information available on alternative energy sources. Don't forget that, in desperate circumstances, "alternatives" also include stealing power from the grid. As long as that grid belongs to the government or to some allegedly private business that holds the gift of government monopoly status, it's a fair target.

Children and education

There are two reasons I didn't provide an entire chapter on children and education. In a sense those reasons are contradictory.

On one hand, homeschooling and alternative schooling are so widespread few people in the Free Community even need to be told about them anymore. Their value is almost universally known among us. Ditto for many other aspects of raising thinking, freedom-loving children.

On the other, the very subject of children divides the world of freedom-seekers into two bitter camps. I had friends who dropped out of the freedom movement claiming, "Our children's lives wouldn't be very good if Daddy were in jail." You probably know such people, too. On the other hand, there are those like Gadsden Minuteman Mike Kemp. Since exposing racist "play" at the BATF's "Good Ol' Boys Roundup" in the mid '90s, Mike has been raided, jailed, defamed and slandered, targeted and spied upon, and woefully misused by his country. Yet Mike will tell anyone who'll listen that the main thing that keeps him going is his children.

He wants a free world for them. He'll live and, if necessary, die to attain it. And if he has to go to jail again, his children will be strong and proud of him — and will learn the value of standing for principles in turn.

Thank heaven there are more like Mike than like my (former) friends. But these are decisions only you and your children can make. And having made the big decisions about whether to subject your children to the hardships of freedom seeking, only you can make the smaller ones about what lifestyle, location, mix of companions, books, toys, etc. will be best for your family.

Sunni Maravillosa of the Liberty Round Table (a homeschooler of three boys) had this to say about children in the Free Community:

> My primary point is that many folx with children are concerned about dropping out like that, because of the potential impact on the children. But, in the scenario you spoke of, part of building the community *necessarily* involves establishing communities for children

as well. (Not just existing kids, but kids to come in the future.)

Using kids as an excuse not to take the step is a cop-out. In my opinion, a community of like-minded individuals, who want their children to grow up in freedom, is the *best* kind of community for kids; the libertarian/individualist message isn't purely abstract and talk there — it's real, it's being worked out. What more powerful education could a kid have? I can't think of a better way to show a child the power of his or her own mind and effort, than to grow up in a community where each individual earns his/her way by their mind and strengths.

The Liberty Round Table's "How to Live Freer Now" Web page also lists many resources for homeschooling. The URL for the Liberty Round Table is listed in the Appendix.

Update 2002
What's New
Since Chapter Ten

Just a brief comment on each of this chapter's major topics. While few of us are yet in the position of having to equip entire communities with utilities and protective services (and may never be in that position), my original cautions about being dependent on government or regulated utility services are even more important today.

Remember that the TIPS Homeland Security program may enlist literally millions of meter readers, furnace repair people, electrical installers, plumbers, delivery drivers, and heaven knows who else in an organized, federally run program to spy on other Americans. Even if Congress kills TIPS or The Injustice Department narrows its scope (which at this point it may), police and bureaucrats have already been using utility workers as informants and spies for years, and this is a trend that will certainly get worse. Police states live on surveillance and the human snitch remains a threat even in the days of the most sophisticated electronic spy wizardry and computer power. So even though few utility services have yet refused entirely to serve the UnNumbered (most cell-phone companies being the major, notable exception), it's a bad idea for many other privacy-related reasons to be dependent on outside services.

Insurance

I listed insurance among the protective services one needs to get along in the contemporary world. It's worth a quick look at what's happening in that area.

It's nearly impossible to pay major medical bills without health insurance — and very difficult to get health insurance without a Slave Number. Some group health insurers (where the risk is spread around among all participants) will accommodate you by enabling you to use a "null" nine-digit number in place of a Beast Number. A very few individual health insurers will similarly accommodate you. But it's harder because they're much more concerned about the specific, individual risk you represent to them. Check out the insurers that advertise on freedom-oriented alternative news sites on the net or in freedom-oriented magazines and newsletters.

This situation hasn't changed that much since *I Am Not a Number!* was written, but the looming presence of the "unique health identifier" means sudden change for the worse is on the way.

In most states if you drive without auto insurance you'll be hassled, fined, and possibly jailed. As long as you can get a driver's license without an SSN, you'll usually still be able to get auto insurance without an SSN — but will very likely have to pay high-risk rates for it. Once the door to a Numberless license is completely closed,[1] the UnNumbered won't be able to get auto insurance and will be at perpetual risk.

The worst change, however, has been in the area of life, property, and other types of insurance. This varies from state-to-state and company-to-company, but nearly all insurers will now charge you high-risk rates (which may be double or more their rate for

more tractable customers) if you won't give an SSN. And some companies will even *refuse to give you a quote on a policy* if you won't submit an SSN. Giving *anyone* (even a potential employer) your SSN before reaching an agreement to do business should be considered a crazy, absurd, and dangerous thing to do, even by people who think there's nothing wrong with having an SS tattoo. But we've indeed reached a pretty pass when American companies won't even discuss business until they see that we're properly labeled and monitored little government slaves.

(Yes, yes. I know their practical reason is to check your credit records — which are databased under your SSN. People with bad credit or no credit history are assumed (those impersonal algorithms, again) to be bad insurance risks as well. But that's bogus. What about your own record as a reliable individual? Shouldn't that count more than a damn algorithm? And if you have no SSN and they can't check your credit record, wouldn't human decency and customer service dictate giving you an alternative way to show your reliability? To simply assume you're an insurance cheat because you have enough principles to refuse to be Numbered, or if your religion forbids it, is outrageous. And that's so no matter what the corporations' stated reasons are for preferring customers to be Beast Numbered.)

You can hope your state insurance commissioner will ban this practice (as a libertarian I hate to see insurance commissioners even exist, let alone ban things, but ...). There have been a *lot* of consumer complaints. The best thing to do, if you must have insurance, is to keep doggedly protesting to the agents and the companies themselves. Pressing the religious issue ("I'll go to hell if I take the Beast's Number") can be helpful; companies are petrified of being hit with discrimination suits. You can make it clear you're going to go to a company that regards you more as a human being, not a number, not a database record. But there are no guarantees.

Increasingly, the companies you do business with, the schools you wish to attend, and even the very police who are investigating you for subversion are relying on consumer credit and consumer-profiling databases that sum you up as Good Sheep (or Bad Sheep) Number XXX-XX-XXXX.

In the meantime, another smidge of good news. If you're *already* insured, the company will probably be

---

[1] And it's important to note again and always that a biometric license is a Slave Numbered license, since a digitized representation of your finger, iris, retina, or DNA pattern is even worse than an SSN. It's not just something you're forced to carry and refer to, but something literally stamped on your head, your hand, or any other part of you at birth.

willing to remove your SSN as your account number and assign you a different account identifier. You have no guarantee that they'll remove the SSN from your records entirely, but this is better than nothing.

Children and the state

Children remain one of the most difficult, yet inspiring, issues for freedom lovers. Do we "protect" our children by being cooperative with the government and thus eliminating hassles and short-term risks in their lives? Or do we protect them more effectively by resisting tyranny and teaching them that freedom and individualism are precious gifts that we and they must never surrender?

One of the first decisions you have to make is whether to get little Patrick or Betsy a Slave Number at birth.

Over the years, the single most sickening message I've received from several people who claim to love freedom (and I've received variations of it several times) is this: "But if I don't get my baby a Social Security number, I can't take him off on my taxes!"

Other readers have simply informed me that I'm wrong when I say there's no law requiring anyone to have a Slave Number. "Yes there is a law requiring Social Security numbers," they protest. "You can't take your children off on your income tax unless they have Social Security numbers."

Let's look at both of these claims. First off, how much is it worth it to you to sell your child's future? Five hundred bucks? Three thousand bucks? Ten thousand? How about the traditional thirty pieces of silver? Because when you give your baby (or schoolchild) an SS number before that young, new, little individual can make an informed decision about whether to carry such a lifelong brand, you're turning your child into a government resource — an Official Citizen-Unit, if you will — who'll be tracked, analyzed, monitored, controlled, conscripted, and generally managed by the state for his or her entire lifetime.[2]

If you decide that *any* amount of money is worth more than your child's liberty, then you've sold out big time and whatever else you do, you ought to stop prating about how much you cherish freedom.

Now, as to that law that requires children to have Social Security numbers. People who claim that are referring to two related things.

GATT and the World Trade Organization. The enabling legislation Congress passed in 1994, when it imposed upon us the newest version of the General Agreement on Tariffs and Trade and created the World Trade Organization, is one portion of this claim. Here's the most relevant portion of that legislation:

TITLE VII--REVENUE PROVISIONS
Subtitle E - (amendments to the U.S. Code)

SEC. 742. TAXPAYER IDENTIFICATION
NUMBERS REQUIRED AT BIRTH.

(b) DEPENDENCY EXEMPTION- Subsection (e) of section 6109 is amended to read as follows:

(e) FURNISHING NUMBER FOR DEPENDENTS- Any taxpayer who claims an exemption under section 151 for any dependent on a return for any taxable year shall include on such return the identifying number (for purposes of this title) of such dependent.

What on earth does international trade have to do with numbering your children? Well, apparently, the Great Powers that cooked up the agreement realized they'd lose tax revenues when the treaty-they-pretended-wasn't-a-treaty went into effect. So they decided that all the signatory countries needed some way of ensuring that good little taxpayers couldn't "cheat the government" by taking Fido or Fluffy as a dependent on their taxes.

What's the best way to ensure that only Legitimate Immature Citizen-Units are tax-deducted? Number them.

IRS policy change. The second thing the "yes, there is a law" people are referring to is the IRS's more recent, but obviously related, policy of refusing

---

[2] Please forgive me for seeming to toot my own horn again, but if you want to see the long-term consequences of government's "benevolent" management of your children's lives, I urge you to read *The State vs. the People*, particularly the chapters "Learning to Obey," "For Your Own Good," and "Privacy is Erased." Also

read the works of the amazing John Taylor Gatto, particularly *The Underground History of American Education.*

to accept anything but an SSN as "proof" of your child's existence. Until a few years ago you could present a birth certificate, family Bible entry, hospital bills, or some other form of documentation showing that your child really was your child. But now (as Scott McDonald explained in Chapter One) unless your child is a Number, your child is a nothing in the eyes and the computers of the Internal Revenue Service. And sorry, but you won't be able to use your child to keep a larger share of your earnings.

So yes. It is entirely, absolutely true that if you don't give your child a Slave Number, you won't be able to use her as a tax deduction.

But no, there is NO law that says you have to go along with any of these statist human-resource management schemes. You will not be fined or jailed for failing to get a number for yourself or refusing to give one to your child. Your life may become more uncomfortable and so might your child's. But that's the way it is.

IF you continue to pay taxes and don't deduct your Numberless children, then you'll pay more of your earnings to the government — which is indeed very sad and unjust. You'll also be giving more monetary support to the very policies that are destroying us — which is not only unjust but forces you to make a terrible moral choice to give even more support to an increasingly oppressive government. But that's *also* the way it is for those who truly want to live in freedom. Everywhere you turn, there are such choices. Your third choice, of course — your alternative to either selling your child to the state or keeping your child free but paying higher taxes — is to face yet another hard moral decision; not to give your labor to support the state.

Choose: The comfort of a slow slide into slavery or the discomfort and integrity of living as a true freedom lover lives.

Part III
Times of Trouble

Chapter Eleven
Free People, Violence, and Alternatives

"Some of our readers — and I pity them — will never be kicked in the jaw with a hard rubber boot heel. Or bashed in the skull with a bicycle pump. Or whipped by their parents until they can't walk anymore.

"You really don't know what you're missing.

"Great souls rarely sprout from happy environments. While suffering may destroy the weak, strong individuals are able to steer their misfortune toward their own advantage. Using a kind of psychic alchemy they're able to take the shit that's been dumped on their heads and turn it into gold. Given the right temperament suffering can create character." — Jim Goad

In the most optimistic of all scenarios, our Free Communities will be left alone. We will simply "live around" those who chronically attempt to control us. We will slip past their notice. The world's control freaks will focus their rule on those who consent to be ruled and leave us alone.

This is a *very* optimistic scenario. Mike Kemp, who reviewed this chapter, called it "our most fond hope and, I fear, our greatest delusion."

For some who find the right hidey-holes or the right facade to present to government, it may come to pass. But we'd be fools to count on it.

We will, of course, be engaged in "illegal" activities on a grand scale. We will be committing such heinous crimes as hairdressing without a license, failure to collect sales tax, building without a permit, using the public highways without a license, building ponds without environmental impact statements, and keeping the money we earn.

These crimes will make us vulnerable. Some of us will be harassed, raided, killed, fined, and jailed. Some of us will have our property seized, to the gleeful profit of local or federal enforcers. Our activities, however peacefully we pursue them, will certainly bring new frenzies of laws, new tracking and surveillance mechanisms, harsher punishments, and yet more demonizing propaganda. We already face an explosion of armed federal agents and an increasing militarization of the equipment, tactics, and mindset of local police.

Yes, noncooperation with authority is dangerous. *But it's more effective and less dangerous than revolution.* It may help us avoid a revolution. There's nothing left to try.

I may be overly optimistic. Mike, who could never be accused of excess optimism, says, "I don't think of your method as an alternative to revolution. It is a method to avoid *firing the first shot*, but which will, in my humble opinion, lead invariably to the same result. Practitioners will be hounded, new rebels will be made, and they will be hounded, till a significant number of us become rebels or are ruined. It still goes to revolt or to slavery."

Mike may be right. But I believe that for both moral and practical reasons, we should try nonviolent noncooperation before violence. If it succeeds, everyone benefits. If it fails, we have nevertheless learned valuable lessons about freedom, self-sufficiency, community, and survival.

Our greatest hope doesn't lie in having our would-be rulers look the other way. They won't. Our greatest hope lies in having so many of us withdraw our consent that governments can't, in all this land, find enough enforcers to send after us or enough jails, prisons, or concentration camps to put us in. Hope lies in being so much smarter and more innovative than they that they won't even know what the hell we're up to, right under their noses.

Nevertheless, we *will* be singled out for the wrath of the ID State. Count on it. And some of that wrath could make the Davidian's inferno look like a summer barbecue party.

Each of us needs to consider that possibility. Each of us needs to consider what we might do when government violence strikes at us or our communities. Each of us also needs to consider when it might be appropriate to strike preemptively against a government that has committed unforgivable acts of aggression against millions.

In this chapter, I'd like to look at a few situations that might arise and speculate about dealing with them. Please keep in mind, I haven't "been there, done that." I have no personal experience with the most extreme forms of government violence — though I have seen many friends raided, jailed, threatened, impoverished, and robbed by government thugs and looters. I have known many people who have been betrayed by federal informants. I have known some whose family members have been cold-bloodedly slaughtered by government agents.

But I haven't *been there*. I'm going to be as startled and terrified as anyone else when the midnight raiders kick my door down. I won't know whether it's time to "shoot the bastards" until the moment my own gut tells me there's no choice but to fire. I may be caught so unaware that I won't have time to make the decision.

So please take these speculations for whatever they might be worth, as those of a writer trying to envision a future that still lies in a haze. But please also conduct some speculations of your own. Your future is very unsafe, but being prepared, even imperfectly, can benefit you.

I'd like to touch on four areas:

- Preemptive strikes against injustice — violent or nonviolent
- Responding to immediate government attacks
- Handling informants
- Nonviolent resistance to authority

Preemptive strikes against injustice

Someday, some ordinary schmuck is going to be stopped at a checkpoint — and he's going to start shooting. This poor, anonymous citizen — who may not even be one of us — is simply going to have felt that last straw smack his back — and is going to react.

Well, similar things already happen without publicity, no doubt. Vin Suprynowicz has pointed out that one reason young black or Hispanic criminals kill cops is that they assume they can't get justice "within the system." For them, blowing away the cop who comes to arrest them might actually seem like the lesser of two bleak alternatives. Small things can trigger such despair and desperation, when you've reached the point of having no options, when you've had enough and don't believe there's anywhere to turn for justice.

A man named Carl Drega recently "had enough" in New Hampshire. After years of struggle over property rights, he blew away a politician who'd been hassling him for years. Got a few other people, too, unfortunately. But do you recall what triggered him? He was tailed and stopped by a cop for — get this — having rust holes in his pickup truck. Local officials were determined to drive Mr. Drega to fury — and they succeeded.

How much more is this sort of thing going to happen when "Your papers, citizen!" has become an American reality? In some places, like Louisiana and New Mexico, it already is a reality. How many ordinary people are going to be driven to extremes when "insurance checkpoints," "pollution checkpoints," "seatbelt checkpoints," "license checkpoints," or general searches might randomly cost them their cars — therefore their jobs and their security, and possibly their freedom?

How much more violence are we going to see when Joe Average gets sick of being mommied-and-daddied to death by the government? Or when we conscientious resisters and freedom seekers get weary of the roadblocks — literal or figurative — that keep getting in the way of our peaceful lives?

Okay, so somebody shoots. A roadblock is a possible place for such things to start, so let's let it stand as an example for all manner of "routine" violations of rights.[1]

Some overtaxed motorist shoots...

And of course, all the cops at the roadblock shoot back. The proverbial hail of gunfire ensues. They kill the motorist very permanently dead. They probably take out the guy's companions, a few fellow cops and people in other cars while they're at it. Blood and the media are all over everything.

So security gets tightened. And there are even more roadblocks because there's even more of a "law and order" problem. But the next time some poor sucker snaps, there are tanks and flamethrowers there. Helicopter support. Whatever.

More repression leads to more anger, which leads to...

Well, nobody here needs to be told.

Some of my friends (and sometimes I) say, "Well, good. Because we won't have enough people with us until more see how bad it's getting. Not until more suffer."

If that's the way it has to be, that's the way it has to be. But isn't there a more efficient, more creative way to handle situations like this?

How about some what-ifs?

- Community Dagny and Kyfho Town, both Free Communities in northern New Mexico, have a joint defense force. They learn — from scanners, CBs, or an alarm sent via messenger — that the DEA-FBI-Army-INS-and-C-O-P-S have set up a roadblock on County Road BG. Their scouts have already scoped out the area. Familiar with the terrain, they're ready to move in. The feddies-and-friends have chosen a spot from which it's hard for approaching motorists to escape. But that means they've also chosen a spot where the road runs through a narrow defile. Motorists can't readily turn and run across country but (unconsidered by the arrogant agents) the whole operation can be observed — and attacked — from above. Snipers or grenade throwers strike from the hill above them, then fade, fade, fade. Hooray for the good guys.

- Unfortunately, the next thing that happens is that a joint cop-military task force burns out Kyfho Town, rounds up everyone in Dagny, and in the future the roadblockers get smart enough to put armed agents up on the hills. And the TV-watching public howls for Congress to *do something* about terrorism. Maybe that's not such a good plan.

- On the other hand, what if resistance is widespread enough that the cops don't have a clue about who hit them? And what if the defense force isn't headquartered in (or identified with) Dagny or Kyfho, but is mobile or operates from an unsuspected location? Eventually, if such things kept on happening, the more sensible law enforcement officers, like the local sheriff's deputies, perhaps, might decide it was stupid to risk their personal butts on silly nanny roadblocks.

- Nevertheless, any such attack is likely to simply lead to greater security at roadblocks. And it would be very difficult to hide any such outlaw justice force for long.

- Now, take a similar scenario, but without an attack on human beings. Warriors on the hills strive to disable vehicles, perhaps. Or to scare and intimidate the officers conducting the blockade.

- Or what if the citizens of Dagny and Kyfho — not a special defense force, but just the women, kids, dogs and old folks — show up, stand at the roadside to sneer and mock the agents? What if they hand copies of the Bill of Rights to motorists waiting their turn at the blockade? What if

---

[1] Another view from Mike Kemp: "Right now, the best chance of their getting a handle on a dangerous (to their plans) individual is by the single traffic stop. Away from home, away from fortification, away from heavier weapons, away from ammunition. On the other hand, the roadblock is largely a psychological weapon, a method of displaying strength and control, catching a few unfortunate souls on minor crap, but most effective in keeping people cowed down. They DO piss people off, but remember your example of Drega — it was a single stop which set him off, not getting caught in the abomination of a roadblock. If there were an outbreak of violence at a roadblock, I would think that the public reaction would be so negative against the poor schmuck that they wouldn't need to up their ante very far. I see the roadblock as building a smoldering resentment. I just don't see it as a flash point."

I Am Not a Number!

every local officer participating in the unconstitutional checkpoint was shunned by everyone who cared about liberty? What if Officer Poltroon couldn't get served in a restaurant or couldn't get her car fixed? What if nobody else's kids would play with his kids — until the roadblocks stopped?

- What if nobody at all interfered with the roadblock…but every time locally based cops participated in such nonsense they shortly thereafter found their vehicles not running, their door locks stuffed with epoxy, their deliveries delayed or sent astray, unordered merchandise showing up on their doorsteps, rumors spread about their sexual habits…

Just some thoughts.

None of this is fail-safe. (There *are* no fail-safes.) Even in the most inherently peaceful scenario — that of townspeople showing up to jeer — there is possibility for terrible harm. Tyrants don't like opposition. It's sort of what makes them tyrants, you know? Even relatively decent cops, by nature and by training, don't like people to stand up to them. They often think they have a right to stomp on protests, however peaceful.

Somebody could get badly hurt. The cops could force the crowd back at gunpoint, could gas them, shoot them with rubber bullets (which can be fatal, or can blind or maim), use one of the new crowd-control techniques (like nets or sonic devices designed to reduce hearers to helpless nausea), push children into the paths of oncoming cars, arrest everyone (charging them with riot, resisting arrest, and assaulting an officer — even if they didn't), start shooting (and of course, blame the victims), run over people with tanks, etc.

All this and more could happen.

In short, there are alternatives to violence that *we* can practice, but there is nothing that can keep violence from seeking us out, even when we abjure it.

We may thwart our oppressors. But some attempts at resistance may result in terrible, futile harm. Others may also result in terrible harm — but shake the conscience of the community or the nation, as did the Ruby Ridge and Waco killings. If consciences are shaken, but no justice comes, new people may join our opposition — as so many did after waiting in vain for justice after the Ruby Ridge and Waco killings.

Of course we should be reasonably cautious and try not to take any actions without assessing likely outcomes and making wise preparations. But that isn't always possible to do. As tyranny grows, we will, inevitably, face situations where the government reaction is totally out of proportion to anything a reasonable person could anticipate.

But ironically, tyranny will get worse whether or not we act. If we act, tyranny will increase in response to our resistance. If we don't act, tyranny will increase — because it feels free to do so when there's no opposition.

As the old saying goes, then: Better to die on our feet than to live on our knees. And, as Mike Kemp adds, "Better yet to *live* on our feet."

So for heaven's sake, let us take some calculated risks for freedom. Yes, we could get hurt. Yes, some people *will* get hurt. And killed. Crispus Attucks never got to enjoy the benefits of freedom after he was killed in the Boston Massacre in March of 1770. He was black and probably wouldn't have had that much freedom, even if he'd lived. But such deaths as his are not meaningless. By dying, Attucks and four others — mere street rowdies — helped drive America toward freedom.

If we can take a calculated risk that might make us more free, isn't it worth it? I think so. Best if we can be nonviolent. But there are times when violence is all an opponent will understand, or all that will serve.

"Only a little guy"

I've never understood the attitude that says ordinary people aren't responsible for their actions.

When I was 18 and watching other 18-year-olds go off boasting they were going to "kill gooks" in Vietnam, I was mystified by people who said the boys had no personal responsibility for the war. Granted some kids faced some very tough choices when drafted. Jail. Canada. Killing. Death. Not a one has the slightest appeal. (Sorry, Canada.)

And granted, absolutely, that the generals and the politicians who sent the boys to war bore a far greater responsibility than any 18-year-old private ever did. And granted, too, I was an 18-year-old *girl* who could be smug in my untested certainty that I'd make a more moral choice than the choice to kill strangers or allow my body to be used as politician-fodder.

If I'm pissing off my Vietnam vet friends now, I apologize, because I realize your choices were more complex and difficult than I ever imagined.

But I looked at those boys and I saw human beings, as capable of moral judgment and ethical action as any others on the planet. I look around me now and I see the same.

Every drone who "just follows orders" has made a choice to do so. Every brute who enforces bad laws makes a *choice* to be brutal and a *choice* to enforce those laws. Every person who becomes a TV zombie rather than an active human being makes a *choice* to do so every time he turns on the TV set, every time she turns her eyes away from some unpleasant reality. Every bureaucrat who practices taxation without representation because it's safe, easy, and lucrative, chooses to perpetuate tyranny. Every bureaucrat who practices taxation without representation because he gets his jollies from control also makes a choice, for his own pleasure.

Every lawyer who goes along with a corrupt system is personally responsible for her cooperation with evil. Every clerk in the county courthouse who willingly looks the other way while citizens are abused is, at best, a parasite and at worst, an abuser.

And yes, the police officer who staffs the roadblock or joins in the raid is as fully, personally, powerfully responsible for every moment of his participation, and every single harm that results. He actively gave his moral sanction to illegal and abusive activity and she should be held fully accountable.

To claim that the individual cop or the individual bureau-cog isn't responsible smacks of elitism. Do you mean to say there is one class of human beings incapable of responsibility or choice, and another, superior, class that makes all the world's decisions and simply moves the lesser humans around as pawns? Bushwah.

There are certainly people — generals, politicians and financiers among them, no doubt — who *believe themselves* to hold that superior status. And they certainly *try* to force us little guys to follow their will.

They put the little cop, the little clerk, the little soldier, and the little citizen into terrible moral binds, forcing terrible, moral decisions.

But dammit, no matter how difficult it is, *making moral decisions is a fundamental aspect of being human.*

I will no more excuse the cop at the roadblock than I will excuse the guard at the Nazi concentration camp. The BATF**k who kicks in your door because you're a gun owner is as responsible as the storm-trooper who came to haul away the Jews. The FBI sniper who shoots the mother is as morally reprehensible and legally responsible as the freelance sniper who gets up in a tower and blasts at strangers.

As long as we make it comfortable for the "little guys" by failing to hold them fully responsible for their actions, then the "big guys" will always be able to find people willing and eager to make the *choice* to be pawns.

If we, *en masse*, as communities of free individuals, make it uncomfortable for so many "little guys" that they refuse to conduct the roadblocks, go on the raids, make the drug busts, confiscate the guns or otherwise take our freedom — our moral choices just might stymie the "big guys'" plans.

We might also — oh wonder of wonders — win some newly conscious moral human beings to our side.

The threat is — *NOW*

A gang of armed strangers is kicking down your door…

A cop has just planted a baggie or a vial on your clothing and is hauling you off to jail…

Your church is under siege…

Your neighbor is being hauled away for tax evasion…

These are also situations in which we have the right to defend ourselves. In some of these, we have an immediate and desperate need to defend ourselves (or our neighbors) — perhaps even a moral responsibility. But accepting that responsibility could be fatal.

I'd rather it be fatal for them than for us. I hope there comes a time when so many midnight no-knockers have been shot dead that nobody will want to go on no-knock raids anymore.

I'd like to see it painful for them in other ways. I hope so many multi-jurisdictional task force members are sued — personally sued — that no agency or

I Am Not a Number!

officer in the world will be able to afford to risk committing a fraudulent or abusive raid.

But of course, as Mike Kemp points out, neither of the last two hopes is possible. Shoot, and you simply give them an excuse to bring in the helicopters, the tormenting search lights, the rabbit screams played at ear-shattering decibels, and ultimately, the flame-throwers and poison gas. Sue them? But the law nearly always protects them from being sued "in the performance of duty."

Interesting, isn't it, that fraud, lies, and brutality could ever be considered part and parcel of one's "duty".

I'd like to see unjust enforcers so cowed by the power of our moral force that all their puffed authority would deflate. I'd like to see thousands of people calmly walk past one of those cop barricades (like the ones at Waco or the Shirley Allen "Ruby Ridge" siege) and peacefully place their own bodies between the police and the intended victims of the police. But that will take numbers. Numbers that we don't yet have in our isolation.

Since the courts will do next-to-nothing to punish government brutality, I'd like to see violent cops punished by vigilante justice or exposed on the Internet, with full details of their crimes. I'd like to see IRS agents so terrified of neighborhood wrath that they'd refuse to risk their own necks arresting nonpayers, ever again.

But I can't kid myself that the homeowner who shoots the invading cops is going to benefit. No, she's going to die. Or go to prison forever for committing self-defense.

Even with the whole nation outraged over Shirley Allen's plight in the fall of 1997, and many fine people mobilized to help Allen (under thirty-nine day siege after relatives made unproven allegations that she was mentally ill), supporters lacked the desire… or the numbers… or the courage… or the foolhardiness… to plant themselves on Allen's front lawn *en masse*.

We don't have the will. And those of us who do usually end up dead or in jail.

At least, that's what happens now. Will it be different after millions have become more alienated from "authority," after we've formed our own communities…when we are more aware of our need of and connections with fellow freedom lovers?

For ordinary protection against ordinary criminals, our free communities might be able to use private defense forces. But what can we use to protect ourselves against unjust government enforcers, particularly in situations requiring *immediate* defense?

Again, I have no sure and certain answers. But again, some thoughts:

- The best time to begin defense is before you need to defend yourself. Or before your neighbor or ally needs help defending himself. That means various forms of preplanning, which might include:
  - Making alliances with other local or regional groups; possibly even defense pacts. (Again, be aware of spurious charges of "criminal conspiracy" and other such nonsense.) Various groups could sign pacts or make informal agreements to aid each other in specific circumstances. You could decide in advance *what* actions to carry out in *which* circumstances. You could designate one group as the lead in area X or radius Y. You could determine which groups would respond in which geographic zones. As soon as an emergency occurs, these groups swing into action. No need to debate or maunder or wonder who's in charge or who should show up. I am thinking primarily of nonviolent defenses here, but not exclusively. Different groups could pledge themselves to different purposes.
  - As an individual, you might have people you could call to witness potentially explosive situations. Some patriot organizations routinely do that, having observers rush to traffic stops, for instance, to watch, photograph, and make sure the police remain within the law.
  - If your local sheriff is at all sympathetic, get him to consider adopting a written policy barring the *federales* from any activity in his county without his written consent. If this sounds idealistic, it isn't impossible. Sheriff Dave Mattis of Big Horn County, Wyoming, was the first to do it, and he has since talked to many other sheriffs about the policy. Your sheriff doesn't have to be a committed freedom lover to take this stand. Remember that these guys have major turf battles with each

I Am Not a Number!

other. Such a policy might simply appeal to a sheriff's power urges.

- Form a self-defense money pool for people who do get in trouble defending their rights against abusive cops or bureaucrats. Your local underground banker could maintain such a fund. The banker could make some contributions painless by using the method credit-card issuers use now — that of tossing in a few cents per every purchase you make on a certain electronic banking system, or with "Ragnar Danneskjold Brand Smart Cards."
- Another means of operating this pool would be for 100 or so activists each to contribute to a fund which any arrested member of the pool could use.

- Some of the above techniques could help a person in immediate need, or could prevent an emergency/abuse from arising. However, there is no help for some situations. When they're kicking down your door, there's not much you can do about it — except remember G. Gordon Liddy's famous advice on where to aim. Or, as a fiery, 5′2″ woman friend of mine says, "Be very nice, ladylike, and totally cooperative until they relax — then kick 'em in the balls!" For other thoughts, see the section on nonviolent resistance, below.

- Get anything you can on audio or video tape — preferably on at least two tapes. Obviously, you aren't likely to be able to do this if they're kicking down your door at 3:00 a.m. Even if you've rigged hidden cameras or audio-recorders, the thugs are likely to find them as they rip apart your house. (If they'll stomp on kittens and shoot dogs, you really don't think they'd have qualms about destroying or stealing your recording devices, do you?) But if your neighbor's being beaten by cops or if you're being shaken down by a DEA agent... or in a myriad of other circumstances, you might be able to record the events if you have the equipment ready and/or properly hidden. This tape could be used as evidence in court. That is, if you still believe in courts (or if courts still believe in any vestige of justice). More likely, it could be used to bring private justice or ruin of reputation against a per-

petrator, or used in the arbitration resolution system of your free community.

- Where you can't halt enforcement abuses before the fact or during the act, vigilantism is an option for making abusers pay after the fact. So are the sorts of shunning, monkeywrenching, and "preventive retaliation" mentioned above.

Finally, and sadly, there will be cases where your neighbors, observing outrages committed against you, will simply shrug — when you can't help yourself and no one else is willing to help you. Neighbors and acquaintances will assume the government "knows what it's doing." After you've been hauled away or slaughtered, they'll read in the paper about what a dangerous extremist you were and they'll mutter, "Well, he *seemed* like a nice guy...."

As Mike Kemp points out, they may even view you as the enemy and cheer your comeuppance.

If your neighbors view you as a criminal, a Gulch may be safer for you than the community you're in. But I'll be optimistic again; I believe that in time, mistrust of authority will be so widespread that most neighbors will come to understand the wrong in government brutality and warrantless raids.

Maybe they won't see it in time to save you. But maybe they'll see it and become the doubting, pissed-off freedom-seeker of the future. As Scott McDonald of Fight the Fingerprint observed in an e-mail that arrived just this morning:

> *When the State categorically mistrusts its citizenry, how can the citizenry any longer trust the State?*

But all I want is to be left alone!

Even if your desire is simply to retreat, don't be surprised if official trouble comes looking for you.

It may come because you haven't paid your taxes. It may come because a neighbor has a dispute with you. It may come because the local government or the *federales* covet your property. It may come because you have a gun purchased in your name and the fedgov has decided it's confiscation time. It may come because you're innocently driving down the road and encounter a roadblock. If you're a hermit in a cave, you could still be dragged *out* of your cave for violating an EPA rule or forgetting to pay your property taxes.

So even if your most devout hope is to avoid all conflict, you ought to have some idea what you'd do or who you'd turn to if conflict arrived upon your doorstep.

Even if you are the most nonviolent individual on the planet, trouble could come looking for you simply because you live by principles of liberty instead of the principle of cowering obedience.

But first, the enforcers are likely to try to turn your friends and neighbors into your betrayers. They are likely to release cockroaches in your midst — their informants and *agents provocateur*.

Handling informants

The really sad fact, so far, seems to be that we in the freedom movement don't "handle informants." They handle us.

As shown again and again — in the Starr/McCranie case in Macon, Georgia, Arizona's Team Viper fiasco, the arrests of the Washington State Militia members, and innumerable others — we idealistic people are easily taken in by *agents provocateur*. Before we even suspect their presence, they've gotten us arrested and are perjuring themselves in a courtroom for the sake of some reward. And we, who may have done nothing except speak incautiously or prepare for self- or community-defense, are in federal prison.

We are naïve. Even though we realize in theory that they're out there, we seldom even suspect that such creatures swarm in our midst.

There is no lower lifeform than the *agent provocateur*. The agent doesn't seek to uncover dangerous criminals. It seeks to *create* criminals out of mere talkers, or to *frame* people as criminals — all for the greater glory of lazy, corrupt police agencies. It performs no useful protective service; it in fact provokes and participates in crimes. (There is at least some evidence that the Oklahoma City bombing may have begun that way.)

It is dangerous to society. It is dangerous to freedom and justice. And it is dangerous to the people who stumble unknowingly into its web.

Even if you aren't actively resisting the government or preparing to defend against it one day, the mere fact that you live and work in a Free Community may make you a criminal and part of a "criminal conspiracy." The government will send its insects boring into your midst. Or will try to turn malcontent coworkers into government-fed vermin.

There are a few obvious ways to avoid such creatures:

- Stay away, away, away from any person in your midst who persistently advocates violence, robberies, bomb-making, etc. Encourage others to do so for their own good. This is typical behavior for an *agent provocateur*.
- Don't blat your own violent inclinations or law-breaking plans randomly about. Not even your vague, unplanned *thoughts* about such things. Your merest angry fantasy can be used against you.
- Stay away from others who can't — or won't — control their tongues or their impulses.
- Be — to whatever extent you can — Caesar's wife. Make it clear that you do not advocate aggression or condone it and that the only thing you and yours want from the world is peaceful coexistence. This is no guarantee. (There *are* no guarantees.) But it makes you a less interesting target.

Here's one thought a little less obvious that I picked up from an Internet message whose author credit got lost in transit. If an old friend or relative — someone you'd trust implicitly — comes to you with a proposal that you do something illegal, always consider that person a likely informant. Most of us would assume the opposite. ("Old Joe, an informant? Couldn't be! We've been buddies for years.") But the writer of the message noted that it's actually a *typical* scenario, not an unusual one. Joe gets in trouble with the law and he's offered a way out if he'll create bigger criminals for the cops to catch. Maybe Joe's got a wife and kids to support or is terrified of going to prison because he doesn't want his precious backside violated. Maybe he's got big debts or a mistress or another secret that makes him vulnerable to police blackmail. Why, his reputation would be ruined, his finances blown. So out of fear — which he can justify in a thousand ways — he'd rather throw you to the wolves than be thrown himself.

There's no way around it. No matter how careful you are, if you are actively seeking freedom and communicating with other freedom seekers, you will encounter informing, trouble-stirring vermin. It will take a certain amount of luck to recognize them. And it will require even more skill and judiciousness to know how to deal with them once you've spotted them.

Once you do recognize them (or think you do), there are new perils. If you make a mistake on the side of kindness or fairness, you may end up in jail courtesy of the person to whom you showed such kindness and fairness. On the other hand, if you make a mistake on the side of vengeance or self-protection, innocent people could be destroyed — and later you might have to pay for that bad decision, as well.

One way of dealing with an informant — someone you're *very* sure is an informant — is to report him to any agency you think he might be working for. Don't expose him as an informant; report him as "this crazy guy who wants to make bombs" or "this weirdo who keeps trying to get his friends to rob banks." That could be enormously frustrating for the agency — although your little deed wouldn't necessarily help turn suspicion away from you or your friends. It might just make the agency mucky-mucks mad enough to redouble their efforts to "get" you.

I also dislike this option because of the risk that you may be reporting a real — though foolish — freedom fighter, not an informant. In that case you're becoming an informant yourself instead of cleverly turning the tables on one.

There have got to be better ways.

Another method for dealing with a suspected informant is to feed her false information. Tell her wild tales that, when she passes them to her handlers, lead to futile stakeouts in empty deserts, searches for evidence that never existed, suspicion that the mayor or the chief of police is a criminal — which is very likely to be true, in any case. (Make sure these tales lead *away* from anyone in your actual circle. Even a "fruitless" search can destroy your life when conducted by vicious thugs.) We're all familiar with the way cop agencies leap into violent, mass raids on the flimsiest of evidence from the most unreliable reports. Let that foolishness work in your favor.

As Robert Heinlein suggests in *The Moon Is a Harsh Mistress*, if you suspect you've got several informants, you can also put them in a cell (or on a project) together and let them inform on each other.

A time to kill?

But what about the time when the only thing to do is kill an informant? What about a circumstance in which, if you don't get rid of the informant, the creature will pull everything you've worked for down around your ears? Your community, your freedom, your crucial plans, your everything will be destroyed if you let this person walk free. Justice will die and tyranny will prevail. What then?

The first thing that comes to my mind is all the times in history when a guiltless person has been tortured and killed by his companions because of some mistaken impression.

What if the person you suspect is an informant really isn't?

What if you were in that position? Maybe you were seen talking with a cop or a bureaucrat in all innocence, and somebody decides you were passing confidential info. Maybe one of your acquaintances is busted and circumstantial evidence points to you as the fink. Maybe it was even *planted* evidence, and you were deliberately set up to look guilty.

Damn! So you get killed and your innocent blood is on someone else's hands.

Or (even worse from my point of view) you are on the other side of the same situation; you kill an innocent and his blood is on *your* hands.

There are ruthless people in this or any other movement who would dismiss the death of innocents as acceptable "collateral damage." I don't consider the death of a single innocent to be acceptable in any sense. That's morally akin to saying it was okay to burn babies at Waco because their parents resisted arrest.

But I do believe that if you have *incontrovertible* evidence that someone is an informant, and if you can't neutralize that person nonviolently, you have every right to throw the human trash into the dumpster.

That's theory.

I've never killed anybody. I never wanted to. I never want to. The few squirrels and rabbits that have met accidental death at my hands are still on my conscience, ridiculous though that may seem.

So there's a certain arrogance and a lot of absurdity in the likes of me talking about the need to kill.

I'd much rather one of my Vietnam vet friends were writing these passages.

Nevertheless, though I can barely contemplate killing a squirrel, I've looked into my heart and I believe it would be easier to kill an evil human being than an animal just going about its natural activities. A human who persistently, knowingly deprives others of freedom is a soul-destroyer, a destroyer of the future. He, she, it merits no respect or fellowship from anyone.

I would do everything I could to avoid having to kill. But I would kill in self defense, and I would also kill in defense of a free, human future if there was no other choice. Increasingly, as laws become more oppressive, enforcement more brutal, and courts less free and just, our masters are pushing us to the point where choices are very, very few.

But I hope, if it's necessary to kill tyrants and their agents, that we treat the killing as a painful necessity, not as an act of pleasure, satisfaction or revenge. It is trash disposal, not a source of emotional satisfaction.

I hope no one who loves freedom would ever stoop to torturing even the worst of creatures. I hope that, if we must ever "send messages" to oppressors by ridding ourselves of their agents, that we would do so by killing the agents cleanly. I hope that no one would ever stoop to tormenting and mangling, as police and guerrillas do in less civilized places. *They* learn their brutality from CIA schools. God, may we learn decency from our own souls.

Because if we can't remain decent and humane when faced with the worst necessities, then we are no better than what we are trying to throw off.

But as I say, it's theory. I don't know. I haven't been there yet.

And unfortunately:

> *In theory, there is no difference between theory and practice. In practice, there is a big difference.* — author unknown

Nonviolent resistance

What if it is against your beliefs *ever* to respond to violence by being violent? Or what if you believe nonviolent resistance is more effective or sensible than violence in a given situation?

There are a number of excellent resources — books, essays and speeches — by the people who've done it. And one of the most important messages they carry is that mindset is even more important than technique when you decide to put your feet down and stand upon principle.

An inspiring example of how mindset enabled a family to maintain their integrity while caught in an unprincipled legal system can be found in the book *No Law Against Mercy* by Barbara Lyn Lapp and Rachel Lapp (Hand of Hope Press, Cassadaga, NY, 1997).

The Lapp family, New York farmers of Amish background (though not practicing Amish), hid a teenaged boy from Child Protective Services. The state had taken the boy from his father, institutionalized him, drugged him, and otherwise abused him. Barbara Lyn, the person most responsible for the boy's rescue, was arrested during a public demonstration. Other demonstrators stepped in to try to prevent her arrest. In the fracas, her sister, father, brother-in-law, and a family friend were hauled in.

The Lapps spent eight months in jail, largely because of their principled refusal to plea bargain or otherwise cooperate with an unconstitutional legal system. So their principles caused them to be punished more harshly than the ordinary criminals with whom they were jailed.

But the same principles also guided them, giving them strength and keeping them on a steady course when they were tempted to waver. The book is, on one level, a simple account of daily life in a jail. But on another, it's a tremendous inspiration to anyone who believes they must be true to principles, even when consistency and honorable behavior carry a heavy cost. When pressured to give fingerprints, when being cajoled, ordered, pressured, or manipulated by judges and jailhouse authorities, the Lapps had their inner something — in this case, their religious convictions and belief in the Constitution — that held them steady even when emotions wavered.

As I write this, several years after their release from jail, the Lapps are in trouble with the IRS — again on an issue of principle. They may need their strength and principles soon as they watch the IRS take their farm away from them, or as they once again face incarceration for refusal to cooperate with evil.

The Lapps have a strong mindset and a devotion to God that keeps them steady. They were also not deliberately brutalized by their jailers. (Which is not to say that their jailers were pleasant, or that jail was anything less than horrible.)

But a young Navy veteran named Stephen Donaldson had an entirely different experience — one for which, in his naïveté, he was completely unprepared. His story demonstrates the importance of knowing the mentality (and the level of brutality) of the people you're dealing with. Unfortunately it also demonstrates how difficult it can be to understand that you may be dealing with monsters.

(As paraphrased from Jim Goad's essay, "The Punk Who Wouldn't Shut Up," first published in the underground zine, *Answer Me!*) Donaldson participated in a peaceful Quaker protest against the Vietnam War, held outside the White House in 1973. He was arrested and refused to pay his $10 bail. Before the protest, he had done some reporting for an antiwar publication, and he naïvely entered his occupation as "journalist" in the jail paperwork. A week later, as he still refused to pay his bail, authorities decided he might be deliberately staying locked up in order to get a story on jail conditions.

One of his jailers determined to show him just how bad jail conditions could be. He assigned Donaldson to a cellblock housing the worst scum of the jail. There, in a large, communal area, the young Quaker was beaten into submission and raped, orally and anally, forty-five times in the first night. The abuse continued.

After being released from jail and recovering from rectal surgery, Donaldson took the courageous step of calling a news conference to report his jailhouse rape. He was the first American male to make his jailhouse rape public. For that he was targeted by the police and eventually jailed again on a minor charge. In jail for the second time, he was raped again.

Stephen Donaldson eventually met a bizarre fate. After being jail-raped more times than his mind could endure, he not only learned to numb himself to the experience, but he came to crave rape as the best possible substitute for genuine human warmth and comfort. (Perhaps in much the same way as hostages come to identify with their captors.)

He became known as "Donny the Punk." He actually sought arrests and, more than twenty years after his first bust as a principled but naïve young man, he died of AIDS.

Lapps or Donaldson? Can you be prepared for where your principles might lead you?

If you're interested in learning more about the techniques and philosophy of nonviolent resistance (both in and out of jail), one of the best possible sources is a three-book series written by Gene Sharp and published in 1973, *The Politics of Nonviolent Action*.

These books were long out of print, then reissued in 1985. They are once again difficult to find. However, they are an absolute treasure of historic information on resistance. Do whatever you must to find them in a used bookstore or from a search service. The awesome online bookstore, Amazon.com, was able to get them for me.

Sharp's books cover everything from consumer boycotts to German women resisting Nazis to save their Jewish husbands. They detail personal incidents and group actions. They discuss the backgrounds and philosophies of resistance movements. And the effectiveness (or lack) of various techniques.

The books are (as you might expect) written from a "left-wing" perspective, and are geared to achieving political goals through mass action. But the information they contain could be useful to anyone who might ever need to hold fast to principles of non-cooperation in the face of brutal or unjust authority.

You'll find more information on these books in the Appendix.

Of course, if you really want to study the techniques of nonviolence, there's always the master, Gandhi. There are many books by and about him, these four good ones among them:

- *Autobiography: The Story of My Experiments with Truth* by Mohandas K. Gandhi (Dover, paperback, 1983, $8.95)
- *Gandhi on Non-Violence* by Mohandas K. Gandhi and Thomas Merton (W.W. Norton, paperback $5.95)
- *Gandhi Wields the Weapon of Moral Power: Salt March* by Gene Sharp (Greenleaf Books, 1993, $8.00)
- *Gandhi's Political Philosophy: A Critical Examination* by Bhikku Parekh (Macmillan, paperback, 1991)

Information on obtaining these books is also in the Appendix.

Like most people, I will be nonviolent as long as it's possible and moral to be so. But I don't believe the technique of nonviolence carries any miraculous moral force. Says Mike Kemp, once again: "You mention the example of Gandhi. Yet the only result of Gandhi's methods is that the Indians traded their British masters for native masters. Nonviolence coupled with ACTIVE, aggressive resistance is fine to set the stage, but sooner or later push will come to shove."

Nonviolence can nevertheless be a strong moral position. As Gandhi wisely said:[2]

> In non-violence, the masses have a weapon which enables a child, a woman, or even a decrepit old man to resist the mightiest government successfully. If your spirit is strong, mere lack of physical strength ceases to be a handicap.
>
> And
>
> The first principle of non-violent action is that of noncooperation with everything humiliating.

Yet Gandhi, though personally committed to total, active nonviolence and love, also made a large number of statements that would astound some pacifists who consider themselves his followers:

> Violence is any day preferable to impotence.

> If the capacity for non-violent self-defense is lacking, there need be no hesitation in using violent means.

> [Injustice must be resisted.] No doubt the non-violent way is always the best, but where that does not come naturally, the violent way is both necessary and honorable. Inaction here is rank cowardice and unmanly. It must be shunned at all cost.

> He who cannot protect himself or his nearest and dearest or their honor by non-violently facing death, may and ought to do so by violently dealing with the oppressor. He who can do neither of the two is a burden.

---

[2] All Gandhi quotes used here are from *Gandhi on Non-Violence*.

Update 2002
What's New
Since Chapter Eleven

In 2000, California meat packer Stuart Alexander shot three government plant inspectors to death. He had just reopened his factory after inspectors had closed it down for health violations. (In 79 years, the family-owned plant had never had a single customer complaint about poor quality product.)

In Texas in the same year, a 72-year-old rancher, Melvin Edison Hale, shot a state trooper to death. Hale had been ticketed earlier for not wearing a seatbelt, and he'd had some angry confrontations with authorities over past-due taxes. In Texas, cops can throw you in jail for seatbelt violations at their own discretion. This time, when the cop stopped him, he figured he was going to be hauled in — and he'd had enough.

Just weeks after Hale reached his breaking point, Gary Watson of Bunker, Missouri shot four city workers who were on his property without permission and who had been warned to stay away after a dispute over easements. Two died, two were wounded, and Watson later shot and killed himself as well.

Like Carl Drega, Alexander and Hale were known to be edgy, fed-up men even before they reached their breaking points. Watson, on the other hand, was called a nice guy and a good neighbor. But they all had one thing in common: They'd had enough of the government shoving itself into their lives.

The great surprise isn't that a handful of prickly, fed-up men have violently attacked government agents. The surprise is that more haven't.

I don't endorse what any of these people did. (It should be fairly clear by now that I prefer adamant, but nonviolent resistance.) But I do understand their outrage.

Unfortunately, if the last decade or so of relentlessly increasing government control has shown anything, it's that Americans have an almost endless ability to tolerate injustice and violations of liberty as long as they themselves remain prosperous, well-fed, and well-employed. Not only do few of us "shoot the bastards," but few of us even rouse ourselves to live as freedom-loving Americans.

Freedom is a great abstraction to most of us. "What's on TV tonight?" is a more important question than "What will we do when the Fourth Amendment is gone?" "How big a raise will I get?" is a weightier matter than "How much of my soul do I have to sell to stay within the system?"

After Ruby Ridge and Waco, the federal government also learned that large-scale violent confrontations against little folks don't bring in the good PR that the FBI and ATF had hoped. And so when dealing with "anti-government cranks," they've taken a gentler hand. Their handling of the Montana Freemen standoff in 1996 is an example of the greater restraint they've been showing.

And of course, since September 11, 2001, we have something far more dangerous (and genuinely dangerous) than "domestic terrorists" and "militia groups" to occupy our law-enforcement people. In fact, references in *I Am Not a Number!* to militias now sound almost quaint and old-fashioned.

International terrorism is a real threat — but imposing greater surveillance on ordinary Americans won't do a thing to halt it.

The government hasn't actually stopped its hasty brutality. Killing fifty innocent people at an Afghani wedding party (as U.S. bombers did in the summer of 2002) because U.S. officials couldn't be bothered finding out whether intelligence received from a warlord was valid isn't morally superior to slaughtering eighty-some men, women, and children in a Texas church. But Americans don't care as long as it's only a bunch of "towel-heads" screaming in agony and watching their children blown to bits before their eyes.

It's also okay, in the eyes of most Americans, to put "rag-heads" and "sand-niggers" into indefinite detention without charges — even when they're American citizens.[3]

In short, we'll tolerate any injustice — as long as it's not done to us. And we'll even tolerate most injustices done to us as long as we're well fed and comfortable. As it's becoming clear, most of us — even most people who *claim* they love freedom — will tolerate the gradual erosion of liberty, and the gradual assumption of government control as long as it's done slowly and politely.

I stand by every scenario in Chapter Eleven. And I continue to hope that true freedom lovers (which includes only those people who actually resist tyranny, not merely those who yap about doing so) will refuse *en masse* to cooperate with evil and will overcome through nonviolent noncooperation.

I don't know to this day whether freedom-community building will ever be the answer, or even *an* answer in the real world, to the dire problem of universal government control through ID and monitoring. It seems logical and even inevitable, but it takes a great deal of energy and commitment, risk and money.

If freedom lovers never gather round each other in sustaining communities as this book suggests, I hope some greater mind than mine comes up with another way.

I'd much, much, much rather be free than right.

In the meantime, I'll resist, with or without companions. What will you do? For yourself? For your children? For freedom?

> *"If you choose not to decide,*
> *you still have made a choice."*
> **— Neil Peart, drummer and**
> **lyricist for the rock band Rush**

---

[3] The U.S. government did this in 2002 with Jose Padilla, a former Chicago gang member. They accused him of being an "enemy combatant" when he fell under suspicion of plotting with the Al-Qaeda terror network. Padilla was not only a U.S. citizen, but as Congress hadn't declared war against anyone, constitutionally there *were* no enemy combatants. Yet this twisted logic was used to totally wipe out Padilla's constitutional rights. Please let's not forget that if we let them take away the constitutional rights of creeps, it's only a matter of time until they take *our* rights, too.

I Am Not a Number!

Afterword
The Prisoner

This book opened with three quotes from the 1960s British TV series, *The Prisoner*.

In *The Prisoner*, a British secret agent, played by Patrick McGoohan, is spirited away to "The Village" after resigning his job. We don't know where The Village is — or even what it is, except that it is a prison. It appears benign, even pleasant; but threats are everywhere, surveillance is omnipresent, and freedom is nowhere. We don't know which are the jailers and which the inmates; all are known only by numbers. We don't know who runs The Village — only that they want "information" and will stop at nothing to get it.

McGoohan, whose character is called Number Six, defies them. And in the end he triumphs. (Or does he? The signs are ambiguous.)

The first two sets of *Prisoner* quotes that opened this book are self-explanatory. But if you haven't seen the program, you might wonder about the implications of the third:

"I'll kill you."

"I'll die."

The words are not negative, as they may seem at first glance, but one of the most positive messages we can deliver to any tyrant.

The words are from the next-to-last episode, "Once Upon a Time." Number Two, the warden, makes the threat to kill Six. Six responds with a shrug. *"If you kill me, of course I'll die."*

Six's acknowledgment that Two can kill him is more than a simple statement of fact. It is also not, in the slightest sense, the statement of a loser. It is a defiant recognition that *killing is not triumph and death is not defeat*. In fact, by dying with his valuable "information" still unspoken and his spirit still unbroken, Six will be the victor.

Death is inevitable, anyway. What does it matter, really, when it comes? It is how we *live* that determines whether we triumph over evil and misrule, not when we die.

Nobody I know wants to die at the hands of tyrants. But to look tyrants in the eye and let them know that their blustering threats of punishment mean nothing when held up against our inner passions — *that* is our victory.[1]

---

[1] *The Prisoner* is an inspiration. If you haven't seen it, I urge you to get the videos, which are widely available through catalogs. There are seventeen episodes. The critical ones, as defined by McGoohan, are: "Arrival", "Free for All"; "Dance of the Dead"; "Checkmate"; "The Chimes of Big Ben"; "Once Upon a Time"; and "Fall Out." These are best viewed in order.

Appendix
Freedom Resources

Here are names, addresses, and other contact information for a variety of freedom resources. Please keep in mind that, except where specified, I can't vouch for the reliability of any business listed here or the reliability of any information presented in books and Web sites. These sources are to help you get started on your own research.

To those without Internet access: I'm sorry, but an increasing number of freedom resources are available only on the net. I've included snail addresses and phone numbers wherever possible. If you have no computer and you're interested in an organization or resource listed here with only a URL, you might try a computer at your local library, a nearby university, or a cyber cafe.

General
The Bill of Rights and its meaning
Jews for the Preservation of Firearms Ownership has the Bill of Rights with modern-language explanations of each article in English and a number of other languages: www.jpfo.org/bor.htm

Chapter One:
The Orgy of Enslavement

Fight the Fingerprint
The excellent Web site of "Fight the Fingerprint" can be found at:
www.networkusa.org/fingerprint.shtml
This site contains many helpful essays and legal cites, as well as a carefully updated chart listing cur-

rent state requirements for driver's license security features.

National ID Card Links
From the Electronic Privacy Information Center, a page of frequently updated news on ID and "security" issues:
www.epic.org/privacy/id_cards/

Chapter Two:
Life in ID State America

The Stalker
The Stalker's web site contains all kinds of fascinating information about privacy — and how little of it we really have.
The Stalker's home page is found at:
www.glr.com/stalk.html
It hasn't been updated recently, but still contains a ton of useful information.
And be sure to check out The Stalker's pages on publicly available Social Security numbers at:
www.glr.com/ssnpub.html

Comprehensive news on new technologies and policies on privacy
Electronic Privacy Information Center:
www.epic.org/privacy/

The Biometric Consortium
This is a bit heavy going for most readers, but anyone wishing to follow new developments in biometrics might do well to watch this industry group.
www.biometrics.org/

Chapter Three:
The Undocumented Citizen

For information on offshore bank accounts, second passports, etc., check out these sources. Please be wary of anyone selling information at high prices, or using fancy verbiage to disguise the fact that they really don't have much to say.

Escape Artist and Cyberhaven

Two great web sites for locating all kinds of offshore resources www.escapeartist.com and www.cyberhaven.com

Escape Artist is a particular goldmine, offering not only banking and investment information, but a vast array of cultural and travel information about potential haven nations. Run by an expatriate American, Escape Artists has highly authorative and well-maintained links to offshore information. Cyberhaven is more oriented to financial and business matters, but in that area it contains (or links to) very useful information.

The Freebooter (newsletter)
PO Box 494
St. Peter Port
Guernsey GY1 6BZ
Channel Islands (Britain)
(+44) 171 223 4295
Web site: www.freebooter.com/

Privacy Alert (newsletter)
561 Keystone Ave. #684
Reno, Nevada 89503
(775) 348-8591
Web site:
www.thespiritof76.com/pa/privacy_alert.html
(Be sure to also see the The Sovereign Society in the section of the Appendix that covers Chapter Seven.)

Articles on legal second-passport programs and alternative residency
www.escapeartist.com/passports/passports.htm

Belizian passport information
www.offshoreworld.com/pass/index13.htm

Fake ID
The Fake ID Man reviews various sites peddling "novelty" ID:
www.fakeidman.org
Keep in mind that most fake ID is geared toward college students trying to buy booze or get into clubs, not for freedom lovers trying to live undetected. "Quality" is in the eye of the beholder. The Fake ID Man gives a scathing review to photoidcards.com (calls it an outright scam) when I've found that company to provide a useful product for casual use.

An inexpensive and (sort of) real second citizenship
The World Service Authority:
www.worldservice.org/
Garry Davis and his organization want world government. Most readers of this book would say, "No thanks." But the World Service Authority does offer a second passport (based on "the inalienable human right of freedom of travel on planet Earth") that's actually accepted as valid by a few — very few — countries of the world.

Outlaws Legal Service
Pro se litigants and those interested in personal sovereignty can find help at the jauntily named Outlaws Legal Service:
www.outlawslegal.com/

Information on the U.S. tax system
Inform America: www.informamerica.com/
Among other things, this site hosts information about the Save-A-Patriot Fellowship and its $10,000 challenge to any bureaucrat, tax authority, CPA (or anyone else) who can disprove certain statements the fellowship makes about the voluntary nature of the U.S. tax system.

One man's experiences without an SSN
Jim Hill has lived without a Social Security number and reports his personal experiences at this site, The Founding Spirit:
www.foundingspirit.com/default.htm
He makes no claim to be giving legal advice and doesn't spend a lot of time making arguments about case law or principles. He just shows you what worked for him.

I Am Not a Number!

And another's ...

Neil McIver has also lived SSNless. He shares his experiences at www.cjmciver.org/

From this site, you can also join Neil's Life Without a Number e-mail message (not discussion) list.

Exploded myths of the patriot community

Larry Becraft's Destroyed Legal Arguments: home.hiwaay.net/~becraft/deadissues.htm

Anyone interested in sovereign citizenship, *pro se* litigation, etc. should definitely read this material early on. Becraft, one of the most noted attorneys in the freedom movement, lists arguments that are known to be legally bogus and others that may be perfectly correct, but that won't help you win in court.

How to create a "null" nine-digit number

Sometimes an insurance company or other business you deal with will allow you to submit a "null" nine-digit number as an identifier on an account in place of the "required" SSN. Sometimes they'll create one for you. And sometimes you just need to fake an SSN. (Not that I'd advise you to do that in any case where it might be illegal, of course.)

Learn the structure of the SSN at the Web site of Computer Professionals for Social Responsibility: www.cpsr.org/cpsr/privacy/ssn/ssn.structure.html

With this information, you can either create a number that looks and is "null" or one that looks like a perfectly plausible number to look good in a case where the number will never be checked. Just be aware that, with all these interlinked databases, even small businesses can, and sometimes will, quickly check and discover your "real" number, assuming you ever use one.

Chapter Four:
The Free American Community

The Rainbow Family

The Rainbow family has been described as "a working anarchy." Family members gather once a year in a National Forest, and hold smaller, regional gatherings, as well. Learn more at:

www.welcomehome.org/rainbow.html

Utopian communities of the past/utopian theory

Men Against the State by James J. Martin, Ralph Myles Publisher, Inc., 1970

Periodical Letter on the Principles of the Equity Movement, Josiah Warren, AMS Press, 1978

The Sex Radicals, Hal D. Sears, University Press of Kansas, 1977.

The individualist anarchist, Wendy McElroy, has also written on nineteenth-century utopian movements:

www.zetetics.com/mac/index.html

Intentional communities of the present and recent past
The Farm

www.gaia.org/farm

Arcosanti

www.arcosanti.org/

Intentional Communities (hundreds of communities, worldwide)

www.ic.org

The Gulchers Guide

www.libertymls.com/gulch/

The Guide is a gathering spot for libertarians and others interested in discussing the requirements of intentional communities.

Twin Oaks

www.twinoaks.org/

The Free State Project

Web site: www.freestateproject.org
E-mail: info@freestateproject.org
Street address:
565 College Drive, C-160
Henderson, Nevada 89015
The FSP's e-mail announcement list:
http://groups.yahoo.com/group/freestate
E-mail discussion lists:
http://groups.yahoo.com/group/freestateproject   and
www.free-market.net/forums/freestate0202/
Web site: www.freestateproject.org/

An article by Claire Wolfe about the Free State Project: "Are You Ready for Liberty in Your Lifetime?"
www.backwoodshome.com/columns/wolfe0207.html

Costa Rica

Movimiento Libertario: www.libertario.org/ (in Spanish)

The political movement fostering libertarianism in Central America.

Costa Rica International Libertarian Network (in English)" www.maxpages.com/ilncostarica/

Links to information about Costa Rica (with emphasis on government and politics): www.gksoft.com/govt/en/cr.html (mix of English and Spanish-language sites)

Chapter Five:
Communications in the Free Community

Anonymous e-mail and web surfing

For more-or-less anonymous web surfing, check out:

> www.anonymizer.com

For e-mail that doesn't point to your physical location, use the anonymizer to go to an online e-mail service such as www.hotmail.com or the more secure www.mailvault.com.

Online encrypted e-mail

> www.mailvault.com

Cookie-management tools

CDT.org Cookie-management tools:
www.cdt.org/resourcelibrary/Privacy/Tools/Cookie_Management/

For PGP encryption software

> www.pgp.com
> www.pgpi.com
> www.web.mit.edu/network/pgp

Broadband Internet access

"The Broadband Breakdown":
http://www.cnet.com/internet/0-3762-8-7287680-1.html

This lively article gives a good overview of the most common or up-and-coming high-speed Internet technologies — some of which are suitable to rural Gulches, isolated homesteads, and small communities. Keep in mind that everything in this area is changing rapidly — and usually for the better. Satellite systems are already less expensive than indicated in this article.

Personal radio services (general)

For brief descriptions of all types of personal radio services, their uses and licensing requirements:

The Federal Communications Commission's Personal Radio Services Page:
> wireless.fcc.gov/prs/

Packet radio

The Tucson Amateur Packet Radio Corporation (TAPR)
Tucson Amateur Packet Radio
8987-309 E. Tanque Verde Rd., #337
Tucson, AZ 85749-9399
voice: (972)671-TAPR (8277)
fax: (972) 671-8716
E-mail: tapr@tapr.org
Web site: www.tapr.org

Ham radio

The American Radio Relay League (ARRL)
1-800-326-3942
> www.arrl.org

General mobile radio service

Personal Radio Steering Group
PO Box 2851
Ann Arbor, MI 48016
(313) MOBILE 3
> www.provide.net/~prsg/

Scanners

"Radio Scanners: Liberty's Ears" by The Owl:
www.doingfreedom.com/gen/0600/ht.scanners.html

An updated (as of 2000) account of how scanners, far from being obsolete, can now give enhanced listening ability in the age of cellphones and police mobile data terminals.

Pirate radio

"An Intro to Pirate Radio" by Necross Sinister and Thomas Icom:

www.iirg.org/ticom/pir8rado.html

Internet radio
SHOUTcast: www.shoutcast.com/
Click on the online docs link where you see the question "Wanna be a broadcaster?"

General underground radio communications
For information on the uses of all types of radio communications in the underground, check out the Internet newsgroup: alt.radio.pirate. The alt.survivalism newsgroup also touches on this topic.

Nationwide paging service
Cue Paging
Nationwide paging and voice messaging service
(800) 824-9755
E-mail: sales@cue.net
Web site: www.cue.com

To be removed from most mailing lists
The Direct Marketing Association
Mail Preference Service
Direct Marketing Association
P. O. Box 9008
Farmingdale, NY 11735-9008
www.dmaconsumers.org/cgi/offmailinglistdave

And to end the plague of telemarketers
The Direct Marketing Association
Telephone Preference Service
Direct Marketing Association
PO Box 9014
Farmingdale, NY 11735-9014
www.dmaconsumers.org/cgi/offtelephonedave

Homing pigeons
The American Racing Pigeon Union
PO Box 18465
Oklahoma City, OK 73154-0465
voice: (405) 478-2240
fax: (405) 670-4748
www.pigeon.org

**Chapter Six:
Travel in the Free Community**

The National Motorists Association

www.motorists.com/
The National Motorists Association also sponsors a national Roadblock Registry:
www.roadblock.org/
where you can read about and report on, known locations of various checkpoints.

Jackie Juntti, The Old Polish Woman
Jackie, who wrote the story of how she boarded an airplane using her Costco Card instead of the required government-issued ID, is an amazing fighter. She also has an interesting web site:
home.earthlink.net/~idzrus/index.html

Alternate passports
Check some of the offshore haven sites listed under Chapter Three, above.
Also visit: www.alteredstates.net for alternate ID of various sorts.

John Gilmore
Lawsuits and protests against travel restrictions:
http://cryptome.org/freetotravel.htm

Underground railroads
For more on the Underground Railroad of the 1800s, try:
The North Star: Tracing the Underground Railroad. This web site located at www.ugrr.org has historic information and leads to more.

Let My People Go
Henrietta Buckmaster
University of South Carolina Press, 1992
A reprint of one of the finest, most comprehensive books on the 19th Century American underground railroad — and the first book to document the slaves' role in their own liberation.
For information on more modern efforts:
Underground Railroad: Practical Advice for Finding Passengers, Getting Them to Safety, and Staying One Step Ahead of the Tyrants, Jefferson Mack, Paladin Press, 2000.
Sanctuary: The New Underground Railroad, Renny Golden and Michael McConnell, Orbis Books, 1986.

No Law Against Mercy, Barbara Lyn Lapp and Rachel Lapp, Hand of Hope Press, Post Office Box 101, Cassadaga, New York 14718.

This book, the story of family members who went to jail for activities in connection with hiding a teenager from the state, is available through Laissez Faire Books and Amazon.com. Don't expect a book of instructions on hiding people; that's only part of the story, with most of the events focusing on their trials and time in jail. Nevertheless, their experience is food for thought and the people are admirable.

Chapter Seven:
Finance and Trade in the Free Community

E-gold
> www.e-gold.com

Alternative money, banking, barter in general
One of the best places to find information on alternative money and banking systems and barter systems is the web site of Roy Davies, science librarian at the University of Exeter:
Web sites:
> www.ex.ac.uk/~RDavies/arian/money.html
> www.ex.ac.uk/~Rdavies/arian/barter.html
> www.ex.ac.uk/~Rdavies/arian/local.html
Also check out the discussion group alt.community.local-money.

Another place with good links to information about money systems is J. Orlin Grabbe's web site at: www.aci.net/Kalliste. Grabbe has written many insightful articles about the whys, wherefores, and hows of Internet banking and money systems.

Ithaca Hours alternative currency
Paul Glover
Ithaca Money
Box 6578
Ithaca, NY 14851
E-mail: hours@lightlink.com or paglo@lightlink.com
Web site: www.lightlink.com/ithacahours/

Offshore banks with (relatively) modest deposit requirements
According to Bob Kephart of Scope International and the Sovereign Society:

"Robeco Bank, the Geneva bank which is cooperating with Sovereign, will open an account for our members with $5,000 minimum. I believe you may also find that Anker Bank in Lausanne will open an account for around $5,000 (fax 01141-21-323-9767). There is also a very good and efficient bank in Jersey that I have done business with for years that will open small accounts. This is Standard Chartered Bank. Also, you can open an account with Anglo Irish Bank in Vienna, also very good and efficient, for around the same minimum (fax 011-43-1-405-8142). All of these banks have many American clients and there are no language problems. And the secrecy aspects, while slightly stronger in Switzerland, are strong in Jersey and Austria as well."

Contact information for the Standard Chartered Bank (now Standard Chartered Grindlays) is:
PO Box 80
Standard Chartered House
13-15 Castle Street
St. Helier, Jersey JE4 8PT
voice: +44 (0) 1534 704000
fax: +44 (0) 1534 704600
Web site: www.standardchartered.com/je/

The Sovereign Society
A membership organization offering information on offshore banking, investment, privacy protection and freedom.
The Sovereign Society
5 Catherine Street, Waterford, Ireland
international phone: +(353) 51-844-068
Fax: +(353) 51-304-561
U.S. service line: (888)-358-8125
E-mail: info@thesovereignsociety.com
Web site: www.sovereignsociety.com/

CASPIAN (Consumers Against Supermarket Privacy Invasion and Numbering)
Hard-working anti-loyalty-card warriors:
www.nocards.org/

Federal Reserve studies on the "unbanked"
"The Unbanked — Who Are They?" *Capital Connections*, Spring 2001.
www.federalreserve.gov/dcca/newsletter/2001/spring 01/unbank.htm

Also see my *Backwoods Home* article, "Bye Bye Banking" at
www.backwoodshome.com/columns/wolfe0201.html

Civil asset forfeiture reform

"Does the Civil Asset Forfeiture Reform Act of 2000 Bring a Modicum of Sanity to the Federal Civil Forfeiture System?" This legal analysis by Peter Joseph Loughlin, J.D., gives a good overview of some of the sanity that was restored to the otherwise entirely insane civil forfeiture field by CAFRA:
www.malet.com/does_the_civil_asset_forfeiture_.htm

Cypherpunks

More than you ever wanted to know about encryption and electronic privacy from the people who are writing the code:
www.csua.berkeley.edu/cypherpunks/

Free markets in fiction

For fictional treatments of free markets, take a look at the agoras in *Alongside Night* by J. Neil Schulman and *The Jehovah Contract* by Victor Koman. Schulman's description is especially detailed. L. Neil Smith's *The Probability Broach* and other books in his North American Confederacy SF series also describe free markets in action.

A booklet, "How to Get a Bank Account without a Social Security Number," is available at
www.livetaxfree.com/products2.asp,
along with other information on how to work, marry, and otherwise survive as a Numberless individual. Again, *caveat emptor*. You may get helpful info from such sources, but never take them as gospel without independent verification.

Chapter Eight:
Medical care in the Free Community

When mainstream medical care isn't available (or when you prefer not to use it), here are some places to begin looking for alternatives. Do it now. When a crisis comes, it may be too late.

Empowerment Resources Online Bookstore (alternative medicine)
www.empowermentresources.com/books/page12.html
Medical self-care archives
www.healthy.net

Online pharmacies

There are probably thousands of online pharmacies. Some, located outside of the U.S. will sell you (without prescription) medications that in this country are tightly controlled by the government-medical establishment. Avoid referral services that charge fees to find these overseas pharmacies for you. If you don't see what you want at the companies below, a Google Internet search and a little asking around will find you everything you need.

PharmaGroup
www.pharmagroup.com
(known reliable; very professional)

Inhouse Pharmacy Europe
www.inhousepharmacy-europe.com/

When all else fails (and if your values allow it):
Hemlock Society
PO Box 101810
Denver, CO 80250-1810
voice: (303) 639-1202
or 1-800-247-7421
fax: (303) 639-1224
e-mail: hemlock@hemlock.org
Web site: www.hemlock.org

Chapter Nine:
Work in the Free Community

Offshore contracting

For more information, check the web sites listed under Chapter Three, above. Many of the same sites that can lead you to offshore banking and second citizenship can also help you find an agent to set up an offshore corporation or trust for you.

Also see www.escapeartist.com/tele/commute.htm for telecommuting and other business resources for expatriates or people who want to establish overseas business contacts.

Chapter Ten:
And a Free World of Things

Self-defense firearms training

For an extensive list of other firearms training centers around the country, check:

www.martialartsresource.com/firearms.htm

or

http://users.erols.com/aglock45/train.html or

Liberty Round Table

Visit their main site at:

www.lrt.org

And check out their "Live Freer, Now" page.

Doing Freedom

www.doingfreedom.com/

This online zine contains practical advice for living free.

Chapter Eleven:
Free People, Violence, and Alternatives

Books on nonviolent resistance

No Law Against Mercy, by Barbara Lyn Lapp and Rachel Lapp., See listing under Chapter Six.

The Politics of Nonviolent Action, Part One: Power and Struggle, Part Two: The Methods of Nonviolent Action, Part Three: The Dynamics of Nonviolent Action, by Gene Sharp, Extending Horizon Books, Porter Sargent Publishers, 11 Beacon Street, Boston, Massachusetts 02108.

YOU WILL ALSO WANT TO READ:

☐ **94281 101 THINGS TO DO 'TIL THE REVOLUTION, Ideas and resources for self-liberation, monkey wrenching and preparedness, *by Claire Wolfe.*** We don't need a weatherman to know which way the wind blows — but we do need the likes of Claire Wolfe, whose book offers 101 suggestions to help grease the wheels as we roll towards the government's inevitable collapse. "Kill your TV… Join a gun-rights group… Fly the Gadsden flag… Buy and carry the Citizens' Rule Book… Join the tax protesters on April 15th… Bury gold, guns, and goodies…" Wolfe's list is lengthy and thought-provoking, as she elaborates on each piece of advice, from generalities to precise instructions. For the concerned citizen who wishes to keep a low profile, protect his or her rights, and survive in the "interesting times" which are sure to come, this is essential reading. *1996, 5½ x 8½, 216 pp, soft cover.* **$15.95.**

☐ **76041 THE OUTLAW'S BIBLE, *by E.X. Boozhie.*** The best "jailhouse" law book ever published — for people on the outside who want to stay there. This is a real life civics lesson for citizen lawbreakers: how to dance on the fine line between freedom and incarceration, how to tiptoe the tightrope of due process. Covers detention, interrogation, searches and seizures. The only nonviolent weapon available for those on the wrong side of the law. *1985, 5½ x8½, 336 pp, index, soft cover.* **$16.95.**

☐ **58095 THE POLICEMAN IS YOUR FRIEND AND OTHER LIES, *by Ned Beaumont.*** America is a society built upon lies, supported by lies, and dedicated to promoting lies. In this astoundingly revealing look at the deceptions that are perpetrated upon us from infancy to old age, author Ned Beaumont peels away the fabric of deception and unveils the hidden untruths that enslave us and poison our perceptions. Policemen, bureaucrats, teachers, politicians, lawyers, financiers, military leaders — they are all part of the system that distorts our most basic freedoms and beliefs, and molds us into unthinking minions of the entrenched power structure. *1996, 5½ x 8½, 160 pp, soft cover.* **$14.95.**

☐ **61129 UNDERSTANDING U.S. IDENTITY DOCUMENTS, *by John Q. Newman.*** The most detailed examination of identity documents ever published. This guide is a must for all new identity seekers and anyone interested in identification, false identification, and alternate ID. You know who you are, your friends know who you are, but thousands of people you deal with in government and business know you only from a document. If you alter your documents, you can evade taxes, regulation and supervision. This book covers birth certificates, Social Security cards, drivers' licenses and passports. It shows how each document is generated and used, and explains the strengths and weaknesses of the agencies issuing them. *1991, 8½ x 11, 212 pp, illustrated, soft cover.* **$27.95.**

☐ **14205 TRAVEL-TRAILER HOMESTEADING FOR UNDER $5,000, Second Edition, *by Brian Kelling.*** Tired of paying rent? Need privacy away from nosy neighbors? This book will show you how a modest financial investment can enable you to place a travel-trailer or other RV on a suitable piece of land and make the necessary improvements for a comfortable home in which to live! This book covers the cost breakdown, tools needed, how to select the land and travel trailer or RV, and how to install a septic system, as well as water, power (including solar panels), heat and refrigeration systems. This new edition covers how to cheaply install and run a hot tub, and reasons why you'll never want to leave your new home. *1999, 5½ x 8½, 103 pp, illustrated, soft cover.* $10.00.

☐ **17032 THE LAST FRONTIERS ON EARTH, Strange Places Where You Can Live Free,** *by Jon Fisher.* This amazing book discusses living in Antarctica, on floating icebergs, on platforms in the ocean, underwater, as a nomad, in an airship, and much more. For each place, the author considers cost of living, the availability of food and shelter, the climate and other important factors. There are places where you can live free — if you're determined. *1985, 5½ x 8½, 140 pp, illustrated, soft cover.* $10.95.

☐ **17091 LIVING NAKED AND FRUGAL, A Handbook for Parsimonious Nudity**, *by Paul Penhallow with Marilyn Lovell.* Author Paul Penhallow's experience of living naked in a non-naked world spanned nearly ten years, and ranged from SunSpace, his 21st floor high-rise apartment in downtown Syracuse, New York, to the many highways and parks of the Northern Atlantic states. Penhallow's "Four Laws of Naturism" (Accept Yourself, Respect Others, Live Simply, and Relax Daily) comprise the springboard for this book, which also contains a comprehensive listing of nudist resorts throughout the United States. If you are considering becoming a nudist, or have already tried the lifestyle and enjoy it, this book provides the naked truth about living a life free of clothing, and how to do so in a thrifty manner. *1997, 5½ x 8½, 86 pp, soft cover.* $8.95.

☐ **14176 HOW TO DEVELOP A LOW-COST FAMILY FOOD-STORAGE SYSTEM**, *by Anita Evangelista.* If you're weary of spending a large percentage of your income on your family's food needs, then you should follow this amazing book's numerous tips on food-storage techniques. Slash your food bill by over fifty percent, and increase your self-sufficiency at the same time through alternative ways of obtaining, processing and storing foodstuffs. Includes methods of freezing, canning, smoking, jerking, salting, pickling, krauting, drying, brandying and many other food preservation procedures. *1995, 5½ x 8½, 120 pp, illustrated, indexed, soft cover.* $10.00

☐ **14187 HOW TO LIVE WITHOUT ELECTRICITY — AND LIKE IT,** *by Anita Evangelista.* There's no need to remain dependent on commercial electrical systems for your home's comforts and security. This book describes many alternative methods that can help you become more self-reliant and free from the utility companies. Learn how to light, heat and cool your home, obtain and store water, cook and refrigerate food, and fulfill many other household needs without paying the power company! This book contains photographs, illustrations, and mail-order listings to make your transition to independence a snap! *1997, 5½ x 8½, 168 pp, illustrated, soft cover.* $13.95.

☐ **17028 HOW TO START YOUR OWN COUNTRY, Second Edition,** *by Erwin S. Strauss.* *Start your own country?* Yes! This book tells the story of dozens of "new country" projects and explains the options available to those who want to start a country of their own. This daring approach to freedom has actually been tried many times in recent years, with varying degrees of success. Covers diplomacy, national defense, sovereignty, raising funds, recruiting settlers, and more, including names and addresses of current new countries. Over 100 pages of fascinating case histories illustrated with dozens of rare photos. *1999, 5½ x 8½, 174 pp, illustrated, soft cover.* $12.95.

We offer the very finest in controversial and unusual books — a complete catalog is sent **FREE** *with every book order. If you would like to order the catalog separately, please see our ad on the last page of this book.*

Please send me the books I have marked below.

☐ **94281**   **101 Things to Do 'Til The Revolution, $15.95**

☐ **76041**   **The Outlaw's Bible, $16.95**

☐ **58095**   **The Policeman is Your Friend, $14.95**

☐ **61129**   **Understanding U.S. Identity Documents, $27.95**

☐ **14205**   **Travel-Trailer Homesteading for Under $5,000, $10.00**

☐ **17032**   **The Last Frontiers on Earth, $10.95**

☐ **17091**   **Living Naked and Frugal, $8.95**

☐ **14176**   **How to Develop a Low-Cost Family Food-Storage System, $10.00**

☐ **14187**   **How to Live Without Electricity — And Like It, $13.95**

☐ **17028**   **How to Start Your Own Country, $12.95**

☐ **88888**   **Loompanics Main Catalog, $5.00**

INN2

LOOMPANICS UNLIMITED
PO BOX 1197
PORT TOWNSEND, WA 98368

Please send me the books I have checked above. I am enclosing $ _____ which includes $5.95 for shipping and handling of orders up to $25.00. Add $1.00 for each additional $25.00 ordered *Washington residents please include 8.2% for sales tax.*

NAME_____

ADDRESS _____

_____

CITY_____

STATE/ZIP_____

We accept Visa, Discover and MasterCard. To place a credit card order *only*,
call 1-800-380-2230, 24 hours a day, 7 days a week.

Check out our web site: www.loompanics.com